CW00734252

THE
RSS

Praise for the Book

The RSS has played an important role in the social, religious and economic life of India since its founding. Its attraction to Indians is based on its patriotism and nationalistic attitude. Despite being a large organization, the RSS is close-knit and opaque to outsiders. With this book on the RSS and its inner workings, Sunil Ambekar is opening a window to the world of the RSS and is bridging the Sangh's past with its potential future role in Indian society.

—T.V. Mohandas Pai, Chairman, Aarin Capital Partners

As a spirited organization which is spread across the length and breadth of India, I wish that the RSS, through its shakhas, serves as a 'firewall' to protect the most marginalized and vulnerable children of our country. I hope that the RSS sensitizes the youth towards a compassionate and inclusive world, which upholds the ethos of Sangachhadhwam and Vasudhaiva Kutumbakam.

—Kailash Satyarthi, Nobel Peace Prize winner, 2014

We should not get judgemental about anything in life without knowing everything about it. This is also true about the Sangh, which is the most talked about subject in political and academic circles today. This book is a ready reckoner for anyone interested in the Sangh.

The RSS: Roadmaps For the 21st Century presents the Sangh from the perspective of the author who grew up knowing it as a swayamsevak. The book also talks about the Sangh's future plans.

—Anand Kumar, Founder, Super 30

THE
RSS
ROADMAPS
FOR THE
21ST
CENTURY

SUNIL AMBEKAR

RUPA

Published by
Rupa Publications India Pvt. Ltd 2019
7/16, Ansari Road, Daryaganj
New Delhi 110002

Sales Centres:
Allahabad Bengaluru Chennai
Hyderabad Jaipur Kathmandu
Kolkata Mumbai

ISBN: 978-93-5333-685-1

Third impression 2019

10 9 8 7 6 5 4 3

The moral right of the author has been asserted.

Printed by Parksons Graphics Pvt. Ltd, India

CONTENTS

INTRODUCTION
THE STORY OF INDIA'S FUTURE

In 2007, when India completed sixty years of independence, a question arose in my mind. What will be the state of our nation in 2047, the year in which our country will celebrate its 100 years of independence from colonial rule. As a long-standing volunteer or swayamsevak of the Rashtriya Swayamsevak Sangh (RSS)—a social organization—and a full-time RSS pracharak or one inspired by the mission, working with the Akhil Bharatiya Vidyarthi Parishad (ABVP)—the largest student organization in terms of membership and university units—the obvious question before me was: what would be the relevance of the RSS in the same time period?

After deliberating with RSS functionaries, the common answer I could gather was that India would continue to march on its mission as a Vishwa Guru, or World Teacher, to provide knowledge and direction to the world, while the Sangh would become indistinguishable from Indian society. The merger of the Sangh and Indian society would be as complete as the mixing of sugar in milk and just as the milk when stirred displays the characteristics of sugar, Indian society as a whole would start exhibiting the traits of the Sangh. So, the Sangh would become coterminous with all of Indian society and the need for it to exist as a distinct entity would be obviated.

The Sangh does not want to be a separate power ruling over society; it wants to strengthen society, so that it can handle its issues constructively. To use a metaphor, just as the mighty rivers fall into oceans and have no separate existence, the Sangh's complete union with society is conceived as the ultimate goal. 'Sangh Samaj Banega' is a slogan, referring to the merging of Sangh with society, which is raised repeatedly in the RSS to reinforce this goal when Sangh and society become one.

The rise of India as a Vishwa Guru is another question that needs to be deciphered. That is why when I was approached with the idea of writing a book on the RSS for the twenty-first century, I grabbed the opportunity with eagerness.

This book is about the process through which the Sangh is re-contextualizing age-old civilizational thoughts in an ever-changing, contemporary society. As one of the most prominent ideologues of the RSS, Pandit Deendayal Upadhyaya once said, 'From the past, through the present, to the future.' Sangh's 94-year-old journey, now into the future, is narrated in this book.

This is a practitioner's book—an insider's account. My association with the RSS dates back to my childhood. It was a natural occurrence. In Nagpur, my family home is next to the RSS headquarters, Hedgewar Bhawan, also known as the Sangh building. The doors of my home open onto the RSS grounds. The Sangh was a part of my daily life. I regularly attended the shakha—the fundamental unit of the RSS and the place where all swayamsevaks assemble daily/weekly as per schedule, where we received instructions and performed physical drills and played games. During holidays, the Sangh premises became a playground for us schoolgoing children.

Mohite Shakha was the shakha of Hedgewar Bhawan. Each shakha has a name and it is usually named after the locality where it is held or after some great personalities. Mohite was the name of the locality and it was also the surname of the original owner of the land. Shakhas conducted in the evening were predicated with shyam (evening).

A network of a vast number of shakas, the primary unit, around the country, constitute the RSS. Shakhas or daily meetings are held in the morning and evening. There are night shakhas for workers to accommodate their factory shifts.

I became a swayamsevak of Mohite Shyam, named thus because it was an evening shakha. The schedule of the shakha became my clock. After attending it, I would go home and busy myself with homework. I would continue till I heared the bell concluding the music or 'ghosh' of the Ghosh Shakha, which imparted training in playing specific musical instruments used in the shakha. The Ghosh group, meaning a music band, played instrumental music and followed our shakha. Only after the gong would go off for this shakha would dinner be served at my home. It was a settled family routine.

So, the Sangh, shakha, getting to know friends there—all of it became a part of my growing-up experience, almost in an organic manner. There are no membership drives or formal initiations in the Sangh. The day one starts going to the shakha, one becomes a swayamsevak. There are no formal initiations. Whoever wants can become a swayamsevak whenever. Thus, it is difficult for me to pinpoint the precise time I became a swayamsevak. As I grew up and began to understand the teachings of the Sangh, I consciously made efforts to become a good swayamsevak and progressed on that path.

Important functionaries, despite their busy schedules, would give us their attention and time. They would narrate to us real life stories of great people who served India and her people. They introduced me to shlokas, or verses, in Sanskrit. We went for picnics and winter camps. It taught me self-discipline and self-management. Critical life skills were thus acquired easily in a natural setting. I was a science student and I found the work ethics of the Sangh logical and scientific.

There was nothing that was artificial, political or mechanical. Work with a pure heart and full effort was the operative principle. For me, these dimensions of Sangh life were very attractive.

SPIRITUAL BROTHERHOOD

There is a natural alignment of Hindu families with the RSS because spirituality is at the core of our family traditions. Crores of Hindu families practise spirituality as a spontaneous daily living conduct that places primacy on oneness with the world, actions for public good and an innately joyful energy.

The spiritual core of RSS expresses itself in easy friendships and genuine brotherhood with people of different faiths. I have many recollections of such relationships—programmatic, individual and personal. Several years ago, the main annual function of the RSS on Vijayadashmi or the Hindu festival of Dusshera, would take place in Kasturchand Park, a famous ground for public meetings, near the Nagpur railway station. In those days, Balasaheb Deoras was the sarsanghchalak, or the guide, friend and philosopher of the RSS. He would conclude his speech with a vote of thanks, and among the many people and entities he thanked, was St. Joseph High School, a famous convent school of Nagpur. Later I learnt that items like furniture and other sundry materials required for the Vijayadashami function used to be provisioned by St. Joseph School. This is the nature of community relationship that the Sangh enjoys with people of all faiths.

Since my college days I have counted among my good friends Cyril Pillai, a Christian from Kerala, and Kaiser Yusuf, who now lives in Mumbai. I was from the Sangh and they used to call me to their house, or they would come to my house—it was natural and open; the fact that was a swayamsevak was not considered odd or different. When Kaiser's father passed away, I walked with him, and as we laid Kaiser's father to rest, I did whatever was ordained by Islamic traditions in such a situation. It was something normal for me and also known and accepted by the top Sangh functionaries. On 3 January 2016, in Pune, a big Sangh event took place, titled 'Shiv Shakti Sangam', an event organized by the Sangh to connect a maximum number of people from different walks of life. This was a big outreach event from an organizational perspective and 80,554[1] swayamsevaks congregated in RSS uniforms and many other people from all walks of life came to listen to the sarsanghchalak. It was a massive gathering of around 1,58,772 people.

So, what did the Sangh do when it came to the list of invitees? It called upon notables from different faiths. Educationists and scholars like Latif Magdum, secretary of Maharashtra Cosmopolitan Education Society in Pune, Dr S.N. Pathan, former vice-chancellor, Anish Chishti, Islamic scholar and writer, Prof. Anna Pratima G. Nikalje, principal of Wilson College, Mumbai, and clerics like Gulzar Sheikh, trustee of Kalewadi Madarsa, Maulana Shakiuddin of Dapodi Pune, Maulana Shaukat of Ravivar Peth, Pune, and Father Francis De'brito attended the event. The guests were effusive in their praise and these reactions were published by print and electronic media. Social media, too, covered it. This event was also attended by a descendant of the social reformer Mahatma Jyotirao Phule's family. Nitin Ranchandra Phule,[2] a 48-year-old swayamsevak and a fourth-generation descendant of the Mahatma Phule family, attended the programme. The Sangh has always had a healthy relationship with members of all communities. This is primarily because the Sangh's definition of Hindu is not linked to any religion but to a national identity of India; it is all-inclusive, a catch-all term that encompasses all communities and faiths in a thriving embrace.

This is the reason why the RSS has become an organization of ordinary people and has expanded like a fast-growing scientific chain

---

[1]Aashay Khandekar, 'Only Constitution Can't Bring Us Equality, Change in Mindset Can: RSS Chief Mohan Bhagwat', *The Indian Express*, 4 January 2016.
[2]Shailendra Paranjpe, Mahatma Phule Family's 4th, 5th Generation Descendants Make It To RSS Show, *DNA*, 11 January 2016.

reaction. It relates to the ordinariness and simplicity of common people. It gives them the confidence that they, the ordinary people, can bring about changes in society and the country. One needn't be a mahatma. The RSS does not espouse distant ideals that only specialists can comprehend but addresses the common concerns and necessary values that are within the grasp of common folks. Out of the ordinariness of the common people, this extraordinary organization is trusted and endures.

RSS work brings infinite joy, which is one of the biggest reasons why people like me stay on as pracharaks and swayamsevaks for the course of their lives. No advertisements are required. The methodology to create a sense of belonging and to connect people with society is personalization, with reliance on people-to-people contact. The importance of each individual is acknowledged and conscious efforts are made to link up with each individual. This open format encourages people with different orientations and from all walks of life to embrace the Sangh. The fabled Sangh discipline ensures that this diverse formation works and moves together, just as traffic rules ensure that a multitude navigates its way to the destination.

The Sangh thought is simple and clear. Though learned scholars have written complicated treatises about it, the central idea is a basic thought: be good and manifest unto society that goodness, through actions to benefit others. Parents want their children to attend shakhas for the inculcation of life's values. It is as simple as that. Even outside the Sangh, everyone impelled by the desire to do something for society and the country, according to one's interest, do not always find the platform. The Sangh has many platforms and each person can find their own fit without leaving their professions or stations in life.

Many people are motivated to undertake labours to bring tangible, visible change but don't want to be in politics—the Sangh is the domain for them. They see honest, good work happening in the Sangh and its many affiliates and make it a field of their activity.

The Sangh speaks a language that everyone understands. It covers all dimensions of humanity, politics, economy, governance, issues of language, religion, social uplift—all are equal in importance. Seva or devotional service to the motherland is its core. Even the sarsangchalak is a humble and ordinary swayamsevak dedicated to seva. That is how and why the RSS grows. With this mentality, it handles sublime social tasks. The Sangh considers society to be the main instrument of change. It believes that only with the complete involvement of society can social change happen. This explains Sangh's enormous focus on society. However, this can be fashioned only through individual preparedness and change, much like the man-making religion of Vivekananda that relies on a harmonious development of the body, mind and soul. The progression is defined as *'vyakti parivartan-samaj parivartan samgra parivartan'* referring to the thinking that changes in individuals will bring change in society, which will further bring complete change. This is because only when individuals bring loftiness in aptitude and conduct does the society change, and a complete and lasting transformation can only take place if there is a major societal change. Parivartan or change permeates Sangh literature. Thus, the RSS is inherently a forward-looking, futuristic organization.

I have had the opportunity of working with the past and present generation of RSS greats. As is our tradition, learning happens not only through teaching sessions and interactions but also through observation. I have known Mohan Bhagwat, the sarsanghchalak of the RSS, since my student days. In Sangh circles, he is addressed as Mohanji. In those days, he was the pracharak for Nagpur and Vidharbha regions. He was always tenacious about time schedules. Even today, Mohanji considers himself a swayamsevak of the Mohite Shakha and is attentive to the instructions of the teacher, or 'mukhyashikshak' leading that shakha. This deferential attitude of an organizational head towards those leading basic units is a valuable attitude.

Another important lesson has been the spirit of genuine camaraderie. Mohanji is a resolute practitioner of dialogue. The RSS training camp is called the Sangh Siksha Varg and its duration is for three years. The camps are held for fifteen, twenty and twenty-five days, respectively. The third year, called Tritiya Varsh, is held in Nagpur and there is a module where questions and answers are posed to the sarsanghchalak by ordinary swayamsevaks. In one such session, an undergraduate swayamsevak unhesitatingly asked Mohanji, 'What is the process for becoming the sarsanghchalak? What is the criteria?' Mohanji candidly explained the consultative process—how the main functionaries confer with each other and then cohere towards a decision. He then added that any swayamsevak could become a sarsanghchalak, while describing the comprehensive discussions that are held regarding the personal qualities of those who can shoulder such a responsibility. I have seen that most decisions in RSS are taken after wide-ranging debates and discussions. The RSS itself was named after a consultative process.

The latest instance of such free-flowing conversations came up on the matter of the RSS uniform, or Sangh Ganavesh. Discussions on this matter were initiated in the Vibhag Pracharak Baithak or the meeting of zonal in-charges. A zone is a group of two or three provinces of India. This matter came up again in the Akhil Bharatiya Karyakari Mandal (ABKM) Baithak, which is the all-India level body, where all office bearers of zonal- and state-level bodies meet. It was again discussed in the baithak of the Akhil Bharatiya Pratinidhi Sabha (ABPS)—the top decision-making body, like the general body of any public organization, having representations proportionate to the number of shakhas and swayamsevaks. Discussions took place over two to three rounds, but there was no consensus. So, Mohanji said that the decision would be paused until a consensus was reached. He decided that five years would be sufficient for a consensual approach and thereafter this matter would be taken up. As scheduled, the discussions resumed after five years. During this time, conversations took place at different levels and many options for the uniform were considered. I saw that many wanted the discussion to be concluded hastily, but Mohanji wanted to include everyone's views, and when most opinions that were recorded leaned towards wanting a change, the RSS general secretary or the sarkaryavah officially declared the change in uniform.

There can be differing viewpoints but when we meet and engage amongst ourselves and conduct dialogue with every section of society, solutions are imminent. Such is Mohanji's leadership. To attain this stature, the most important prerequisite is to get rid of one's ego. It is also the fundamental precept of organizational life. I have seen this quality in the top Sangh functionaries. The paraphernalia and rituals of leadership do not impact their consciousness. As a matter of habitual practice, they stay with ordinary, simple people. I experience the subtleties of this ethos every day in my work as the national organizing secretary of ABVP.

THE SANGH UNIVERSE

There is no generation gap in the Sangh. In the early 1990s, when many economic perspectives were being debated, as a young ABVP delegate to Swadeshi Jagaran Manch (SJM)—an RSS-affiliate body that is a platform for activist organizations to safeguard national economic interest—I used to have long conversations over cups of tea with the workers' movement stalwart and thinker, Dattopant Thengadi. Certain recollections stand out in my memory.

In 1990, Dr Babasaheb Ambedkar's birth centenary was celebrated, which coincided with the punya tithi (passing away) centenary of Mahatma Phule. Both these events were combined as 'Samajik Samrasta Sandesh Yatra' (nationwide march for social justice). In Maharashtra, the march began from Mahatma Phule's residence in Pune and terminated in Deekshabhoomi in Nagpur.

I was the organizer for the Nagpur leg of the march. Dattopant Thengadi had deep knowledge about Dr Ambedkar's life and a sworn commitment to social justice and he bequeathed this vision to young swayamsevaks like me.

Madan Das Devi, the previous sah sarkaryavah (joint general secretary) of the RSS, was the national organizing secretary of ABVP when I was a university student. He was a man of strict discipline. From him, I acquired the stamina and temperament for personal austerity. I have spent a lot of time working with Dattatreya Hosabale, the present sah sarkaryavah of the RSS. He is very interested in student networks and is always eager to know about what the students think and feel. He is very particular about expressive language and the profoundness of thought. It may just be a poster or a mere statement, but to pass Hosabale's scrutiny, the content has to be innovative and creative.

So, the Sangh universe is a very vigorous place to be a part of. After handling numerous responsibilities and extensive work, I became the national organizing secretary of ABVP in 2003. I travel to all corners of India for my work, and have been doing so for many years. There have been many memorable experiences— meticulous work in the northeast and southern parts of India, national security campaigns like the anti-infiltration agitation involving highly accurate surveys of 1000-km border areas and the launching and revamping of many student forums. The ABVP forum for international students, World Organization of Students and Youth (WOSY), was revamped in 2005–06 and is currently a robust body. It is a network of international students who come to study in various Indian universities and has developed a well-connected alumni community as well. It started an initiative to work with national institutes like the Indian Institutes of Technology, the Indian Institutes of Management and national law schools, and in the past ten years, it has experienced outstanding growth.

Among the youth, there prevails an environment of ideological awakening and the pursuit of debates. There are issues of globalization, nationalism, social justice for students, and equality for all castes and communities. ABVP has focused on these matters in a sustained manner and has contributed to the maturity of these social conversations and transformation.

None of this is easy and there are challenges. But we are trained to be undaunted, to have high perceptual intelligence and clarity of the goal.

The Sangh runs on the basis of good personal relations and teamwork. There are no rigid hierarchies of posts or seniority. It is a key RSS management principle. Decentralized and autonomous in form, collaborative in spirit, the Sangh's dynamism is distinctive and matchless.

This book explores many themes—RSS principles, governed by the values of Indian culture and its compatibility with modern notions of liberty. The Hindu identity of India, the regeneration and organization of Hindu society, views on the changing social trends impacting family, marriage, parenting, homosexuality, and various other subjects are discussed candidly. Since many words used belong to the RSS lexicon, a separate glossary of technical terms has also been appended.

The book delineates several roadmaps. All RSS roadmaps follow the basic premise of building on India's strengths and rectifying her weaknesses. Hence, the projects of poverty alleviation, social harmony, equality and unity, women's empowerment, history writing, education, culture, security and preservation of cultural values are important and elaborate.

The Sangh is a vehicle of unity for a powerful India. This is the story of India's future. This is the story of the RSS.

I

TRACING THE ORIGINS

Anyone attempting to understand the Sangh must get to know about the life of its founder, Dr Keshav Baliram Hedgewar, or Doctorji as he was reverentially known in his lifetime and even today. Anyone keen to understand the thinking pattern of swayamsevaks must visit a shakha. Doctorji has a tremendous influence on each and every swayamsevak of the Sangh, and the various incidents of his life provide extraordinary inspiration. Every swayamsevak voluntarily meditates on one life instance or value from Doctorji's life, discussed in every shakha, to refine his understanding of the Sangh and draw the direction and purpose of his own life.

Doctorji lived in a two-storey house in Nagpur, where he held his meetings with friends before the formation of the RSS. He was particular about cleanliness and orderliness, and even a small crease on a bare mat was not acceptable to him—such was his fabled discipline. Photographs of Lokmanya Tilak, Samarth Ramdas and Shivaji Maharaj adorned his meeting room. He lived a simple life, and as was the custom in those days, carried a walking stick embellished with a miniature lion and an inscription of the Sanskrit proverb, *'Na abhisheko, na samskraha; simhasya kriyate vanae, vikramarjita satvasya svayameva mrugendrata'* (No official ceremony is held nor any greetings sounded to declare that the lion is the king of the jungle). His resonance with the proverb that one becomes king by his own attributes and heroism reflects his brave temperament, as evidenced in multiple instances in his life.

FORMATIVE YEARS

Doctorji's residence in Nagpur was close to the palace of the erstwhile ruling family of Bhonsle. From childhood, he was aware of the British encroachment of the Bhonsle territory and heirlooms, and the atrocities that followed after the end of the Peshwa rule in Pune. His family belonged to a tradition of Hindu piety and was steeped in religious learning. Studying the Vedas was a tradition. Doctorji, too, was exposed to this knowledge system. But as a schoolgoing boy, he was more interested in the developments taking place in the real world.

He was a born patriot. Once, in his childish intensity, he formulated a plan with his school friends of digging a tunnel to the Sitabuldi Fort in Nagpur, from the house of Vaze Guruji, his teacher. The fort was a British garrison. In those times, the whole country was swept by a nationalist fervour, and for a young Keshav, the sight of the Union Jack was an unbearable visage. He wanted the Union Jack to go and the national flag to be hoisted in its place. When his teacher came to know of this plan, he dissuaded the children. However, he was silently pleased with Keshav. It may seem like a small incident, but it reflects the fierce attachment for the motherland that young Keshav bore in his heart. His patriotic fervour was not triggered by any personal encounter or a reactionary spurt but remained a stable emotion all his life.

Nagpur at the time was a fertile territory for nationalist activities. Doctorji, since childhood, was deeply influenced by Lokmanya Tilak, whose thoughts, writings and work held sway over Vidarbha and the surrounding regions, which were home to influential Congress committees.

As an enslaved nation then, India was bound by British laws and tied to a British monarch. The year 1897 marked the sixtieth anniversary of Queen Victoria's coronation. The British wanted a celebration, and so, on 22 June that year, sweets were distributed in schools to mark the occasion. To an 8-year-old Keshav, this was repulsive. He asked his brother how he could celebrate a monarch that held India captive. Young Keshav refused to eat the sweet that other children were accepting, and threw it in the dustbin. Similarly, he boycotted the celebrations marking the coronation of Edward VII in 1902. For a 12-year-old Keshav, participation in such celebrations was a matter of utter shame. Spellbound by the life of Chhatrapati Shivaji Maharaj, he absorbed the minutiae of Shivaji's life during class lessons and was eager to imbibe his valour.

Two impulses governed Doctorji's mind from an early age—respect for India and an antagonism towards foreign rule. He was profoundly affected by Tilak's writings in the newspaper, *Kesri*, and the clarion call of 'Swaraj is my birthright'. His longing for the motherland was so immersive that he placed India and the Indian society above everything else. He hardly thought about himself; it was always nation first.

Various accounts about Doctorji by his contemporaries reflect that nationalism was an innate quality he possessed. Writer and RSS Pracharak Naryanhari Palkar's descriptive account[1] details these characteristics of Doctorji's personality.

Doctorji lost his parents when he was very young. Nagpur was hit by a devastating plague for two years (1902–04), and on the same day, he lost both his parents—Baliram Pant Hedgewar, his father, and Revati, his mother. After this, the family, comprising his brothers and sisters, fell into financially trying times, which only made him more resilient.

The British government announced its decision to partition Bengal on 29 September 1905. This had a tumultuous impact throughout India and there was a vehement reaction. Bengal observed 16 October as a day of mourning, and it was supported by people in different parts of the country. Doctorji was an

[1]Narayan Hari Palkar, *Doctor Hedgewar Charit*, Lokhit Prakashan, Lucknow.

adolescent of 16 years at that time, and youngsters of the same age with nationalist inclinations would assemble at the residence of Dr Munje, an eye surgeon and freedom fighter. He was a prominent leader of the Congress in Central India, who later became the All India President of Hindu Mahasabha from 1927 to 1937. He was a respectable fatherly figure in Nagpur and Doctorji shared a good relationship with him.

'Vande Mataram' had become a nationalist mantra, a patriotic salute, and this mantra was reverberating in Nagpur. This was the backdrop for the Congress session of 1906 held in Calcutta (now Kolkata), when the movement against the partition of Bengal was at its height. While returning from this session, Lokmanya Tilak halted at Nagpur and addressed massive meetings there. 'Vande Mataram' was banned; raising the slogan could result in police action. The Risley Circular issued by the colonial administration prohibited students from participating in political activities. Alongside this political awakening, the age-old traditions of Hindu society acquired a patriotic hue.

In Maharashtra, as part of Dusshera celebrations, there was an old ritual of assembling in a procession and crossing the village frontier. During such a celebratory communion in Rampayli, a small village near the Madhya Pradesh and Maharashtra border, a young Keshav addressed the gathering and raised the slogan of 'Vande Mataram'. From that time onwards he was marked by the local police of the area and a case under Section 180 IPC was registered against Doctorji. But he remained undeterred and his nationalist leanings kept on increasing.

Doctorji was popular both with the students and teachers of his school—City High School. In 1908, the school inspector was greeted with 'Vande Mataram' by the schoolboys, the students being organized by Keshav. Naturally, an enquiry was ordered. All the students were roughly probed and asked to identify their leader. As pressure tactics, the students were dismissed from school. After student strikes and subsequent conciliatory efforts, most of the schoolboys yielded verbally. But Keshav refused to give in.

The development of the national education system was an outcome of the Swadeshi Movement along with other boycott movements in the wake of the Bengal Partition. It led to the setting up of a non-colonial school system. In 1909, Keshav was admitted to one such school—Vidyagriha Rashtriya Shala, Yavatmal—at the insistence of Dr Munje, Bapuji Aney, an educationist, freedom fighter and Congress leader who became the member of the Lok Sabha from 1950 to 1967; Shivram Paranjape, the founder of the Vidyagriha, and other notables of the province. Later, Dr Munje introduced Keshav to his childhood hero, Lokmanya Tilak, in whose house in Pune, Doctorji stayed for a while.

Information about Doctorji's interactions with Bengal revolutionaries is limited, yet comprehensive. Indian revolutionary and freedom fighter, Trailokyanath Chakravarty made multiple references to Doctorji in his book, *Jail Mein Tees Varsh* (30 Years in Prison), on Anushilan Samiti, a famous revolutionary organization that believed in armed struggle against the British. Anushilan Samiti was active in Bengal in the first quarter of the twentieth century. Its members were young, highly committed and had linkages with other like-minded revolutionary groups in Punjab and Maharashtra. The British feared the Samiti freedom fighters. In his lectures too, Trailokyanath Chakravarty, also a government of India awardee, recalled Doctorji as a bosom friend and a close associate in revolutionary activities. Doctorji was part of the drive that collected funds for the defence of the revolutionaries of the Anushilan Samiti who were facing trials in the Alipore Bomb Case.[2]

THE CALCUTTA YEARS

In 1910, it was not just medical education that drew Doctorji to Calcutta but also the patriotic ferment that had taken hold of the

---

[2]Narayan Hari Palkar, *Dr Hedgewar Charit*, p. 47, Lokhit Prakashan, Lucknow.

city. He was in touch with the revolutionary, Pulin Behari Das, who became the founder-president of the Dhaka Anushilan Samiti.

Trailokyanath Chakravarty, in his book, has presented the portraiture of his fellow freedom fighters, one of them being Doctorji. While he was in Calcutta, in 1913, the Damodar River floods wrecked large parts of Bengal, and many social organizations were active on the field to provide relief. Doctorji participated in the relief work done by Ramakrishna Mission and was lauded for his steadfast service on several accounts.[3] Similarly, in times of epidemics, Doctorji was an eager volunteer and used his medical degree for serving the poor and humble.

Makar Sakranti fairs are held in January in Gangasagar, which brings India's multitude to the Bay of Bengal. It is an ancient festival, an unbroken tradition of the observance of the solar cycle, marking the end of winter solstice and the beginning of longer days. For thousands of years, Indians have travelled from faraway distances to reach Gangasagar, an island in the Ganges delta. In colonial India, public health was dismal and massively neglected, and diarrhoea outbreaks were frequent in such gatherings. During such times, Doctorji went from hut to hut treating the affected people.

Doctorji popularized the Ganapati Festival in Calcutta during his stay in the various hostels of the city, which was transformed into a celebration of patriotism and identity. Following the completion of his medical education in Calcutta, Doctorji returned to Nagpur in 1915.

RISE OF THE YOUNG LEADER

Doctorji was to strengthen the Anushilan Samiti work in Nagpur—this was the thinking in the Samiti circles of that time. He started a gymnasium for the youth, with his close friends Bhauji Kawre

---

[3]Narendra Sehgal, *Viplawi Swatantrata Senani, Bharatvarsh Ki Sarvaang Swatantrata*, p. 86, Prabhat Publication, Delhi.

and Anna Khot, who, like him, had faith in revolutionary struggle. The gym exists to this day near the Sangh headquarters. Such gyms were commonly called akhadas or vyayamshalas. Doctorji and his associates organized debating clubs and undertook tours to raise awareness. He convinced a few businessmen and some big farmers to contribute to his patriotic work. 'Narendra Mandal' was the code name given to this group and the contributions raised were used to buy arms and ammunition for the revolutionaries. Freedom fighters were trained to become human couriers and were sent to Calcutta, Hyderabad and Goa to fetch this cache. One of his associates, Dada Saheb Bakshi, was a technical expert for fixing jammed revolvers, and gun repair work for revolutionaries operating in different provinces was carried out by this group.

Doctorji was in close contact with Punjabi and Bengali revolutionaries and volunteer youth couriers were used to ferry arms to freedom fighters. This task was fraught with risk, mandating the use of disguise and masking techniques. Doctorji personally ran this security drill. The revolutionary oath before the Hindu icons, Chhatrapati Shivaji Maharaj and Samartha Ramdas, was administered and lessons in patriotic literature were conducted to mentally prepare the volunteers to carry out grave tasks. Bhagat Singh's comrade Rajguru was sheltered by Doctorji. During this phase of his life, Doctorji developed a close bond with a Nagpur-based advocate, Appaji Joshi, who later went on to play a crucial role in the founding of the RSS.

India's struggle for independence produced several strands of thought and paths in which Doctorji was deeply involved. He worked with a diverse group of freedom fighters and the Indian National Congress (INC) as well, in the freedom struggle under the leadership of Gandhiji. Doctorji was even jailed during the Gandhian Satyagraha movements, as a part of the state committee of the Congress.

Doctorji's participation in Gandhiji's Non-cooperation Movement provoked the British to book him on charges of sedition. In those days, freedom fighters would generally not argue cases but Doctorji thought differently. He said that while readiness for the hangman's noose when working for the country was important, a jail sentence should not be interpreted as a sought-after sublime achievement. So, he prepared his arguments in the cases filed against him, and ultimately on 19 August 1921, he was sentenced to a one-year prison term.

While Doctorji was still in prison, Gandhiji[4] was arrested on 10 March 1922 and charged with sedition for writing articles against the British colonial rule in his weekly journal, *Young India*. Gandhiji was given a six-year jail sentence to be served in Mandalay prison and the entire country stood up in homage.

Upon Doctorji's release from jail on 12 July 1922, a rousing function was organized in an auditorium, Vyanktesh Natyagriha, in Nagpur, where top Congress leaders, Pt. Motilal Nehru, Vithalbhai Patel, C. Rajagopalachari and Dr S.A. Ansari were present. Pt. Motilal Nehru and Hakim Ajmal Khan also addressed the gathering. Doctorji was appointed the joint secretary for the 1922 state session of the Congress.

Meanwhile, some of his close revolutionary friends at the time were trying out social experiments of a different nature. Dr N.S. Hardikar[5] began the Hindustani Seva Dal. But some leaders in the Congress opposed this as they thought it had a military orientation and ran counter to the Congress discipline. This organization went on to become the Congress Seva Dal in later years. Ganga Prasad Pandey began a wrestling training club, Rashtriya Mallavidya Shalla, which taught traditional Indian

---

[4]Years of Arrest and Imprisonment of Mahatma Gandhi, mkgandhi.org, https://www.mkgandhi.org/arrestofmahatma.htm

[5]V.S. Narayana Rao, *Dr N. S. Hardiker*, p. 29, Ministry of Information and Broadcasting, Government of India, Publication Division, Delhi, 1982.

martial arts. Doctorji presided over the trust for this organization. Govind Ganesh Cholkar started a student orphanage, Anaath Vidyarthigriha, which was frequently used for underground revolutionary activities and in preventing conversions being carried out by missionaries. In January 1920, Doctorji's close friend, Dr L.V. Paranjpe started the Bharat Swayamsevak Mandal, with Doctorji as his chief colleague. The aim of the organization was to help in arranging public programmes, for which recruitment of youth was conducted through participation in study circles (swadhya mandal), anti-liquor protests, Ganesh Mahotsav, etc.

This was an intense time for Doctorji as he realized that revolutionary activities alone were not enough to gain India's freedom. Speaking at a gathering, where people had collected to register their protest against Gandhiji's arrest, Doctorji said, 'For establishing swarajya, it is necessary to acquire the physical strength of the opponent and then speak the language of peace. Only then it is reasonable. If you have to follow Mahatmaji, anoint yourself with tulsi (an auspicious Hindu ritual), forsake everything and join the nationalist struggle.' Doctorji believed that it was important to be strong to defeat the British and strength came from unity. In his experience, he had seen many organizations, including the Congress, fail due to infighting. Hence, he favoured an organization strong and free from frailty, with everyone fully devoted to the cause.

After Gandhiji's ascendance in the Congress, a new definition of Swaraj emerged for which Hindu-Muslim unity was a prerequisite. British machinations of the 'divide and rule' policy imposed the condition that Hindus and Muslims should come together for negotiations, whether related to administrative reform or representation in provincial assemblies. The Congress allowed itself to be trapped in this British conspiracy. The separatist group within the Muslim community utilized this as a device for practising two-nation politics. Thus, the benign-sounding phrase 'Hindu-Muslim unity' became a prerequisite. It was repeated in all the meetings of the Congress. The British exploited this theme—as did the fundamentalist Muslims—who sought the partition of the country. The absolute Congress support for the riotous Khilafat Movement in 1920 was a point of reckoning for Doctorji.

Accounts left by Doctorji's associates show that he found it unacceptable that a personality cult should become the basis for a national movement and regeneration. Gandhiji led powerful national movements, in which common people were also involved. The commitment of the people and workers was centred around Gandhiji.

Doctorji also observed that the Swadeshi Movement and Swadharma Movement, ignited by Lokmanya Tilak's towering personality, had petered out once he was jailed, although, people held on to Tilak's values. He realized that even the best leadership was subject to mortality.

Doctorji was convinced that the basis for liberation of the motherland and national service could not be located in any one personality. It was his firm belief that national service should be a determined system and process, and not personified.

The colonial epistemology that 'India was a nation in the making' was being planted firmly in writings and educational institutions. The contributions of Maharana Pratap, Chhatrapati Shivaji and Guru Gobind Singh to save India from the depredations of the invaders was sought to be erased systematically. To Doctorji, these historical stages were the fountainhead of India's independence strivings and her deep sense of sovereignty, and could not be compromised in any manner. He felt that whittling down the memory of India's great men and women was a dangerous portent, which would have a cascading effect on India's Hindu identity and ideals, and would harm the national purpose. India would end up bearing an insurmountable cost. He discussed these points with his brother colleagues.

INTELLECTUAL INFLUENCES

Doctorji received intense intellectual inspiration from books, especially two Marathi classics—*Dasbodh,* meaning advice to the disciple by Saint Samartha Ramdas; and *Geeta Rahasya,* a commentary on Bhagavadgita written by Lokmanya Tilak entirely from his memory of the sacred text while in prison. Ramdas was a great saint who lived in Maharashtra during the medieval period and was Shivaji Maharaj's spiritual preceptor, while Tilak was the nationalist hero.

Like Ramdas, Doctorji believed that anyone engaged in the work of society must be strong and possess the purity of body, mind and intellect. This required austere practice, a manifestation of high character, value-laden actions, hard work and an infinite commitment for the well-being of society. The organization of society for warding off attacks was a key principle of Ramdas, and the seer himself had established 1,100 maths, or monasteries, in his time. Doctorji was determined to raise swaymasevaks in this image and made his plans of bringing about change in India through the work of swayamsevaks.

From Ramdas and Shivaji, he also learnt the lesson on uniting the Hindu society. He believed that India was enslaved not only because of external forces that attacked her but also due to internal discord and divisions. A place was required where everyone could meet and conduct dialogues without discrimination and hierarchy. From this idea rose the concept of shakhas in the later years.

Since before the formation of the RSS, Doctorji would write a daily diary and the works of Ramdas were frequently cited in his notes, in the form of quotes. 'Without action, words are meaningless, without hardships and severe labour, a kingdom cannot be won,' were some of Ramdas's teachings that he valued highly and scribbled in his diary. A diary entry of 4 March 1929 on Ramdas notes: 'Sri Samarth did not want anything for himself. He mindfully guarded against self-pride which can flow from success and greatness. Ingraining this discipline, he devoted himself to the welfare of his people and a higher self-realization.'

Doctorji was fond of listening to the narrations of Shiva Charitra. Chanting of shlokas like *'Shubham karoti kalyanam'* (I pay my salutation to the light/lamp which brings auspiciousness; prosperity) and reading of *Ram Raksha* verses written by Ramdas were constant influences in his spiritual and temporal life. The saffron flag of the RSS can be traced to this thinking process. When Doctorji wrote letters, he always began with the auspicious Hindu signage of 'Shri' and quoted Tukaram, another great saint of Maharashtra, on the letterhead itself. One such letter, dated 6 April 1940, quoting Tukaram in the letterhead, states, *'Daya tiche nanwa bhutanche palan, aanik nirdalan kantkache'*, meaning 'compassion is not only the welfare of all living beings, but also includes protecting them from harm's way'.

BASIC SANGH PRINCIPLES

The first half of the twentieth century was a tumultuous time as India was overtaken by a national movement for freedom from colonial rule. The formation of the Sangh at the height of the freedom struggle in 1925 was influenced by these factors bursting forth on the national landscape apart from the unfolding developments and experiences that weighed on Doctorji's mind and influenced his perceptions about the basic principles of the Sangh, its formation and structure. His apprehensions, concerns and ideas during the course of the Sangh formation are extensively reported in the book, *Development of Sangh Methods*,[6] written by Bapurao Varanhapandey, a young swayamsevak from Nagpur who worked with Doctorji.

The principles on which the Sangh is shaped flowed from Doctorji's experiences. First, for the purposes of longevity and

---

[6]B.N. Baranhadpandey, *Evolution of the Sangh* (*Sangh Karyapadhati Ka Vikas*), Shreebharti Prakashan, Nagpur, 2016.

stability, movements needed to have a life of their own and strive for permanence beyond the lifespan of great personalities. Second, Hindu society for centuries was disorganized and in a state of perennial surprise attacks. It, therefore, required consistent work of several decades to instil confidence among commoners, for them to visibly become assertive nationalists. Third, the comprehensive awakening of national character was not possible on the basis of the qualities of a great leader alone. Many individuals, thus, had to work and tire themselves out continually because this was an unceasing process. Hence, such tasks could not be personality centred. What was required was a method that would invigorate the hearts and minds of many, who would become so steeped in this consciousness that they would give everything up to serve the causes of society. Good work ethics were required to stimulate lifelong commitment.

Doctorji was the originator, the seed, and like a seed, he buried himself deep in India's soil. He neither wanted control over the process nor displayed any ambition for popularity. With exceptional management acumen, he set his mind on only one thing—the need to get volunteers in thousands for national service, in every field of work and in every nook and corner of the country.

The idea of physical fitness originated when Doctorji was the secretary for the volunteer division and the head of logistics for the 1920 Congress session that hosted 14,583 delegates, 3,000 members of the reception committee and an audience of around 8,000 people. Many of his volunteers in khaki uniform manned the arrangements. These were early days, and Doctorji could assess that the volunteers required training and bodily fitness to measure up to their tasks.

Doctorji was a Congressman devoted to volunteering. Yet, he came out of it to start the RSS. This was because Congress's characteristics were entirely political and did not suit Doctorji's high ideals of selfless service for society. As Doctorji revealed in an honest, no-frills converzation with Gandhiji, who praised his methods of youth training, 'It was not possible to begin an organization like RSS within the Congress. It was not the question of money, but a question of Antahkarana.' Antahkarana is the Vedantic description of the psychological process that combines the subtle elements of mind, consciousness and intellect to go beyond the limitations of ego and self. Doctorji said that problems arose because the Congress leadership did not have the 'udaar antahkarana'[7] that was required for this purpose. Congress had many good people but since its foundational philosophy was purely political, every action was driven by politics and power play. Due to this framework, the Congress could not produce spontaneous volunteerism—instinctive dedication for an all-around national development. Therefore, Doctorji said, he created the RSS.

It was on the auspicious occasion of Vijayadashami on 27 September 1925 that the RSS was founded with the objective of strengthening society. This was followed by another meeting in which they conducted a discussion to determine the first task, which was to carry out some voluntary service activities on the occasion of Ramnavami festival at Ram temple in Ramtek, about 60 km from Nagpur. Doctorji founded the organization by defining its aims and objectives and developed an understanding about these aims among other swayamsevaks.

About seven months later, on 17 April 1926, a resolution for the name of the organization came up in the discussion held at Doctorji's residence. There were twenty-five members who voted, out of which twenty members approved the name 'Rashtriya Swayamsevak Sangh'; five were in favour of a different name, 'Jaripataka Mandal', while nobody supported the third option, 'Bharatodharak Mandal.' Finally, they adopted the name 'Rashtriya Swayamsevak Sangh', or the RSS. Raghunathrao Bande was appointed its interim or acting secretary[8] and was authorized to

---

[7]Register No. 001, p. 281, RSS Archives.
[8]Narayan Hari Palkar, *Dr Hedgewar Charit*, p. 152 (Fifth Edition), Lokhit Prakashan, Lucknow, 2014.

select two joint secretaries. Eventually, it was felt that the Sangh needed a leader, a family head and guide, in order to ensure simplicity in decision-making. At the end of the discussion, the choice fell on Doctorji. Although Doctorji continued to guide the RSS, he did not want to take on any post. However, over time, the RSS structure was formalized, and on 10 November 1929, on the request of all members, a post was created and Doctorji assumed charge as the sarsanghchalak. As a member, he was duty-bound to accept the post.

Reflecting its belief system and attitude, the word for 'post' in the Sangh is 'responsibility'. Work is more important than the person assigned to it. The same is taught to the swayamsevaks.

Doctorji laid great emphasis on self-reliance. Since the beginning of the Sangh, he started the practice of monetary contributions in the form of guru dakshina to run the Sangh. On the occasion of Guru Poornima in 1927, the swayamsevaks offered guru dakshina before the saffron flag for the first time. According to the records of the Sangh, a total of ₹84 and some annas were collected. Even today, in every shakha, the swayamsevaks follow this tradition. They offer contributions of their own free will, depending on their economic ability. Many times, I have seen poor swayamsevaks queuing up with the rich to offer their contributions. Expenses of the organization are met with this money. Due to this clean and self-reliant financial arrangement, the Sangh continues to work without depending on any individual or party. This spirit is the true basis of the Sangh's strength and Doctorji's vision.

The quest for permanence, certainty and the need to avoid crests and troughs of growth and decline led Doctorji to enshrine two consecrated symbols—the saffron flag and the slogan 'Bharat Mata ki Jai'. From time immemorial, the saffron flag has defined India and her eternal values of sacrifice, renunciation, valour and learning. All great warriors, from Maharana Pratap to Chhatrapati Shivaji, carried it, scholars wrote odes to it and mystics meditated on it. The saffron flag became the RSS flag. The phrase *'Bharat Mata ki Jai'* consecrates India as Sacred Mother. With these twin inspirations, swayamsevaks started humbly and built the RSS courageously.

2

DOCTORJI'S VISION: IDEAS THAT SHAPED THE SANGH

When Doctorji established the RSS, he was 36 years old. He had no aspirations for personal leadership because if he would have, then with the enormous hardships and privations he subjected himself to, he would have founded a political party, which was not his motivation.

Doctorji was chosen to become the leader because of his demonstrated ability. He was the first sarsanghchalak and was conscious that he was creating a template of behaviour and personality for the rest of them. So, he always stayed in the background while the organization, the RSS, came in the foreground and centre stage. He was forward-looking and went beyond conventional thinking. He knew that many organizations disintegrated when their leaders were at the end of their lives. So the 'babugiri' culture was shunned. The RSS was intended to live through its swayamsevaks.

He placed his faith in the common people. From amongst them he raised his swayamsevaks and through them he carried out his struggle against the British colonial rule. Prior to India's independence, a sworn pledge of every swayamsevak before the RSS saffron flag included the words, 'freedom for the Hindu Rashtra'. After India won its freedom, this was changed to 'comprehensive development of Hindu Rashtra'. An immeasurable love and respect for India and her people was at the core of his being. Doctorji was focused on the organization of the Indian nation on the basis of its values, culture and traditions. Thus, a preliminary quality for anyone wishing to become a swayamsevak is to bear a feeling of brotherhood towards his/her fellow country people. This gives rise to the ethics of service, called seva. This vision gave primacy to the work of the Sangh. To this day, Doctorji's life and vision deeply influence each and every swayamsevak as much as it had influenced the second sarsangchalak, M.S. Golwalkar, fondly called Guruji.

INVALUABLE CONTRIBUTION

Whenever Doctorji visited other parts of the country, meeting up with the notables of those regions was an important part of his itinerary. Only meeting kindred people or those associated with Sangh activities was not a part of his mentality. A worthy Hindu belonging to any party or ideology was a person of interest for him. He reached out to such people to explain Sangh's activities and also to attract them to the Sangh fold. Therefore, he met even those who were opposed to him or placed hurdles in the way of his work.[9]

The influence of the Sangh gradually widened. Celebrating its reach and strength, the Sangh celebrated Independence Day on 26 January 1930 at all the Sangh shakhas formed till then. Thousands of swayamsevaks actively participated in India's freedom movement and the Sangh openly supported them. In 1930, Doctorji led thousands of Satyagrahis during Gandhiji's Civil Disobedience movement, known as Jungle Satyagraha in Maharashtra. Along with nine senior swayamsevaks, Doctorji was incarcerated and had to spend one year in prison.

The Sangh also played a significant role in Chimur during the Chimur-Ashti Movement. Swayamsevaks participated in the historic

---

[9]Narayan Hari Palkar, *Dr Hedgewar Charit* (Fifth Edition), p. 193, Lokhit Prakashan, Lucknow, 2014.

Quit India Movement in which Ramakant Keshav Deshpande, a lawyer and social activist, was sentenced to a life term, which was later converted to a jail term. It was after independence that Deshpande started working for the Janjatiyas or tribal people in Chhattisgarh and founded the Vanavasi Kalyan Ashram for tribal people in 1952. Goa's liberation and integration with India was marked by peaceful satyagraha by swayamsevaks. Dadra and Nagar Haveli also saw the commitment of swayamsevaks to the motherland, where hundreds of them controlled the situation.

The RSS views participation in the freedom struggle as a natural duty that the daughters and sons of Mother India performed.

LEADERSHIP CHOICE

Today, most people know about the RSS but very few know about Doctorji. What made him special? There are great leaders who have a vision but it is limited to their lifespan. Then there are leaders who are far-sighted, but cannot create an instrument in their lifetime to either implement their vision or carry it to the next generation. And then there are leaders like Doctorji who had a long-term vision and were able to create an instrument that not only worked in their lifetime but was powerful enough to carry the work forward into the future generations as well.

Doctorji was a unique personality. His vision was not encumbered by the limitations, prejudices and ideas of the present. He visualized the strengths and weaknesses of both the past and the present. And thus, an instrumentality was created that was realistic, futuristic and balanced. It was not a theoretical model but a practical method that was not dependent on him. This self-driven instrument was the Sangh Shakha—its methods and thoughts. It has stood the test of time; it is a robust, organic movement. The growth and stability of the RSS movement verifies Doctorji's hypothesis. He had hypothesized correctly that the problems are chronic and cannot be solved by any one political party or government, but instead by the involvement of common people.

Important problems, Doctorji felt, could not be solved by administration as the solution lay in social consensus, which had to be brought about by the voluntary determination of the people. He believed that volunteerism of the common masses would build our nation and this required strong character. Therefore, the RSS was never meant to be an elite club or governed by specific interest groups; it was conceived essentially as an organization of common people. It has continued to remain beyond caste, profession and social status; and as it expands, it has an inbuilt capacity to involve people from all walks of life.

It was this thought that brought in the remarkable unconventionality in the Sangh's leadership choices. When the time came for succession, Appaji Joshi, considered to be Doctorji's right hand, was asked why he had not been chosen as the next sarsanghchalak. Why was Guruji, who was only 34 at that time, given this responsibility. Affirming his closeness to Doctorji, Appaji said, 'If I am Doctorji's right hand, Guruji is his heart'. Guruji knew how to implement Doctorji's vision; he was the best person. Guruji was meritorious and young. Doctorji had spotted this ability in the time that both spent traversing the country. So, there are no straitjackets or preferential treatment. Even today, anyone with proven ability can lead the Sangh.

Network expansion in the RSS does not only mean increase in the number of shakhas but also the inclusion of different streams of people and beliefs. It is only a matter of time before Muslims and Christians, too, start feeling that the RSS is an organization for all of us. This is the assimilative current of Hindu society, which is the basic characteristic of India. Therefore, when the Sangh advances, it is not to imperil others or strike fear. The Sangh is India's biggest assimilative and integrative force.

Doctorji often said, 'The British should go but we must analyse why we were subjugated and why we were not able to overcome the invaders.' This question nagged him. After deep thought, he concluded that it was because we had lost our cultural unity and our sense of identity as Bharatiya that India was repeatedly enslaved. The restoration of that identity, the unity of people and connecting India's past to her future became his life's task and mission. From this central idea the core postulates of Sangh thought emerged. These postulates are cultural nation or Rashtriyata, spiritual unity or Ekatmata, and oneness or Samuhikta.

Rashtriyata or Cultural Nation

The Sangh considers language to not only be a medium of communication but also a carrier of culture. It firmly believes that all languages and dialects should get their space and respect, especially ancient languages like Sanskrit and Tamil, which have a history of thousands of years and have been fellow travellers of Bharat's glorious history. It is necessary to promote all Indian languages.[10]

Many fear that seeking inspiration from the past will also mean revival of the inequities of the bygone era, but the Sangh has clarified on numerous occasions that, 'We want to bring back the best traditions of the past and also change the wrong practices that have crept into society.' The Sangh does not view the past, present or future as separate or disjointed but believes in a continuum that links all three. It believes in using the accumulated knowledge and experience of the past as a foundation and reference point for its present and future activities. The stronger this foundation, the better will be the progress.

---

[10]'ABPS Resolution: Need to Protect and Promote Bharatiya Languages', http://rss.org//Encyc/2018/3/10/abps-rsolution-2018.html, Access date 12 July 2019.

The Sangh has always believed that while adopting modern ways of life, the ancient tradition and practices should not be abandoned. Hence, the Sangh has continuously strived to ensure, both before and after independence, that ancient symbols and traditions are given appropriate place in society.

Sangh critics have presented this as the 'Hindutva' viewpoint and, therefore, contemptible. Let us examine what these Hindutva traditions are, the dharma practices considered sanatan or eternal.[11] These are the virtues of honesty, refraining from injuring living beings, purity, goodwill, mercy, patience, forbearance, self-restraint, generosity and asceticism. Barring asceticism, which is the terrain of a few, most qualities are an absolute set of duties or religiously ordained practices incumbent upon all Hindus, regardless of class, caste or sect. Can we justify the rejection of the symbols and practices of a civilization thousands of years old just because of its Hindu roots?

Ekatmata or Spiritual Unity

Everything in the universe is connected with each other; each separate living being has a link with all other life forms. This includes human beings too. This is the essence of Indian knowledge, which has been expressed in different languages, in numerous scriptures by sages and others in eras gone by. It is this philosophy that the Sangh propagates. This leads to a culture of mutual understanding, of forging links between different groups of people. In my opinion, these linkages bind the entire society in a common culture despite its diversity. That's why Sangh says that India is a cultural nation and its foundation is in Ekatmata. The Sangh has expended much energy in restoring this and wants to guide the entire society along this path.

---

[11]Rakesh Sinha, 'Hindutva movement and Politics', https://www.academia.edu/29166068/Hindutva_movement_and_Politics

My experience with the Sangh has proved that it is an integrative force trying to create harmony, trust and mutual respect. The fundamental purpose of Sangh work is the addition of new people and reaching out to more. If a decision requires four people, an attempt is made to consult eight, or if it requires eight, sixteen are involved. The idea is to involve the maximum number of people. The Sangh's ethos is to act with a collective spirit. The manner in which its meetings are held supports a consultative process.

Similarly, critical feedback is never discarded as being incorrect. The Sangh doesn't determine its opinion or action on the basis of the view of the majority alone. It makes realistic decision on the basis of fact and logic. Hence, the Sangh's temperament is scientific and its decisions are logically derived.

We are committed to instil this element of oneness in society as well. The Upanishad verse, '*Sam gachhwadham, sam vadadhwam sam vo manaansi jaanatam. Deva Bhagam Yatha Poorve sanjaanaanaa upasate*,' which means 'Let us come together, let us speak together. Let our minds be of one accord as the gods of old sat together in harmony to worship' is a mantra of the RSS. The doctrine of samuhikta stipulates that only when society irons out its internal differences can a nation progress. Thus, reaching out to people is a task of national interest.

ON RELIGION

According to the Indian tradition, the truth is one, but the wise ones call it by different names—'*Ekam sat, Vipra Bahudha Vadanti*'. Therefore, no one should be discriminated against because of differences in the modes of worship. This is a critical difference between the Sangh and The Hindu Mahasabha. Hindu Mahasabha, a nationalist group formed in 1905 to give Hindus a stronger voice in politics during the British rule, wanted representation of people on the basis of religion.[12] The Sangh, on the other hand, made no such demand at any stage. It always propounded the idea that Bharat belongs to all who were born here and continue to live here, irrespective of religion, faith or the school of thought they may belong to.

After the Partition of India, Guruji, the second sarsanghchalak, gave a call to all swayamsevaks to work for the victims of partition irrespective of their religion, saying that it was a tragedy for everyone and that the Sangh would treat it as one. Swayamsevaks worked tirelessly, providing relief to all. The Sangh's relief work during the Partition was taken note of by every Congress leader, including Gandhiji.

Pt. Jawaharlal Nehru's speech, as the first prime minister of India, in the convocation ceremony of the Aligarh Muslim University on 24 January 1948, is a powerful corroborative evidence of an awareness of a common cultural inheritance. Raising some valid questions in this speech, he said, '...I am proud of our inheritance and our ancestors who gave an intellectual and cultural pre-eminence to India. How do you feel about this past? Do you feel that you are also sharers in it and inheritors of it and therefore, proud of something that belongs to you as much as to me?' He added, 'You are Muslims and I am a Hindu. We may adhere to different religious faiths or even to none; but that does not take away from that cultural inheritance that is yours as well as mine. The past holds us together; why should the present or future divide us in spirit?'[13]

Admittedly, at the time of the country's partition, religion became a reason for much violence. The Sangh opposed the division on religious lines, and so, when Gandhiji agreed to the Partition, the Sangh was disheartened and condemned the decision. Later,

---

[12]Rakesh Sinha, *Aadhunik Bharat Ke Nirmata* (Fourth Edition), p. 126, Prakashan Vibhag, New Delhi.

[13]J.L.N. Nehru, Nehru AMU Convocation Speech, https://www.scribd.com/doc/67416161/Nehru-AMU-Convocation-Speech-24-Jan-1948, 1948.

when certain individuals assassinated Gandhiji, Sangh detractors saw the tragedy as an opportunity to blame the Sangh, although investigations and enquiries later negated this viewpoint. In fact, Gandhiji had praised Sangh activities on various instances. On 16 September 1947, Gandhiji visited a shakha in Valmiki Basti, an enclave of so-called lower castes, where more than five-hundred swayamsevaks were present. He praised the Sangh for its work, as he had done earlier in 1934. This news was published in *The Hindu* newspaper on 17 September 1947.

Sardar Patel, too, debunked the negative perception about the Sangh. During his 6 January 1948 address on the All India Radio in Lucknow, he mentioned the swayamsevaks, 'They are patriots and they love their motherland.' After the assassination of Gandhiji, in a letter to Pt. Nehru on 27 February 1948, he wrote, 'After the examination of all accused, it is clear that the RSS has no role in the assassination of Gandhiji.'[14] But despite this, Pt. Nehru, due to political reasons, was biased and the ban on the Sangh was withdrawn only after a countrywide Satyagraha conducted by swayamsevaks on 12 July 1949.

Once, Deen Dayal Upadhyay, one of the Sangh thinkers and co-founder of the Bharatiya Jan Sangh and the precursor to the Bharatiya Janata Party (BJP), was asked about the fate of Muslims in Bharat. The questioner implied that as the Sangh was engaged in aggregating the Hindus, it would weaken the Muslims. He replied that as the Hindus in India were known for their coexistence values, Muslims would come to no harm and they needed to be free of fear.

India was partitioned mainly because of the Muslim League, which wanted a nation of their own. Muslims living in India are better off here than any other place, they have more democratic freedom and representative rights than any other place in the world. In India, there are various sects of Islam who practise their beliefs without fear, which is not possible even in Islamic states.

---

[14]"Prakashkey Evam Lekhak Ki Baat', Archives of RSS, www.archivesofrss.org

Religious conversions and secessionist activities in some parts of the country, particularly in tribal-dominated regions, present a fundamental threat to the values, ideals and principles of India. In the beginning, the Congress was alive to such issues but gradually developed a clear disconnect and disregard. For instance, to resolve and address the threat arising out of the religious conversion of the Hindus into Christianity, engineered by the Christian missionaries through money, coercion and deceit, the Congress government of Madhya Pradesh had set up the Niyogi Committee on Christian Missionary Activity (1956), but it did not implement the committee recommendations.[15]

Another example of a similar conversion activity of the Christian missionaries and secessionist insurgency arose in the northeast. The then information and broadcasting minister of India, Indira Gandhi, wrote a letter to Swami Ranganathananda of the Ramakrishna Math. In her letter, dated 21 July 1965, she requested the Math to open schools in the region for the tribal people.[16] This was requested because Christian missionaries ran educational and health institutions in the tribal hinterland and used it as a springboard for conversion. As a prime minister, Indira Gandhi too, had expressed grave concerns on the spurt of religious conversions of the Hindus to Islam in Meenkashipuram, Tamil Nadu.

What successive governments have acknowledged in a muted manner, the Sangh announced loudly. Conversion is a threat, particularly in tribal and underprivileged areas. The Sangh has expanded its footprint in these spheres. It is a high-priority focus. The Sangh runs a wide range of diverse programmes through its Vanavasi Kalyan Ashram, a social welfare organization, dedicated to the tribal people, and is headquartered in Jashpur, Chhattisgarh.

---

[15]'The Niyogi Commitee Report', Vishva Hindu Parishad, http://vhp.org/dim5-the-niyogi-committee-report/
[16]'The Beginning', Golden Jubilee Celebration 2018, Ramakrishna Mission, Viveknagar, Aalo, http://www.ramakrishnamissionaalo.org/

The Sangh is not a political party but a social organization. It has no political intent nor does it work for any political outcome but it has a political impact on national political life. Even though it stays away from politics, its shakha system has produced swayamsevaks who are now in politics and have attained high positions. These are incidental facts. The general line in Sangh is that the RSS will do nothing other than running shakhas but the swayamsevaks will enter every sphere of activity. The swayamsevaks work in all domains of society—education, politics, economy, security and culture.

RSS has only one goal—making India great. It is dedicated to the cause of a corruption-free Bharat. The Sangh works for uniting all castes and for establishing a strong Hindu society. Some people want mechanical imitations of the Western model of education, industry, administration and health services, while the Sangh wants to create new systems that are in line with the native ideas of this land.

The Sangh leadership has always been aware and conscious of new technologies, particularly the ones related to nuclear weapons and satellite communications. It also puts a premium on the development of indigenous technologies to prevent dependency on other countries. It believes that we should modify technologies developed elsewhere in the world to suit our conditions. Two things must always be kept in mind while adopting technologies. One, technology should never replace human beings because though it may be faster than humans, it cannot be a substitute for human beings. Whenever human interest has been overlooked in favour of machines, the consequences have been adverse and undesirable. One such example is the mindless adoption of technology, causing environmental pollution. The Sangh advocates the use of eco-friendly technologies, particularly those that have an indigenous origin.

In the RSS worldview, social change is a time-consuming process and must be based on a realistic assessment of the preparedness of society and its surrounding environment. That makes the change stable. Therefore, it does not believe in spontaneous and random revolutions. Its activities are plan-driven, directed by experience, conviction and pragmatic imagination.

In summation, the RSS philosophy is the eternal spirit of Bharat. It is based on the following lines:

Om Sarve Bhavantu Sukhinah
Sarve Santu Niraamayaah |
Sarve Bhadraanni Pashyantu
Maa Kashcid-Duhkha-Bhaag-Bhavet |
Om Shaantih Shaantih Shaantih ||

Om, may all become happy,
May all be healthy (free from illness)
May all see what is auspicious,
May no one suffer in any way.
Om peace

3

SHAKHA SYSTEM AND STRUCTURE: HOW THE RSS WORKS

When Doctorji began the Sangh on Vijayadashami in September 1925, he did not make any grandstanding speeches, nor were any of his announcements printed in the papers. He did not offer any blueprint or programmes. The RSS has no written constitution as Doctorji gave primacy to the creation of the organization, not paperwork. Publicity was shunned as a matter of principle. With rare self-assuredness forged out of great personal hardships, Doctorji embarked on his mission with a band of twenty-five young swayamsevaks.

The first acting secretary of the Sangh, Raghunathrao Bande, diligently recorded the details of the meetings of the Sangh and prepared the minutes for its formation and the incorporation of his name. After the constitution and naming of the Sangh, the first meeting of the RSS was held at Doctorji's residence on 9 May 1926. It resolved the basics—to assemble every fortnight, and set up physical fitness gymnasiums. Discussions were conducted on the uniforms for swayamsevaks and the logistics for the Shiv Jayanti festival, an important highlight of the RSS almanac. The meeting on 21 June 1926, held at a students' orphanage, deliberated over its working methods.

A key meeting on 12 December 1926 to impart military education to the swayamsevaks. The day and time were fixed at six O' clock in the morning of every Sunday. It was around this time that the structure of the RSS emerged. A meeting on 19 December 1926 averred that for the ease of decision-making and for discipline purposes, one person needed to be the reference point. The nomenclature for this was 'person of authority.' A consensus resolution gave this position to Doctorji. He assumed charge as sarsanghchalak on 10 November 1929. 'Our national identity is Hindu identity' was Doctorji's grammar of nationalism. The RSS was formed to re-establish this identity.

THE FIRST SHAKHA

The shakha seen today went through phases of evolution. Nana Hari Palkar's book describes the first shakha. In Doctorji's house, there was an assemblage of twenty teenagers. Bhauji Kawre, Anna Soni, Vishwanathrao Kelkar, Balaji Huddar and Bapurao Bhedi were some of the attendees mentioned. The term 'baithak', denoting meeting, is traced to this phase.

Doctorji used to frequent the local gymnasiums like Nagpur Vyayamshala and Maharashtra Vyayamshala to recruit swayamsevaks. Vyayamshala was a revolutionary tradition in Bengal and Maharashtra. Swami Vivekananda who taught Raja Yoga to the West was its great votary. In Bengal, 'byam samities' were connected to freedom struggle leaders like Rishi Aurobindo, Jatindranath Mukherji alias Bagha Jatin, and many Anushilan heavyweights. Wrestling and stick-fighting exhibitions were common in the meetings of the time. The gymnasiums were the identified catchment areas where nationalist youth congregated, so Doctorji decided to look there.

Soon after, Itwar Dwara Prathamik Shala (now Aditwar Darwaza), Sangh's own physical fitness programme, began. Anna Soni began teaching the lathi drills. After 28 May 1926, the content of shakha schedules was systematized. Beyond Nagpur, the shakha footprint was first planted in Wardha. The famous khaki shorts uniform was also instituted during this phase. This uniform was designed by Doctorji and was worn originally by the volunteers of Bharat Sevak Samaj that he created for the 1920 Congress Nagpur session.

SHAKHAS: MICROCOSMS OF INDIA

The precursor of the shakha system was the swadhyaya mandal or study circles. Later, physical fitness programmes were added and training camps began. As these gradual layers got added, the daily shakhas commenced.

The shakha timetable is an hour long. Its main components are standardized and have been the same since the time of its commencement. These are sharirik physical drills, boudhik intellectual or academic discussions, khel games and samta practice sessions for systematic parade. The RSS flag hoisting at the beginning of the shakha is protocol driven and swayamsevaks are taught to stand in attendance. The shakha closes with a prayer. There is a fair bit of localization in the choice of games to be played and subjects to be discussed. The Sharirik Vibhag (Department of Physical Fitness) and Boudhik Vibhag (Department of Intellectual and Cultural Affairs) are dynamic, as they study feedback and absorb changes. Those assigned as 'shikshak' or teachers in the shakhas go through a vigorous training process. To ensure that the shakha system works efficiently and regularly, regional and national 'adhikari' or office-bearers of the RSS tour extensively.

Just like the cell is the basic unit of a living organism, the shakha is the basic unit of the RSS. Every swayamsevak has a shakha to which he belongs. In my case, as a child growing up in Nagpur, I was part of the Mohite Shakha. When I moved to Sitabuldi, I was part of Choti Dhantoli Shakha and then Congress Nagar Shakha. When I moved to Mumbai in 2003, Shivaji Udyan Prabhat became my shakha.

Although, the discussions in the shakha are just for an hour, for the swayamsevaks, the timeline is twenty-four hours. Every swayamsevak is available 24x7 on call for the organization/society, especially during a natural calamity or an accident. Their duties don't end by merely visiting the shakha. There are no deactivated swayamsevaks. The shakha system ensures that everyone remains spirited. This means that no swayamsevak becomes a swayamsevak for a particular duration like members in other organizations. Swayamsevaks voluntarily commit for their lifetimes, which influences their families as well.

Shakhas are held in the morning, evening and night to cater to the increasing numbers and to incorporate diverse time schedules for people of various age groups. Weekly get-togethers called 'saptahik milans' are also held. Those who cannot come to the shakha can come to the monthly 'Sangh mandalis' or groups. These are non-shakha formations, informal setups convertible to shakhas on maturation. If Sangh mandalis gain critical mass in terms of engagement, they are moved up the value chain into weekly meetings, and if these experience traction, they progress to become daily shakhas and acquire a more formal structure. Through such sequential progression, the shakha network expands.

In March 2019, there were 37,011 shakha assemblies held throughout the country, and the total number of shakhas on the said date was 59,266. Saptahik milans were around 17,229 and 8,382 'masik milan' or monthly meets were accounted for. These statistics were presented at the ABPS by Suresh Joshi, the RSS sarkaryavah, fondly addressed as Bhaiyyaji by the people.

The captain of a shakha is the 'mukhya shikshak' or the head teacher. While travelling across the country, national and regional office-bearers of the RSS conduct reviews with the mukhya shikshak and discuss how to improve the shakha system.

DOCTORJI'S DIALOGUE WITH GANDHIJI

In December 1934, the Sangh training camp was held in Wardha, where Gandhiji was on his visit to Wardha Sevagram Ashram.

Gandhiji sent a message through his personal secretary, Mahadev Desai,[17] expressing his inclination to visit the Sangh training camp. So, on 25 December 1934, at the appointed time of six O' clock in the morning, Gandhiji visited the camp, along with twenty-five Wardha Sevagram Ashram inmates. Around 1,500 swayamsevaks were present in their uniforms at the Sangh Wardha training camp. According to archival sources, Gandhiji appreciated the manner in which welcome salutations were expressed, along with the uniformity, equality and cleanliness of the camp. He told Appaji Joshi, a close associate of Doctorji, 'I am very happy. I have not seen a more alluring scene than this.' Gandhiji observed that within an hour, everyone's meal was taken care of. He asked about the costs, adding that in the Congress, the expense per person was ₹1 for two meals. He was surprised and wondered how the Sangh managed with such a small budget—₹1 for nine meals. Appaji responded by saying that everyone who attended the Sangh training camps brought their own rations, useable items and minor subscriptions; therefore, everything could be conducted at nominal costs. On co-mingling and co-working of castes, Gandhiji asked the swayamsevaks how they interacted, to which he got a response in Hindi—'Hum sab Hindu hai aur hum sab bandhu hai,' meaning 'We are all Hindus and we are all brothers'. When Gandhiji wanted to know what the Sangh did to get rid of caste inequities, everyone pointed to Doctorji's training, which stressed upon everyone working together.

The next day, on 26 December, Gandhiji met Doctorji at the Wardha Ashram where he praised Doctorji's work and asked him about the RSS's constitution. When Gandhiji asked Doctorji the definition of a swayamsevak, Doctorji replied,

> One who would happily, of his own free will and with goodwill towards all, succeed in submitting everything for the national cause, I would consider him a swayamsevak leader.

---

[17]'Fundamental Works', *The Diary of Mahadev Desai* Volume I, Gandhi Heritage Portal.

My target is to raise such swayamsevaks. In this organization, there is no difference between a leader and a swayamsevak. We are all swayamsevaks. Bearing equality towards all, we make no distinctions and have no place for hierarchies.

Even today in the RSS, no task is high or low. Everyone has to handle the tasks assigned to them.

When Gandhiji probed Doctorji about the budget and asked whether help was provided by the house of Bajaj, Doctorji clarified that financial help was not sought. The RSS ran with the gurudakshina money—modest contributions of the swayamsevaks. Despite the clarification, Gandhiji was still sceptical about this model working when the work would no longer be limited and small. Not to be cowed down, Doctorji added that when people would realize that the RSS's work was vital for society's sustenance, they themselves would come forward with wealth contributions. At such a time, financial help would not be opposed or refused.

SHAKHA TEACHINGS

In all the shakhas, the most important lesson taught is—India is a Hindu Rashtra. India developed on a profound understanding of unity which finds expression in the conduct of relations and behavioural patterns. This is the tradition of Indian knowledge systems and culture, and is Hindu in essence. Preservation and development of these values and symbols are a high-priority task. Pride in India's culture and history, propagating it as worthy of emulation and recalibrating this ancient wisdom in the modern times is key to the Nation First theory. From this flows the paramountcy of unity and integrity of India. This is the principle of Akhand Bharat, or national integration.

The Sangh believes that prejudices and differences based on caste, region and wealth should not exist in society. Diversity is celebrated as different manifestations of Hindu culture. Cooperation, mutual respect and peace in the conduct of world affairs is the message it wants to convey. These fundamental precepts constitute the Hindu Rashtra and are explained in a simple form.

The Sangh seeks inspiration from India's heritage and classical learning. It is modern because it is adaptive and has the capacity to absorb the changes that are taking place in the society. This creates its connectedness with the next generation.

The shakha system is a juggernaut for service to society; it has no desire to be hegemonic or overwhelm society with its ideas, policies and practice. It is inherently responsive, mirrors society's requirements and is aware that change is a complex process.

By 1940, the Sangh network had reached all parts of the country. Doctorji had predicted the intertwining of the Sangh and India. In his last speech at the Sangh Shiksha Varg or training camp, Doctorji said, 'I am seeing a microcosm of India today.'

Doctorji passed away in 1940. He was only 51.

TO THE DEFENCE OF SOCIETY

By the time Doctorji passed away in 1940, expansion had taken place and a structure for transmitting Sangh ideas was fully functional. The political climate was stormy. India was in the throes of its freedom struggle; World War II had begun and swayamsevaks were participating in the Quit India Movement led by Gandhiji. According to British records, in a place called Asti near Nagpur, eight freedom fighters were hanged, and two of them were swayamsevaks. At the same time, the dark clouds of communalism were gathering. The appeasement of the Muslim League and the accommodation of two-nation politics by the Congress was an attack on Hindu society. Direct action, increasing violence against the Hindu community, Gandhiji's consistent instruction to Hindus for peace while embracing the likes of Suhrawardy, the butcher of Calcutta killings, emboldened Jinnah and the Muslim League. It turned the apparition of Pakistan into a reality. India won its independence but Partition was the heavy price it paid for it.

In such a situation, M.S. Golwalkar or Guruji, who was the sarsanghchalak at that time, rose like a 'parivrajak saviour', or a monk who travels for doing public good. It was the patriot-monk's greatest challenge and he gave every fibre of his being to it. As he led with yogic self-mastery and élan, thousands of swayamsevaks followed him to defend Hindu society in the bloodlands of West Punjab and the North-West Frontier Province (NWFP), both of which are now in Pakistan.

Guruji expanded the Sangh work in West Punjab, travelling frequently to Lahore and Karachi. In Punjab, there were 1,500 shakhas comprising 84,820 swayamsevaks. Each shakha had attendees within the range of 80–100. Punjab was divided into seven regions, or kshetras—Multan, Rawalpindi, Lyallpur, Jammu, Jalandhar, Amritsar and Lahore. In July-August 1947, two Sangh training camps were conducted. The training camp in West Punjab drew 1,937 swayamsevaks, and 338 attended from Lahore. However, the Sangh training camps were terminated prematurely because of the Partition. Swayamsevaks in all the shakhas were issued directions to fan out, protect imperilled Hindu families, transport them to safety and run camps in the east for the refugees from West Punjab.

Relief and rescue missions in different localities and towns were undertaken by a Punjab relief committee formed for this purpose. Since March 1946, this committee had started its work for Hindu refugees streaming from the NWFP into Lahore. From Sindh, an influx of Hindu refugees came into Rajasthan, in Kota and Ajmer; and to Gujarat and Mumbai. In all these, places the shakha network was galvanized to protect the Hindu society and defend the honour of Hindu women who were the routine targets of abductions and insensate violence. Islamic raids were common in Poonch and Rajouri sectors of Jammu and Kashmir (J&K). Here, too, the shakha system was working in a concerted pitch.

The book *Jyoti Jala Nij Pran Ki*,[18] written by Manikchand Vajpayee and Sridhar Paradkar, gives a 572-page account of how Guruji led his heroic swayamsevaks. On 5 August 1947, Guruji reached Karachi. A big public meeting was held in the Karachi Fire Brigade maidan. Karachi's population of 6 lakh was evenly distributed between Hindus and Muslims. Guruji's meeting was attended by 1.5 lakh people—the entire Hindu society of Karachi came to listen to him. Similarly, in Hyderabad, Sindh (now in Pakistan), where the Hindu population numbered 65,000, a big meeting was organized and was attended by 35,000 people. The RSS became the stoutest defender of Hindu society during this dark phase of the holocaust and ethnic cleansing of Hindus.

The RSS sah sarkaryavah for many years, H.V. Sheshadri has written extensive accounts of how bravely the swayamsevaks worked in the areas of West Punjab, Sindh and the NWFP to protect the Hindu community, and how many perished while doing so. The official machinery was in doldrums; the exodus of Hindus and RSS relief camps became the dominant narrative. Popular-genre films, the likes of *Bhaag Milkha Bhaag*, have referred to these camps.

The RSS network in Bengal and Assam was not as extensive as in Punjab, Sindh and J&K. Yet relief and rescue efforts were mounted. The Vastuhara Sahyata Samiti or Relief Committee for Displaced Persons was set up in Calcutta. Refugee help centres were put up at major stations like Howrah, Sealdah, Murshidabad and Malda. A big centre was started in Kalna in the Burdwan district. Help centres came up in Bankura, Midnapore and Hooghly districts. In Assam, too, a Vastuhara Samiti was constituted. Shillong, Silchar, Tinsukia, Dibrugarh, Agartala, Nowgaon, Tejpur, Dhubri, Lamding and Karimganj became centres of relief action.

---

[18]Manikchandra Vajpayee, Shridha Paradkar, & Paradkar, Shridha. *Jyoti Jala Nij Pran Ki* (Third Edition), Suruchi Prakashan, New Delhi, 2016.

The Partition-era work helped in further developing the working methods of the Sangh. Guruji's biggest contribution was the sculpting of a nationwide Sangh network with defined processes and systems.

Guruji was brought into the Sangh's fold by Doctorji. He was a professor who became a monk of the Ramakrishna order of sanyasis, having been initiated by Swami Akhandananda, a brother monk of Swami Vivekananda. In deference to Akhandananda's wishes, Guruji pledged to work for society and was inducted by Doctorji. The RSS has been fortunate in terms of its leadership bank. All those who have moved on to become sarsanghchalaks have been moral stalwarts amongst men. This is a rare achievement.

Doctorji once said that an organization should not wake up to occasional activity, and in the fifteen years that he led the Sangh—from 1925, when the Sangh was established, to 1940, when he passed away—Doctorji set everything on a firm footing. He was an extremely gifted talent scout and he found and groomed high-calibre activists, who had India in their soul. Two of them in this series, who were guided by Doctorji and held important responsibilities under him, were Guruji, who was the sarkaryavah, and Balasaheb Deoras,[19] who became a pracharak in 1939 and moved to Calcutta. He was asked to return to Nagpur when Doctorji's health deteriorated. Both of them went on to become sarsanghchalaks in cataclysmic times. Guruji was the sarsanghchalak for thirty-three years and his work is the stuff of folklore. Balasaheb Deoras was the sarsanghchalak for twenty years and led independent India's struggle for the restoration of democracy. Both battled bans on the Sangh as well as repression. In Guruji's time, the ban on the Sangh after Gandhiji's murder was a political conspiracy. A section of politicians tried to link the RSS with Gandhiji's murder. Legal redress was sought and achieved, when Satyagrahis forced the

---

[19]'December Janam Diwas', vskbharat.com

government for a fair enquiry that proved the accusations wrong and exposed the political conspirators who were keen to suppress the RSS. In Balasaheb Deoras's time, the ban was part of the overall repression in the country and was lifted once democracy was re-established through the anti-Emergency struggle. After every ban, the Sangh has arisen to build itself more stoutly, in the spirit of 'Punascha Hari Om,' or pledge for revival—Guruji's catchphrase for every crisis.

The pracharak (or full-time worker) system was started in 1942. The divisions of prant (or province) and kshetra (or region) came into existence in 1950. The structure of ABPS, an all-India body of representatives from all levels, was also created during this time. It is the highest decision-making body of the RSS regarding policy and priorities. Before this system was established, there was a core committee of senior members of all regions, which collectively made decisions, a process Doctorji had instituted. At a ten-day meeting held in Sindi near Nagpur in 1939, a year before Doctorji's demise, a decision was taken regarding the titles for office-bearers, the departments, the RSS prayer and the 'Ekatmata stotra' (Verse of Oneness).

THE SANGH PRAYER

The initial RSS prayer and several dimensions of Sangh practices are deeply influenced by the works of Samarth Ramdas. This prayer began with 'Bharat Mata ki Jai' and concluded with 'Rashtra Guru Swami Ramdas Maharaj ki Jai'. It was a combination of Marathi and Hindi stanzas. As the Sangh expanded, the RSS prayer was changed to Sanskrit to reflect its national representation and ended with 'Bharat Mata ki Jai' once again. This has been recited with fervour by swayamsevaks all over the country from 1940.

The change was brought in with Doctorji's consent. He was remarkably focused on constructive agendas, even in the selection of words. There was a popular prayer in Hindi which stated,

'Render us free from our faults soon'. Doctorji felt this had a negative connotation and changed the line to 'Fill us with good qualities and render us purna (complete) Hindus'. He was a self-aware swayamsevak. As Doctorji said, 'Though Sangh was started in Nagpur, Sangh's home is all-India, its work sphere lies in each and every village of India.'[20] In 1945, delivering his Vijayadashami speech, Guruji said, 'Sangh has the nectar of values with which it is busy in its work, peacefully. There is no place for provincialism in Sangh's thought. The Sangh is a factory for expanding human greatness.'

The Ekatmata Stotra (*Om Sacchidanandrupay Namostu Paramatmane*), a collection of thirty-three verses, is recited in all Sangh offices and gatherings. It is a record of all who distinguished themselves in their service for India. It is a tribute that covers thousands of years of history—kings, queens, warriors, saints, scientists, scholars, philosophers, artists, musicians, poets and all the hallowed geographical sites of India. It is a daily remembrance through which attachment to the nation is instilled. Ekatmata mantra *(Yamvaidikamantradrishah Purana)* and the mealtime prayer *(Brahmarpanam Brahmaharvi Brahmagnau Brahmana Hutam and Sangh Prarthna)* are key elements in the daily life of a swayamsevak. It is the ethics driving the functional tasks that they perform for society's welfare.

AN ECOSYSTEM OF INTEGRATION

From an organizational perspective, the Sangh currently comprises forty-four provinces. Each kshetra is comprised of some prants, each prant is further segmented into a collection of districts called vibhag, each district has some towns and villages called nagar, and each nagar has a collection of localities called basti.

The main working departments of the RSS are Sharirik Vibhag (physical activities department), Bauddhik Vibhag (ideological

---

[20]K.B. Hedgewar, 13th Vijaydashmi Mahotsav, Patrak Number-45, p. 10, 1938.

training department), Pracharak Vibhag (full-timer department), Prachar Vibhag (propagation department), Sampark Vibhag (outreach department), Seva Vibhag (public service department), Vyavastha Vibhag (logistics department) and some activity-related departments like Kutumb Prabodhan (work among families), Gau Seva (cow welfare), Gram Vikas (village development), Dharam Jagran Vibhag (religious discourse department), and Samrasta with local, regional and national coordination for the strengthening of national spirit. Planning, implementation and review is an ongoing process and tours are undertaken across all tiers by local, regional and national office-bearers.

There are six festive highlights in the Sangh almanac: Varsh Pratipada (Hindu New Year), Hindu Samrajya Diwas, coronation of Shivaji Maharaj, Guru Poornima, Raksha Bandhan, Sankranti and Vijayadashmi.

The Sangh training camps are an ecosystem of integration. For twenty-five days, trainees stay together. They are divided into groups of around eighteen people. For purposes of physical training, these groups are called 'gan' and when they assemble for intellectual discourses and other activities, they are called 'gatt'. Groups are named after famous national heroes or social reformers belonging to different states. For instance, a group in a training camp in Maharashtra may be named after social reformers like Narayan Guru or Sant Ravidas, who worked to end injustice and caste discrimination. The groups get together for practice sessions of patriotic songs from different languages. In this manner, swayamsevaks are given national exposure. In the third year of training in Nagpur, one group usually has swayamsevaks from nearly ten states, thus further deepening the engagement for an all-India perspective. Thus, Ekatmata becomes a behavioural practice. The famous Bengali poet Dwijendralal Ray's lyrical ode to the Motherland, 'Shokol Desher Raani Shey Je, Amar Janmabhoomi', is learnt by all swayamsevaks and is a popular rendition.

Technology is used in Sangh training camps for a variety of

functions—accounting for headcounts, patriotic song selection and registration apps. But the mainstay is person-to-person dialogue.

From Shakha to the all-India level, dialogue, outreach and social works for society are discussed. How to reach every village, town, district and family is a constant occupation. In present times, discussions are held on how to reach every apartment bloc. The working of ABVP was systematized by Yashwantrao Kelkar. A book on his life and teaching, *Towards Man-making*, explained how lasting expansion takes place by educating public conscience through debate and deliberations. Dattopant Thengadi's famous book *Karyakarta* also dwells on the same subject.

At the latest meeting of the RSS, held on 29–31 October 2018, the major discussion was on how to improve the areas adjoining the shakha sites. Self-management systems in society should be developed; everything does not need to be driven by government bodies. As the truth needs no varnish, the focus is not on any kind of marketing blitz even in this age of blaring advertisement campaigns, but only on work and quality assurance.

LESSONS FROM THE EMERGENCY

In independent India, the biggest democratic movement for civil liberties was undertaken by the Sangh. As prime minister, Indira Gandhi, who ran an almost dictatorial government, smashed democracy and declared a twenty-one-month emergency, from 1975 to 1977. Part XVIII of the Constitution of India states the Emergency provisions (Articles 352–360) which are there to deal with abnormal situations where normal governmental machinery set up by the Constitution cannot function. Mrs Gandhi had the Proclamation of Emergency declared on the ground of 'internal disturbance.' The press note relating to the Proclamation, stated, 'Certain persons have been inciting the police and the Armed Forces against the discharge of their duties and their normal functioning.'[21] This Proclamation of Emergency was made on 25 June 1975 under Article 352 of the Constitution in response to the anti-corruption and anti-price rise movements sweeping the country against her government. Mrs Gandhi wanted monolithic control, tried to destroy the basic features of the Constitution and brought in the 42nd Amendment Act, 1976, imposing it under Emergency. Subsequently, such provisions of the amendment were struck down by the Minerva Mills case judgement in 1980. The 44th Amendment, 1978, substituted the words 'internal disturbance'[22] with 'armed rebellion'. After 1978, it was not possible to issue a Proclamation of Emergency on the ground of mere 'internal disturbance', which does not constitute an armed rebellion. This is still very much the constitutional position today.

Soon after the Proclamation of Emergency, Mrs Gandhi and the president of the Congress party, Dev Kant Barooah, pronounced their intent to destroy the RSS.[23] At a meeting of Central Secretariat officials held on 27 June 1975, Mrs Gandhi declared the RSS as the root cause of the internal disturbance. Simultaneously, Baruah, addressing a conference of youth congress leaders, said, 'We want to completely destroy the RSS. They should not be given an opportunity to re-organize.'[24] The Indira Gandhi government banned the RSS on 4 July 1975. All fundamental rights were suspended under Emergency; the right to move the courts for enforcement of rights was also suspended. So, mass mobilization and struggle were the only options left. To protest against the Emergency, all political parties got together and formed the Lok Sangharsh Samiti led by veteran Gandhian freedom fighter, Jayprakash Narayan. For ten days,

---

[21]D.D. Basu, *Introduction to the Constitution of India* (Twenty-third Edition), p. 361, Lexis Nexis, Delhi, 2018.
[22]Ibid, p. 365.
[23]P.G. Sahstrabudhhe and M. Vajpayee, *Satyagrah Aapaatkalin Sangharsh Gatha (1975–77)* (Third Edition), p. 57, Suruchi Prakashan, New Delhi, 2018.
[24]Ibid.

from 15 to 25 July 1975, a nationwide satyagraha was planned. The operationalization of this plan was delegated to Nanaji Deshmukh, a Sangh stalwart of the time. For the swayamsevaks, fighting the repression and the tyranny of the Congress government was the foremost task. In these difficult times, Balasaheb Deoras led the RSS, as sarsangchalak.

The ban did not invoke fear but only increased their grit and the RSS led the anti-Emergency movement with spectacular strength. After the incarceration of Nanaji, the entire coordination was taken up by Madhavrao Muley. Fifty years of continuous work had yielded a rich harvest of swayamsevaks. A big efficient team was available despite jail sentences for top leaders. There were 1,356 pracharaks. Out of this pool, 189 were in jail, and the rest were underground and working actively. The fabled Sangh division of work was pressed into action. From an operations perspective, the whole country was divided into six zones, or kshetras that, prior to the Emergency, were compressed into four. Among the pracharaks, Bhaurao Deoras—the younger brother of Balasaheb Deoras and a senior functionary of RSS, in-charge of coordination with the BJP— and Moropant Pingle, the man behind the Ram Mandir movement, began working as associates of Madhavrao Muley who now ran the Lok Sangharsh Samiti.

A Nagarik Swatantra Morcha, or Citizens Freedom Movement, was formed. Its work was directed by the fourth sarsanghchalak, Prof. Rajendra Singh, fondly called Rajju Bhaiya. Foreign relations were looked after by Balasaheb Bhide and Chaman Lal, pracharaks in the Sangh. Protest literature preparation was based out of Delhi and handled by Bhanupratap Shukla, editor of *Panchjanya*, a weekly magazine. In Nagpur, this work was overseen by Anant Kumar Gokhale and Madhu Limaye, a socialist leader who also coordinated movements against Emergency. Relations with religious heads were maintained by Dadasaheb Apte.

Apatkalin Sangharsh Gatha is a compendium on the Sangh's role in the anti-Emergency movement. It was put together by

K. Nagraj, Prof. Dasi Desai and Narendra Modi, the prime minister of India. While Narendra Modi and K.S. Nagraj were pracharaks at the time, Dasi Desai retired as principal of Kirti college, Mumbai.[25] Even though the shakha was banned, the shakha system functioned efficiently. No shakhas could be held anywhere in the country where swayamsevaks could do their drills, salute the saffron RSS flag and participate in intellectual discourses. But the shakha is not simply a spatial-physical construct; it is the RSS work ethic, which remained rock solid as did the code of obedience to orders of duty. This was fully utilized during the anti-Emergency movement. Those swayamsevaks who were jailed conducted their shakhas even during their imprisonment and all jails became shakha sites. In fact, most felt that jail was a privilege because every morning they could loudly render '*Namastey sada vatsale Matrabhume*,' which means, 'Forever I bow to thee, O Loving Motherland.'

Sangh training camps were held inside jail compounds. Those who were outside became the welfare custodians of those who were jailed, looking after their families and court cases. Swayamsevaks held on to each other and fought the most tyrannical regime to restore life and liberty to India.

ABVP played a key role in this movement. The social anger was represented by the student community. This was a rerun of the student activism in the days of the freedom struggle. The students' movement in Gujarat, followed by the Bihar movement, demonstrated the resolve of young India for democracy. Students' protests in Gujarat began with rising dining bills in hostel messes. This soon spread to Bihar and other states as anti-price rise and anti-corruption movements against the Congress government and its repressive policies. ABVP played a key role in both the Gujarat and Bihar movements. Due to its Sangh roots, ABVP retained its character as a students' organization and did not merge in party politics, which was a big propensity for most student organizations of that time.

---

[25]Ibid.

The anti-Emergency movement held heavy lessons for the future. It showed that no matter how difficult the times were, the Sangh would not veer away from its social agenda. Since many swayamsevaks are today seen in one political party—the BJP—surely, RSS values will impact the nature of Indian politics. The RSS has an idea and imagination about politics and of good political parties, but it does not involve itself in politics. About India's political future, the RSS feels that there will be many political parties but they will all be proud of India's ancient lineage and symbols. They will be united on matters of fundamental values and Hindu cultural heritage. Differences will exist but they will be in the context and contest of ideas and models of development for the country.

THE TWENTY-FIRST-CENTURY SHAKHA SYSTEM

The RSS uniform, or 'ganavesh', has been and is much discussed. It has been modified; for example, khaki shorts have given way to trousers. But contrary to general perception about the Sangh Shakha, the uniform is not mandatory. Only on festive occasions which are more formal, the uniform is worn. On other regular days, one can attend shakhas wearing everyday clothes. Shorts were worn as they were conducive for physical exercises. After the changes, the expectation is basically still the same, that the clothing worn should be suitable for workouts.

In terms of timings, flexibility and local convenience are considered. There are early-morning shakhas at 5:00 a.m., morning shakha slots are from 6:00–8:30 a.m., evening shakhas from 6:00–8:30 p.m. and night shakhas till 10:00 p.m. For students, shakhas are assigned according to their timetables. Schedules are flexible but there is strict adherence to the decided time slots and the conduct of shakhas is disciplined, whether they are held in the morning or at night.

On festive occasions, there has been a commencement of

women's participation as guests, particularly for the show of physical drills and parade. This presence is large. At times, women also participate in Sangh mandalis and saptahik milans.

The RSS website has a link, 'Join RSS', and this is witnessing a surge. Almost 50,000 people per month are becoming part of the RSS movement. The local swayamsevaks are given the coordinates who then contact the entrants and hold introductory meetings, called Sangh Parichay Varg. In Bengaluru, at one such introductory meet, more than 3,000 people from the IT industry participated. The Sangh hosts IT milans in big cities like Mumbai, Bengaluru, Pune, Hyderabad and Delhi. This has been a unique experience where professionals have built shakha networks using technology, overcoming time and traffic constraints through e-shakhas for debates and discussions. Online material is disseminated on India's history and issues of national importance. Patriotic songs are also circulated. Many such innovative experiments are underway. People from all walks of life are clicking the 'Join RSS' button. Since 2012, 601,950 have clicked the button.

REDEFINING NARI SHAKTI

While it is true that women are not a part of the shakhas, there are many women in the RSS. Doctorji inspired the formation of the Rashtriya Sevika Samiti; it began soon after the founding of the Sangh. It is a mirror image of the Sangh, in terms of programmes, priorities and departments. In the savage days of the Partition, when Guruji was rousing swayamsevaks in Karachi, Mausi Kelkar of the Sevika Samiti was on a tour of Lahore. Many women of the Sevika Samiti and Sangh Parivar were working to bring the Hindus to safety.

Women today are a part of the major departments of the Sangh—the Seva Vibhag, the Sampark Vibhag and Prachar Vibhag. Sangh activities—village development, cow protection, religious affairs, family ties—are all areas of massive activity for women. Stree Shakti is another women-only organization of the Sangh. Major parivar organizations like ABVP have several woman leaders. Sushree Geetatai Gunde is a leader in the team of all-India RSS office-bearers. Geetatai quit a lucrative corporate career with Glaxo in 1984 to become a full-timer. She went on to spend long years in ABVP, becoming its vice-president. She currently heads all the activities and work related to women's issues. Her focus is the coordination and development of leadership among female students, workers and politicos in all organizations under the Sangh umbrella. It is a responsibility she has held for fifteen years. Both the sarsanghchalak and sarkaryavaha support this work and the Sangh is working methodically to enhance the participation of women in the public sphere.

The overseas shakhas of RSS are conducted by the Hindu Swayamsevak Sangh (HSS). These are family shakhas and include both men and women. They are held weekly and for a longer duration. Groups of both men and women are formed. Each has physical training and intellectual curriculum in common. General programmes are also held where the attendance is combined.

In the coming days, the Sangh will become a user-driven network. The shakha attendees improvise according to their needs and preferences while strictly retaining the core properties. It is the people who connect the shakhas to the communities they live in; for they, the people, own and run the shakhas.

THE PATH AHEAD

When it comes to contemporary issues, the state of the planet is an important twenty-first-century concern for the RSS. Environment, drinking water shortage, global warming, healthy lifestyle, etc. are important subjects. Among sociological issues, marriage in modern times, position of women in families, upbringing of children, confluence of modernity and tradition, etc. are discussed. The focus of study in India is science. India's technological achievements, future roadmaps, national security challenges, concept of Hindutva in a contemporary format, economic programmes of the government, employment, investment, poverty alleviation, and basic quality education for all are important programmatic agendas for the twenty-first century.

At the individual level, the Sangh's training of personal qualities like diligence, moral imperatives, productive work, expenditure accountability, executing good programmes on small budgets, saving costs, and reflecting oneness with society and the country in one's management etiquettes, will continue. Ethics must be put into practice. You can elevate others only if you are elevated yourself. Therefore, the Sangh's mission of man-making, or 'vyakti nirman', remains as forceful in the twenty-first century as it did when it first began.

4

THE HISTORY OF BHARAT

History is a serious subject. It constructs the identity of the present, which further determines the vision for the future. Our present has a historical context. When there is a confusion regarding the contexts, an identity crisis emerges, making clarity of goal impossible. Therefore, for any society, it is imperative to gather a realistic assessment of one's own history.

Most of our history, however, is still taught through the British colonial lens. Marxist and Macaulayist historians, guided only by the Western prism, exercised a totalitarian control over the educational infrastructure—universities, research bodies, curriculum and authorship of the books to be taught. Over the years, they created a pipeline of historiographers with colonial attitudes and prejudices. Many such leading stalwarts did not even know Sanskrit, but wrote the history of India's past based on British commentaries. As a result, despite being one of the oldest civilizations in the world, the history teaching of India dwells mostly on the last 400 years.

For masses receiving this instruction in schools, colleges and universities, it led to the internalization of colonial mindsets and the 'otherization' of India, whereby only the principles of Western culture were deemed knowledge, and everything Indian was despicably native and backward. Savarkar used two words— 'swatantra', meaning freedom, and 'swadharma', meaning one's own dharma. Dharma here does not mean practices of ritualistic worship but certain values, thinking, systems and a way of life known as 'Bhartiyata', or the Indian way of life. This dharma is the foundation of India. Without it, there is no Indian way of life. For instance, the world has seen terrible conflicts in the name of religion, race and brazen bids for power and wealth. Human greed has caused environmental exploitation to the level of extreme depredation. The Indian way of life offers an antidote to stall such behaviour and promote harmony both in the personal and national life. Therefore, for the preservation of the world, the protection of the Indian way of life is necessary. And one can protect only when one is free. This is the swatantra-swadharma matrix.

However, Marxist-Macaulayist history is the complete antithesis of swatantra-swadharma. It is the rulebook of the invading classes which deemed everything Indian as inglorious. It superimposed judgemental and derogatory perspectives and experiences of the invading classes to life in India. Consequently, India's freedom struggle is still defined by British terminologies.

DISTORTED AND COLOURED

The 1857 revolt was India's first war of independence. But, Veer Savarkar's book by the same name was banned by the British. This was a war Indian peasant soldiers waged against a rapacious imperial rule. But generations of Indians reading Marxist-Macaulayist history grew up learning about it not as a revolution, but as a sepoy mutiny—a British-rule classification. These historians made the nondescript Bahadur Shah Zafar, a Mughal descendant, the icon of 1857, when in reality, this was a war of independence fought in many parts of India. The main stalwarts of 1857, Rani Lakshmibai, Tantia Tope, Kunwar Singh, Nana Saheb Peshwa, Begum Hazrat Mahal and Jhalkaribai etc. are mere names mentioned only in passing. Mangal Pandey, the first martyr of the First War of independence, is a footnote. The misery and suffering of the people due to the atrocities wreaked by the British following the war is passed over and all one reads is how the British 'reformed' their administration by ending the rule of the East India Company and replacing it with direct rule by the Crown through the Proclamation of 1858.

Tilak's tract in the Marathi newspaper, *Kesari*, dated 14 September 1897, explained why the killing of Afzal Khan by Shivaji was correct. For this piece of writing, the British jailed Tilak for one and a half years. The important question is: will this incarceration be narrated from the British colonial view or will there be an Indian rendering of the event? The history of Azad Hind Fauj and the contribution of Subhas Chandra Bose are unparalleled developments in the national liberation struggles of the world. Creating an army out of prisoners of war, comprised of soldiers from all regions of India, was an extraordinary feat, but the event has been excluded from our history. Students know about Alexander and Napoleon, but they learn about Baji Rao only through films.

OBLITERATION OF TRIBAL HISTORY

Likewise, our village and tribal histories, too, have been obliterated. If tribal histories are considered, Rani Durgavati, who fought against the conquest of Akbar, is absent from school textbooks and mainstream history. Her memory survives only because the Gonds of Gondwana kept her alive in their folklore, and children's literature publications like *Amar Chitra Katha* narrated it as a folk tale. Other tribal freedom fighters, like Tilka Manjhi, the first Janjatiya (tribal) leader among the Santhals, who took up arms against the British in 1785; or even Veer Budhu Bhagat, the Oraon leader supported by the Mundas, who revolted in 1832 for independence, are lost to us. Even today, in schools in Jharkhand, the life of Birsa Munda, the first tribal revolutionary, religious leader and Santhal folk hero is mentioned in just one sentence although his fight was a classic example of people's struggle. He fought against the dual might of the Church and British colonial system. He went against the conversion activities by Christian missionaries and the land revenue system of the British, apart from working for the preservation of the tribal mode of living, and above all, for independence. He died in jail in Ranchi in 1900. The Ranchi airport in Jharkhand is named after him.

Other leaders like Sidhu and Kanu, the tribal-brother duo who became freedom fighters; Govind Guru from Banswara, Rajasthan; Raghunath Shah, the king of Gondwana; Tantiya Bhil, and many other warriors who, in the pre-1857 era and during the war in 1857, stood up and took the cudgels against the British are nowhere to be found—neither in books nor in the nation's landmarks. There were multitude streams of struggle, which got India its freedom, yet only the Congress and Gandhian movements are presented as a monolith and are credited for making this possible. All other streams have been excluded.

The perspectives which went into writing Indian history have been based on the sidelining of Indian heroes. They must be given the prominence they deserve. Hence, the project of writing or recording history becomes a major reclamation effort.

HISTORY MISSION

History also means the history of people. A comprehensive history of the Indian people is yet to be written. The history of prosperity, the cultural expansion of Hindus, the trade history, the commodity exports, its healthcare systems, architectural advances, and Indian successes as a maritime nation, are at best, known scantily. India's military history suffers from similar neglect, and when it appears, it is a recital of setbacks. It is known that India was wealthy among nations. Such wealth presupposes a mature economy, advanced material sciences, a security apparatus, a settled administrative setup and high compliance. There is much that needs to be investigated. These details lie at the core of the Sangh's historical concerns. Some of the details and reasons have been presented by the Indian Gandhian thinker and author, Dharmpal, in his books on pre-British India, eighteenth-century science and technology, and economy in India.

The project of writing Indian history is important. All sources, oral traditions, folklore, archaeological excavations, written treatises, and unread ancient manuscripts have to be considered. Much ground remains to be reclaimed.

In February 2003, during NDA-I, Prime Minister Atal Bihari Vajpayee had instituted the National Manuscript Mission,[26] which could collect manuscripts and tap into them.[27] According to its records, the Manuscripts Mission conserved 4.3456 crore folios of manuscripts. A large number of manuscripts—43.16 lakh—have been documented and 2.96 lakh manuscripts (2.61 crore pages) were digitized.[28] It is through these efforts that Sidhha medicine has come into existence after the study of Tamil and Grantha manuscripts.[29]

The project of history writing has to narrate achievements, high points, slippages and mistakes honestly. It has to state facts in an unembellished form. This is necessary for future generations to learn from the past and build the future with confidence.

BHARAT BODH: COMPREHENDING INDIA

What were our values? Today, we hear about life values, which have a long evolutionary history. Our values become our social reality. Truthful conduct, probity, respect for women and raj dharma (or duties of the government) are social values that can be traced

---

[26]National Mission for Manuscripts, 21 August 2019, https://www.namami. gov.in/about-us-0
[27]Ibid.
[28]'National Mission for Manuscripts (NMM) Has Digitized 283 Lakh Pages of 2.96 Lakh Manuscripts Till Date: Dr Mahesh Sharma', Press Information Bureau, Ministry of Culture, Government of India, 23 July 2018.
[29]Government Oriental Manuscripts Library and Research Centre, www. tnarch.gov.in

back to the earliest times of Lord Rama, King Harishchandra of the Ikshvaku dynasty, and the grand verses of the Upanishads, or sacred Hindu treatises embodying the doctrines of Hindu philosophy. Other ancient Indian treatises on statecraft and strategy commented elaborately on these values and books like *Arthshashtra* and *Harshachartia* shed light on these values. As India has always been considered—and aspired to be—a Vishwa Guru or World Teacher, it is important to write the history of Indian values.

India has a tradition of knowledge and learning. Tomes of scholarly works, covering every field of human enquiry, have been produced in India. Scouring literature belonging to diverse fields is the work of several generations. Many texts still have to be excavated, deciphered and explained. There is a great thirst in the world to drink from the fountain of Indian wisdom. *Sama Veda* which talks about music and arts, Patanjali's *Yogsutra*, Charaka's *Charaka Samhita*, Vishakhadatta's *Devichandraguptam* (drama), Panini's *Ashtadhyayi*, Parashara's *Krishi Parashara*—all these texts represent the intellectual history of India. Books have been written on science and mathematics, which are among the first scientific works in history. Yet, many original texts have been lost over time. For instance, the contribution of Kalidas in Indian and world literature is immense, but it came to be known much later.

The Upanishads are one of the greatest intellectual assets of our history. Upanishads are dialogues between the knowledge seeker (disciple) and knowledge provider (teacher). It is a knowledge dive into the mind-body complex and the functioning of the world. The Upanishads are vigorous in their tackling of complex concepts and excite contemporary interest. They also signify how Indian philosophy and knowledge system has evolved through scepticism, enquiry and questioning. Another source, Dharmpal's *The Beautiful Tree*, is a collection of records on India's education system[30] in

---

[30]Dharmpal, *The Beautiful Tree: Indigenous Indian Education in the Eighteenth century* (Second Reprint), Collected Writings (Volume III), Goa Sidh Publication, 2007.

pre-British India while another work, *They Said About India*, is a compilation of foreign travellers' accounts[31] about India, which are important works for understanding India's history.

An understanding of India's history has to be based on readings of the original sources, devoid of subjective interpretations influenced by Westernisms and straitjackets. For example, Western history of nationalism which yielded strife, racism and world wars, is not India's experience of nationalism. Similarly, Western history of religion, marked by interference in matters of state and civil wars, is in total contrast to what happened in India. In the West, the clash of the church and the state, spanning centuries, led to secularism or complete separation of the church and the state. In India, the domain of religion is society; its objective is dharma, peace and nation-making for global welfare. Religion in India has never been located in an institution; however, religious persecution was a state policy in the West. It was unknown in India before Islamic invasions. Even when India was enslaved, first under Islamic rulers and then under British rulers, Hindu religion remained full of regenerative energy, be it the Bhakti and the Vaishnava movements during the Muslim rule or the Arya Samaj movement during the colonial phase of British rule. Throughout its thousand years of slavery, Hindu society preserved India's history and culture through its religion. This it did through its social actions in the face of a hostile state. All other geographies where the cross and the crescent went lost their culture. Even the memory of what their ancestors had been was smashed and lost to future generations. The most notable museums of the Western world display the magnitude of this destruction.

In India, the recurring idea through the ages has been: *'Nagar, gram, vanavasi, hum sab hai adivasi,'* meaning, 'city dwellers, villagers and forest people are all original inhabitants or adivasis'. The worship of certain trees as sacred by janjatis, or tribals, and

---

[31]Jain Meenakshi, *The India They Saw*, Vol. II, Delhi Ocean Books Pvt. Limited, 2011.

the worship of basil plants in urban residences is a continuum as is the ritualistic veneration of rivers, mountains and other forms of nature. India's religious history is a treasure in dialectics and rich yields of investigations and answers.

Ignoring India's intellectual history will lead to ignorant history writing. The Sangh's treatment of history is conceived as a purely academic venture driven by 'Bharat Bodh', or a deep spiritual awareness about India. Without Bharat Bodh, one cannot comprehend India, nor have a vision for the future.

STUDY OF SOCIAL HISTORY

Our country is based on social systems, which have withstood the test of time. India's family system, festivals and religious fairs like the Kumbh, are precious sociocultural inheritances. This is our culture. Their experiences and journey are important subjects for research. India is dotted with pilgrimage centres, which are crucibles of rituals, traditions and philosophical values. Indian families queue up at these centres and having done so for centuries in the quest for peace, prosperity, happiness and salvation; many do this out of reverence for ancestors. The Sangh has encouraged and supported many people who have records of Vanshavalis, or family genealogies—by networking and organizing conferences—so that people can trace their roots and can connect with their individual origins and histories. An effort has been made to create a country-wide network of writers who have preserved and collected such records in a historical manner. Besides, every religious place has its history of political events, socio-economic transformation, and legal and knowledge systems. Through such localized and innovative methods, too, the Sangh is trying to study history.

Latest researches into the functioning of village councils and experiences of evolving political and democratic systems such as administrative ethics of monarchs like Shivaji Maharaj, Maharana Pratap and Chanakya's statecraft are on our curriculum. The king was a custodian of public interest; his basic duty was the protection of his people and their welfare. He was judged by how well he performed this duty. This was the rajdharama of the king. Chandragupta Maurya, Asoka, Maharana Pratap and Chhatrapati Shivaji are metaphors for the political ethics of India, i.e. rajdharma.

Decision-making through consensus and dispute resolution were achievements of the governance and are relevant for present times. We have to draw lessons from our history of political ethics. We do not want to live in the past but we do want to learn from the past. The chronology and periodization of history into ancient, medieval and modern is incorrect. It is a colonial hangover in historical research. This needs to be Indianized and divided as: an antiquity phase with the earliest recordings of human history, as in the epics and Vedic texts; the classical era, when fundamental and spiritual experiences narrating the primary framework for human life was laid down; and the golden era when civilization reached sustainable prosperity in all walks of life.

ONGOING HISTORY PROJECTS

To definitively decide certain historical questions, the Sangh has undertaken certain historical projects. The Baba Saheb Apte Smarak Samiti, a body of the earlier days, was given a new form in 1994 as the Akhil Bharatiya Itihas Sankalan Yojana[32]—an RSS-inspired organization that seeks to scientifically correct the distortions in Indian history. It shifted its base from Nagpur to Delhi. The foisted Aryan-Dravidian divide theory of the colonials has been busted by several scholars like Shriram Sathe, Vishnu Shridhar Wakankar, P.N. Varal Pande, Michel Danino,[33]

---

[32]Akhil Bharatiya Itihas Sankalan Yojna, 9 July 2019, https://www.abisy.org/
[33]Dinsa Sachan, 'Aryan Invasion Debunked', DownToEarth, 4 July 2015.

David Frawley,[34] and Dr Shivaji Singh.[35] It was also reported 'in a path-breaking study by Harvard University and indigenous researchers on ancestral Indian populations that there is a genetic relationship between all Indians and the hitherto believed "fact" that Aryans and Dravidians signify the ancestry of north and south Indians respectively might after all, be a myth.'[36]

Another important research project taken up by S. Kalyan Raman was the origin and course of the Saraswati River and the civilization that thrived upon its banks. The findings were published in two volumes titled *Saraswati*. This is validated by later scientific discoveries narrated by K.S. Vaidya of the geodynamics unit of Jawaharlal Nehru Centre for Advanced Scientific Research, Bengaluru, in his book *Prehistoric River Saraswati, Western India: Geological Appraisal and Social Aspects*. In Haryana, the re-emergence of Saraswati is located at Adi Badri, Yamunanagar. Satellite images suggest that Vedic Saraswati originated from a group of glaciers in Tons river basin at Naitwar (Netwar) in Garhwal Himalayas. It flows through Himachal Pradesh, Haryana, Punjab and Rajasthan.[37] The archaeological excavation of Dwarka is underway to unearth the antiquity sites. The Indian system for measurement of time, chronology, calendar and the study of stellar paths for ritual observances and mathematical calculations involved thereof, is another project of massive proportions. The history of old towns is related with epoch events and great personalities like the Great War of *Mahabharata*, Lord Buddha, Chanakya, and Shankaracharya. To re-establish this history in mainstream curriculum is the work of Itihas Sankalan Yojana. Indian history writing methods, of which there are many accounts,

---

[34]David Frawley, 'The Aryan-Dravidian Divide is a Political Myth', Swarajya, 13 April 2016.
[35]Dinsa Sachan, 'Aryan Invasion Debunked', DownToEarth, 4 July 2015.
[36]'Aryan-Dravidian Divide a Myth: Study', *The Times of India*, 25 September 2009.
[37]Richard Mahaptra, 'Saraswati Underground', DownToEarth, 19 September 2018.

are being studied. Sanskrit Bharati,[38] an RSS-inspired organization that works to promote Sanskrit language, has delved deep into Sanskrit studies and the Government of India has also prepared a vision document on Sanskrit. This is a foremost requirement because vast amounts of knowledge related to Ayurveda, volumes on medicine, astronomy, archaeology and music is written in Sanskrit language, and perusal of original sources is a research necessity.

INDIANIZATION OF EDUCATION

ABVP's ongoing movement for the Indianization of education is an important review of the history-writing process, which will usher the correct understanding of our history from an education system based on Indian experiences and perspectives and it will be free from a colonial legacy.[39] It has four components, of which three are academic in nature and scope and one is agitational and legal— first is to identify and isolate falsehoods and misrepresentations; second is the inclusion of important events, developments and personalities with the weightage that they deserve; the third is the reclamation of Indian history through university researches; and the fourth is that many times, perverse imagination masquerades as historical-literary works. ABVP keeps a tough scrutiny on this aspect and even organizes movements against those who try to portray India and Indian civilization in a bad light through writings completely shorn of facts.

ABVP works in many ways to present the right perspective before the university community, even with the help of legal action if necessary. This has in the past led to changes in university curricula of some subjects, which now include indigenous knowledge, traditions and perspective. An example was the teaching of A.K. Ramanujan's essay 'Three Hundred *Ramayanas*', as part of Delhi

---

[38]Samskriti Bharati, https://www.samskritabharati.in/
[39]Balasaheb Apte, *Nation First*, Prabhat Prakashan, New Delhi, 2013.

University's history syllabus in 2008. ABVP launched a movement against it. Dinanath Batra, the convener of Shiksha Bachao Andolan Samiti, petitioned the Delhi High Court, and in 2008, this case was filed in the Supreme Court (SC)—Dinanath Batra and others versus University of Delhi. On 19 September 2008, the apex court passed the order that advised the University of Delhi to get the matter examined by a few experts and stated that expert opinions be considered by the Academic Council (AC) of the university for the decision. Accordingly, the views of four experts were invited. The AC noted that the essay had been approved for study only up to 2009 and the continuation was unauthorized. By a majority of 120 members, the AC passed the resolution to drop the essay from the syllabus. They opined that it hurt religious sentiments. Only nine members dissented.

Books from the National Council of Educational Research and Training (NCERT) regularly parroted colonial historiographers, describing Bhagat Singh and Tilak as extremist leaders. NCERT books (Page 35, *Ancient History*, Class VI) gave incorrect interpretations of the *Rig Veda* on castes. Insulting statements were written about the ninth Sikh guru, Guru Tegh Bahadur (Page 119, *Social Sciences Part-1, Medieval India*, Class VII). In five books, errors, faults and misrepresentations were reported. These books were *Ancient History*, Class VI; *Social Sciences Part-1*, Class VII; *Social Sciences, Part-1*, Class VIII; *Ancient India*, Class XI; and *Modern India*, Class XII. As a pursuant to ABVP's nationwide agitation, Shiksha Bachao Andolan Samiti was formed. It petitioned the court on several matters—*Three-Hundred Ramayanas* and NCERT—for correctives.

Bodies like the Indian Council of Historical Research (ICHR) and the Indian Council of Social Science Research (ICSSR) should shed light on Indian methodologies, to give currency to the works of genuine historians who have plodded through the facts. It should re-examine history writing that has been based on prejudices, distortions and manipulations. Remedial action must be taken.

The Sangh does not consider the rewriting of history as a political project but a national one. An enslaved country has to bear many blows, but an independent nation has to look at these injuries and take curative measures. Therefore, rewriting of textbooks is not only desirable but an urgent necessity. Prof. Shivaji Singh's work on the history of Saraswati river, Vasant Shinde's[40] work on Rakhigarhi, the ancient Harappan archaeology site dating to 2600 BC, in Hisar district, Haryana, located 150 km from Delhi, or the spread of the Indus Valley civilization, Kalyan Raman's work on River Saraswati, Deenbandhu Pandey's book on the antiquity of Ram Janmabhoomi temple, K.N. Dixit's study of the Mohenjo-Daro site, and Satish Mittal's study of Azad Hind Fauj must be circulated widely. Archaeologists like Swaraj Prakash Gupta and K.S. Ramchandran who have studied temples in India, have produced some notable works that must be accorded appropriate placement.

The history relating to earlier times, mostly passed through generations by oral traditions and folklore, has been dismissed as myth. This needs to change, for ours is not just a textual civilization. Oral histories have to be paired with archaeological findings and linkages established in academic methodologies. We have many folk bards in our country and the Government of India has a good plan on cultural mapping, which must soon be set in motion.

PRAVASI NARRATIVES

East Asian, South-East Asian and Silk Road countries have a rich crop of Indian cultural export represented in art and architectural forms—the *Ramayana*, the *Mahabharata*, and Buddhism. The first Buddhist temple, dating to 68 AD and built on the Silk Road transmission route, is found in Luoyang, Henan Province of China. The *Ramayana* is staged in many languages across the world. Indonesia has a grand range of fine arts and performing arts history

---

[40]'Archaeological And Anthropological Studies on the Harappan Cemetery of Rakhigarhi, India', Plos One, 21 February 2018.

in the *Ramayana* traditions.

All neighbouring countries in our region—Nepal, Bhutan, Myanmar, Afghanistan and Sri Lanka—also bear the Indian cultural heritage. Nalanda University attracted students from outside India, who would today be known as foreign students. Indian maritime history touched many shores. The maritime silk route was created during the rule of the Chola dynasty from ninth to thirteenth century. In 1025 AD, the powerful Chola king, Rajendra I, led his forces and defeated many kingdoms, including Sumatra and Malay Peninsula. Under Chola dynasty, the Indian naval force was one of the strongest in the region and remained unchallenged.[41] Cholas controlled the Indian Ocean and were security providers, the guardians of the sea route for the merchants. Interestingly, the Indian Ocean was known as the Chola Lake and their naval expeditions protected the interest of merchants. Many scholars trace the weakening of the Indian nation to the fall of the Chola dynasty. As long as they ruled the Indian Sea, there was no threat against the nation. Not only India's, even China's fall happened when the Chola naval presence weakened in the sea lanes.

Excavations and literary sources on India's relations with Indian Ocean littoral states need to be brought into focus to show that India had a well-developed mercantile class engaged in overseas trade, whereas what has been projected is that Indians were inert and did not travel due to caste taboos of ritual pollution resulting from travelling on the seven seas. India had a robust merchant and naval fleet. The navy developed because trade had to be conducted on secure lanes, guaranteed by the state and king. Various swayamsevaks who work in the history departments of different universities are scrutinizing these trends. The purpose is to document the real history of India in elaborate detail. For far too long, invalid views, speculative distortions, unfounded opinions and colonial prejudices

---

[41]Herman Kulke, K. Kesavapany, Vijay Sakhuja, *Nagapattinam to Suvarnadwipa: Reflections on the Chola Naval Expeditions to Southeast Asia*, Institute of South Asian Studies, Singapore, 2009.

have occupied the history establishment in India. They succeeded in entrenching the falsehood that the Indian nation was non-existent, that India was backward, that science came to India only with the advent of Europeans, particularly the British, and that there was not a shred of education in society. They propagated that administration was disorganized, that people had no say in governance and that India was ruled by indolent weaklings.

The Pravasi narratives came into popular reckon only after the efforts of the NDA-I government of Vajpayee. Populations of indentured Indians, who went to slave on colonial farms and plantations in Africa and the Caribbean, held on to their Hindu customs, traditions, values and beliefs amidst back-breaking labour. Many of their descendants went on to hold high public offices and even became heads of state. Through their work and conduct, they created an appreciation about India in the societies where they assimilated. They now live as good citizens of those countries which eventually became their homes. This is an evolving field of study and a subject matter of immense importance. Overall, Indian diaspora studies have come into sharp focus due to the sustained efforts of swayamsevaks for the past twenty years. The Pravasi Bharatiya Diwas (PBD) was started by former Prime Minister Vajpayee to celebrate the contributions by overseas Indians, and has reached greater heights under Prime Minister Narendra Modi. Establishing connect with future generations through youth PBD ensures that the relations are evergreen. Pravasi communities belonging to different regions, like the Girmityas of UP and Bihar, and the Marathi community in Mauritius, are already preparing their anthologies.

BIGOTED INTERPRETATIONS

Today, what we have as our 'official' history is a mix of the colonial approach and the Marxist interpretation of our history. Both these enterprises were produced and propagated by state-sponsorship.

Both the colonial state and the Nehruvian Congress, deeply embedded with colonial elites, had certain objectives behind the kind of history they narrated to us. The objective of the British is not difficult to understand. They were foreign imperialists and it was natural for them to manipulate Indian history and historical records to suit their interest for prolonging their rule. Also, they were buoyed by a sense of racial superiority, which stopped them from accepting some of the facts of Indian history that could contradict their superior status. Most importantly, the British had great epistemological and methodological limitations to study events, ideas and phenomena, which were typically Indian in nature.

After the British, Marxist historians took over history writing under full state-patronage. History writing to them was a political enterprise guided by their restrictive epistemology of historical materialism and class struggle. This framework was flawed in the Indian context. Furthermore, they added a double coat of Hindu-bashing, thus causing more damage to our understanding of our own past than the Europeans. They refused to see evidence-based claims as legitimate history simply because that did not suit their politics. They established their opinions as facts while the facts expressed by others were branded as communally motivated opinions.

RAM MANDIR: EVIDENCE VS CONTROVERSY

The most compelling example of this premise is the issue of Ram Janmabhoomi Temple, where Left historians have consistently tried to waylay archaeological evidences with their bigoted interpretations aligned with fundamentalists.

K.K. Mohammad, ASI director of North region, studied the evidence about the Ram Temple in Ayodhya. His report stated that twelve pillars with Hindu ritualistic sacral vases and figurines were found. These archaeological finds were conclusive proofs that the Ram Temple in Ayodhya stood at the place where the invading armies of the Mughal emperor Babur had built the Babri Masjid by destroying the temple.[42] But several Left historians, who were established names in history writing and teaching, consistently stonewalled these archaeological discoveries. Successive ASI findings met the same fate and professional archaeologists were labelled communal.

K.K. Mohammad in his autobiography in the Malayalam language, *Njan Enna Bharatheeyan*, which has been translated into Hindi as *Main Hoon Bharatiya*[43], has written that there is solid evidence of a temple (eleventh and twelfth century AD) under the Babri Masjid. He states that their team, headed by Prof. B.B. Lal, found the remnants of a Hindu temple during his excavations in 1976–77.

He states that in the earlier days of excavation, the Indian Muslim community had agreed to hand over the land to Hindus but the Left historians opposed it. Dr Mohammad opines that the Muslim community should reconcile and concede the rights of the Hindus to the janmasthan.

The ASI report cites three points categorically. First, there is 'archaeological evidence of a massive structure' below the ground where the Babri mosque was destroyed in 1992. Second, the structure bears distinctive features associated with the ancient temples of northern India. Third, there is evidence of building work from as early as the tenth century.[44]

The second excavation of the Ayodhya site took place in the presence of Wakf Board representatives. It yielded fifty Hindu temple pillars. While archaeologists and ASI reports cite that they have found evidence of a temple at the disputed site, Left historians and intellectuals have chosen the path of diversion by saying that the site also has ruins of Buddhism and Jain stupa temples. They

---

[42]K.K. Muhammed, *Main Hoon Bhartiya*, pp. 81–82, Prabhat Prakashan, New Delhi, 2018.

[43]Ibid.

[44]'Ayodhya Verdict Based on ASI Report: Archaeologist, *Hindustan Times*, 28 October 2010.

label Muslim invasion as a colonial idea floated by James Fergusson in the first half of the nineteenth century. In the early twentieth century, E.B. Havell revised this idea and made a distinction between the early Muslim constructions in and around Delhi and the modern constructions in the regional areas where the Delhi Sultanate had expanded. These are the standard subterfuges of minority appeasement pressed into action by the Left.

ERASING THE ANTIQUITY OF INDIAN NATIONHOOD

For these particular historians, the destruction of Hindu sites did not happen. Their sole focus has been on how to present India as the losing side, a place of strife and internecine quarrels, a cradle of superstition and repellent practices.

When Sanskrit learnings and texts—the original sources— were disregarded, it became easy for such falsehoods to flourish. Sanskrit language and literature were defamed in casteist terms. The cartel of Left historians outlawed the 'Hinduness' of India. The hatred was not plainly ideological but pathological, and used to snuff out Sanskrit from curriculums. If you take out Hinduness from the historical scholarship of India, you not only harm India, you also harm humanity. This is because the Hinduness of India is a record of advances in human culture, and a treasure trove of knowledge, which is rational in nature and universal in scope. Equally importantly, if the history of past events is not narrated clearly, truthfully and comprehensively, the subject of history itself suffers from severe impairments.

At the time of Independence, leading historians like R.C. Mazumdar, Jadunath Sarkar, Neelkanth Shastri and others were painted as 'communal' or 'saffron' historians by the Marxists. K.M. Munshi, founder of the Bharatiya Vidya Bhavan (BVB), had embarked on a major programme of historical research that gave us the monumental eleven-volume history and culture of the Indian people. Simultaneously, major discoveries were being made in archaeology at places like Lothal, Kalibangan and others, which added significantly to our knowledge of the past. So, by 1960, conditions could not have been better for an aspiring young generation to make a mark in history.

But, unfortunately, a bunch of historians in cahoots with colonial elites formed a cartel and cemented its monopoly on the Indian history establishment. This influential group made no significant contribution to the history of India and the central theme of their work was to denounce the greatness of Hindu civilization. Almost everything they have produced, from the history of Vedic and Harappan civilization to the freedom movement, has been proved wrong.

Adapting from the old imperial theory that India is a mere geographical expression, they propounded that India was a nation made by several waves of migrations, and that invasions never happened. With this formula, they colonized the intellectual atmosphere of India. For the Sangh, the challenge is to decolonize the Indian mind. Historical narratives create national consciousness. Deen Dayal Upadhyay said that the nation is a pulsating entity; it has a physical body infused with prana, or vital life force. The prana is the history of a nation. Just as the prana gives strength to the organs of the body, refreshes the intellect and keeps the body and soul together, the history of a nation directs the government's programmes and inspires its worldview. Indian history writing has to be liberated from the Marxist-Macaulayist methods.

NEW MUSEUMS: HOME OF LOST HISTORY

Though India has a spread of museums nationwide, a lot of ground still needs to be covered. In Delhi, there are sixteen museums, Mumbai has eighteen, Kerala has nineteen, Gujarat has thirteen, Telangana has seven, UP has eight, and every state has around two to four museums of repute, housing art and culture exhibits. There are science museums, too, with galleries on marine life, zoology and engineering.

Museums exist to document national history, preserve ancestral memory, advance consciousness about events and situate the country's contribution in the march of the world. It records the past to create a legacy for the future. This, by and large, is the job of museums the world over. In India, we find major exclusions like the historical fort of Raigarh; Azad Hind Fauj, India's armed force that challenged British rule; and Ambedkar memorial, etc. These parameters have to be addressed because museums, through their displays of permanent and special exhibitions, fulfil the mandate of mass education both for our national population and international visitors.

New museums are required in India for disseminating knowledge about India's immense contribution to the civilizational development of the world. They are required in different parts of the country, to recount their history and achievements. For example, the Raigarh Fort of Shivaji was the seat of a new state structure after the victory against the Mughals was achieved. A form of governance with people's participation was set up. In the days of authoritarianism and revenue exactions, Shivaji gave a uniquely modern revenue administration to the people and is hailed as a farmers' leader. But there exists no museology that commemorates this great feat. Other great personalities like Chandragupta Maurya, Chanakya, Maharana Pratap and other revolutionary leaders are left bereft. There exists no national museum of the First War of Independence in 1857. Till recently, the founding father of the Constitution of India, Dr Ambedkar, shared the same fate. It is only now that the Narendra Modi government has started gathering all collectibles on Dr Ambedkar's life from diverse places associated with him—Mumbai, Baroda, London, America—to raise a big museum in his honour.

The revolutionary thread of India's freedom struggle has also been excluded in the existing museums. Those who served sentences in the dreaded Andaman jails have no national presence.

Their memories, curated in Andaman only, are required to be brought into the mainland areas. Azad Hind Fauj was willed into the wilderness, its valour and sacrifices for the motherland banished from public memory. It is only under PM Modi's government that the Azad Hind Fauj has come into sharp focus. On 21 October 2018, Prime Minister Modi declared that a museum for the Azad Hind Fauj would be set up in the premises of the Red Fort. Work is underway on new museums under BJP-ruled states. The Maharashtra government is constructing a Shivaji memorial museum. The 'Statue of Unity' has been built by Gujarat government which is experiencing great footfalls.

Since early times, India has seen many forms of government. Svarajyam-vairajyam (people's participation or self-rule), samarajyam (a large empire ruled by a king), bhaujyam (a kingdom of abundant comfort)—all conceivable forms of governance have been tried, at times it happened simultaneously and at times this took place in succession. The primacy of ordinary people's welfare is deeply rooted. There is a high requirement for a people's museum to exhibit these democratic traditions.

The grandeur of Indian knowledge systems has been suppressed. Indian philosophy, the fountainhead of logic and enquiry, was rubbished as otherworldly, and its health systems of Ayurveda and Yogasutras were lampooned as quackery, all because of its Hindu heritage. An intense process of negative internalization was implemented. But this scholarship remained alive through the dedication of certain individuals and in the life choices of ascetics. When the West and many non-Western countries despairing of modernity, turned to India for a prescription of holistic life and wellness, this knowledge was imparted to them. The whole world has now embraced yoga, meditation and Ayurveda. Yoga missions and retreats are universal, just the way they were meant to be. The world hungers to know the wisdom of Sanskrit texts.

Museums on Indian languages, festivals, spiritual traditions, grammar systems, the education and university systems dating back to 3,000 years—the whole gamut of their curriculum and literary landscape are required. Science museums with specialized galleries on material sciences, mathematics and astronomy, agriculture, mining, chemistry and armaments must take shape.

EXPANSION OF THE NEHRU MEMORIAL

The new museums will retrieve decades of lost history, but they alone cannot provide all answers. Expansion of existing institutions has to proceed apace. Therefore, the structural reform of Nehru Memorial Museum Library (NMML) was taken up and is one component of this augmentation strategy. NMML is now the museum of prime ministers of India and it is important to understand this issue in the right perspective.

The NMML is housed in the Teen Murti House in Delhi, designed by British architect Robert Russel in 1930, who planned the Connaught Place. Teen Murti was Nehru's home from August 1948 till his death in 1964. The Teen Murti was earlier the flagstaff house of the commander-in-chief of the British Indian Army. General Sir Roy Bucher, the last C-in-C, vacated the house soon after India's independence. Nehru in many of his correspondences with N.V. Gadgil, who was the minister of public works (also commerce, mines and power), expressed his desire to move from his residence on 17 York Road (now called Motilal Nehru Road) to Teen Murti and make it his official residence. Outside the bhavan stand the three Indian soldiers (Teen Murtis) sculpted by Leonard Jennings from the three princely states of Hyderabad, Mysore and Jodhpur, who died fighting in West Asia during World War I. It is now called the Teen Murti Haifa Chowk.

After Nehru's death, the Government of India converted the thirty-room Teen Murti house into a memorial that would perpetuate Nehru's memory and work. On 14 November 1964, marking Nehru's 75th birthday, the president of India, Dr S. Radhakrishnan, formally dedicated Teen Murti to the nation for housing a museum and library, known as the NMML, which was inaugurated in 1968 by Indira Gandhi.

In 2016, Prime Minister Narendra Modi expressed keenness to construct a museum dedicated to the legacy of all former prime ministers. At the 43rd annual general meeting of the thirty-four members of the NMML society in July 2018, chaired by the then minister for home affairs, Rajnath Singh, the vice president of the society (the prime minister is the president), the plan to change it to a museum on prime ministers of India was endorsed by a majority of the members. Six members of the society opposed it, calling it a bid to tarnish Nehru's legacy[45]—the logic behind which remains unclear as the Nehruvian documents, personal papers and artefacts will remain the way they were. Other prime ministers are added, Nehru is not deleted. In the AGM, amendments specifying the task for having a museum for all PMs were proposed in the Memorandum of Association. Earlier, the memorandum stated that the purpose of the museum was 'to acquire, maintain and preserve the personal papers and other historical materials pertaining to Jawaharlal Nehru and papers relating to his life and work.'[46]

Now, a subsection added, reads as: 'To acquire, maintain, preserve and exhibit the personal papers and other related papers, video audio photographs and other material relating to the lives and works of all Prime Ministers.'[47]

The clauses specifying the task to have a museum for all prime ministers has been added, which was not there earlier. The NMML will also work towards becoming a repository of documents and research related to 'nationalism' and not just limited to the 'freedom struggle'.

---

[45]Vasudha Venugopal, 'NMML to stay as it is; Museum for PMs at Teen Murti Complex', *The Economic Times*, 26 July 2018.

[46]'Objectives', Nehru Memorial Museum and Library.

[47]Eram Agha, 'Foundation Stone Prime Ministers' Museum at Teen Murti Bhavan to Be Laid Today Despite Congress Objection', News18.com, 15 October 2018.

The Bhoomi poojan to house the museum for the prime ministers was held on 15 October 2018. The site is behind the Nehru Memorial and will be part of the 25.5 acres of Teen Murti estate, which belongs to the Government of India and will be built at a cost of ₹271 crore in a span of twelve months.

The legatees of the Gandhi family have objected to the reform of the NMML. The Indira Gandhi Memorial Trust (IGMT), headed by Sonia Gandhi, has demanded the return of all documents of the late prime minister, which are housed in the museum.[48] The management of the NMML has refused to hand over the papers on the ground that once documents are transferred to a library for the avowed purpose of access to scholars, they cannot be withdrawn. The IGMT insists that the library was simply 'the custodian' of the papers and the ownership rights remain with Indira Gandhi's family, as per her will. Before the Modi government, researchers were allowed to examine the Nehru and Indira papers only with the express permission of Sonia Gandhi.[49]

The revamp of existing museums is necessary as many untold histories have to be made known. The past has to be narrated with factual accuracy. Crucial moral lessons must be illuminated to instil self-esteem and a sense of purpose. Institutions of this genre must serve as a guide for the vision of a future.

THE PARTITION AND EMERGENCY: HIGH-PRIORITY FUTURE PROJECTS

Just as it records and classifies the past, history also communicates concepts, complex information and knowledge.

Two events in history writing must be immediately prioritized. The first is the Partition of India. It was one of the most disturbing

---

[48]Vasudha Venugopal, 'Nehru Memorial Says Not Possible to Part With Indira Gandhi's Papers', *The Economic Times*, 26 September 2018.
[49]Ibid.

events of the twentieth century. It was a political decision but the cataclysms were borne by ordinary people; the displacement and exodus of populations at such a large scale made it the bloodiest event in Indian history. Thematically speaking, it was the zealotry of one section of the Muslim leadership, the shrewdness of the imperial British and the helplessness of the Congress leadership, because of which India was partitioned in this way. Inclusion of details in history books and memorial museums on the Partition is extremely important.

The second is the deadly assault on Indian democracy through the imposition of the Emergency, barely twenty-five years after India's independence. Ordinary people struggled in the face of harsh government repression and authoritarian rule for the restoration of democracy in our country. The Emergency and the anti-Emergency struggle are a lesson for the future on issues of personal liberty and democratic rights. It is also a lesson for those aspiring to assume decision-making positions, that if public offices are used to destroy democracy, they will face an avalanche of protest from the common people of India.

The RSS fulfilled a historical role in protecting public interest in both these events.

TEACHING SANSKRIT

In RSS's theory of knowledge and education, Sanskrit occupies a pivotal place. It is the most ancient language of the world and is the pride of India. The Sangh feels that it is important for the teaching of Sanskrit to commence from the school level whilst students are taught in their mother tongue and obtain modern education. Through instructions in the mother tongue, students will integrate with their local environment while Sanskrit will integrate them with the entire India and other Indian languages, acquainting them with Indian knowledge systems.

In a historic judgement, the SC stressed the need to promote the language in the field of education.[50] It said, 'Sanskrit is not just a language, it is a vocabulary of our culture.' Pointing out how the Chinese system of writing and modern Hebrew served to unify the newly formed nations of China and Israel, respectively, it queried why Sanskrit could not be expected to play a similar role in India. Therefore, the promotion of Sanskrit is a must for the rejuvenation of the Bhartiya vichar, or Indian thought.[51]

Programmes and short courses for familiarization with Sanskrit held by Sanskrit Bharti have taught ten million people reading and speaking skills in the Sanskrit language. The Sanskrit Bharti's efforts are to design courses that make Sanskrit comprehensible to large audiences.

Sanskrit is the language of culture and fine arts, drama and literary display, and ancient Indian science, medicine and philosophy. In its historic heritage, there is a contemporary relevance. *Charaka Samhita* has become the bedrock of the holistic health movement that one sees growing in influence the world over. Sanskrit-speaking Ayurveda and yoga practitioners are rising. Equally important are the Sanskrit texts covering physics, chemistry, metallurgy and psychology. Therefore, several universities are organizing Sanskrit workshops for conducting deep data dives for research purposes, such as IIT Hyderabad, Hyderabad University, Jaipur University, and Osmania University. These initiatives aim at making students familiar with India's knowledge history.

RENAMING PLACES TO RECLAIM HISTORY

History inspires pride in one's nation and that instils self-confidence in each and every being of that nation. Only a self-confident, self-assured people and nation can shape a robust future.

Some people think that renaming of places like Allahabad to

---

[50]Santhosh Kumar and Others vs The Secretary, Ministry of Human..., indiankanoon.org, 4 October 1994.
[51]Ibid.

Prayagraj, Faizabad to Ayodhya, Victoria to Chhatrapati Shivaji terminus is pointless. Aurangabad in Maharashtra, which was Devagiri, the centre of a flourishing Hindu empire, was named after the fanatic Mughal ruler, Aurangzeb. After Shivaji, his son Sambhaji grappled with Aurangzeb for nine long years, at the end of which he was cruelly put to death by Aurangzeb. We still continue with the name Aurangabad though Aurangzeb's rule is a psychological wound in the mind of India. Aurangabad must be renamed Sambhajinagar.

Renaming is an important part of the reclamation project. There are tangible cultural products flowing from this reclamation project, like the Ramayana Express, trains on the Ramayana route and restoration of Nalanda University. Renaming is only one part; the reclamation project demands massive research output. Our universities and students must rise to this task of rediscovering and reclaiming India. Popular-genre formats of short films, plays, documentaries, cinema and songs should also help in spreading this awareness.

This has taken the form of a national movement today and is far bigger than politics or polemical debates. It is about a confident, self-assured India telling its story to the world, free from external influences. The boards of study of different universities need to review their syllabi. Unhistorical representations and narrations have to be expunged. This is not the work of any one individual or organization. There has to be societal involvement in identifying and examining issues.

The Sangh feels that every community and faith must be able to locate its history in India. It is time we tell and write our Ekatmata history with people's participation. Of course, this has to be organized and delineated in an academic format and structure, which is the task of scholars and universities. In this manner, a proud and prejudice-free history of India has to be written. This is the Sangh's approach to rewriting history.

5

RISE OF SANATAN HINDUTVA

Hindutva is a way of life. It is 'sanatan' in nature. Sanatan is a word used to explain certain values and life principles that are eternal, an accretion of wisdom that has held sway beyond the vagaries of time and tumult of historical events. This philosophy of life is pervasive, complete and humane. It is a force of goodness and an idea of welfare for all. The great scholars of yore investigated the mysteries of creation; they queried about the purpose of life and the methods by which life ought to be lived—these findings aggregated and came to be called Hindutva. The fundamental principle, the basic structure of this, was oneness. It is an understanding that though reality is expressed in different forms, inherently, there is an underlying unity and oneness or Ekatmata. This was a comprehensive realization; it was not a reaction but primal knowledge of the early evolutionary times of humankind. The behavioural manifestation of this oneness was Hindu dharma, or the Hindu way of life, which is self-evolutionary and also known as Hindutva. It is universal because the Divine can be invoked in any form and in any manner. Etymologically speaking, the word 'Hindutva' as we know it today was coined by Chandranath Basu, in 1880. Basu, a deputy magistrate and an author, was the president of Bangiya Sahitya Parishad—a literary society in West Bengal. He conducted a comparative study of different doctrines located within the Hindu realm of philosophical and political thinking in his most important book, *Hindutva* (1892).[52] Unfortunately, his original work is not available in English and the actual Bangla version is perhaps lost too. However, his work has been referred to by many contemporary scholars.[53]

During the freedom struggle, the first stirrings of national awakening came from Hindu cultural traditions. Nabogopal Mitra, a thinker and patriot, started 'Hindu Mela,'[54] a national fair to promote indigenous art, nationalist views and work for uniting India, and raise awareness against cultural colonialism. A newspaper named *National Paper* was started in Calcutta in 1867 to educate people about the best ancient Hindu practices for instilling self-pride and to fight the imperial stereotyping of Indians as backward natives. It was richly supported by the Tagore family. Rabindranath Tagore first participated in the Hindu Mela, a platform to unite Indian people, at the age of 14 in 1875. The gathering was open to all who wanted to express their views on the nation, irrespective of their occupation, social group and religions. Hindu icons, theatre and religious plays were used to cultivate attachment to the motherland—'Bharat Bhumi.' Hindutva and the nationalist struggle went hand in hand. The Sangh is curating the works of this phase of our freedom struggle.

Bankim Chandra Chattopadhyay's patriotic novel *Ananda Math* is a historic work narrating the armed uprising of the sanyasis (monks) against the British rule. The purest form of national consciousness was seen in the personification of Bharat as Bharat Mata. For Bharat Mata, all Indians are her children, or 'santaan.' Marking the most powerful phase in India's modern history, 'Vande Mataram', a song authored by Bankim, was woven into *Ananda Math*.

---

[52]Ankur Barua, 'Vedantic Variations in the Presence of Europe: Establishing the Hindu Dharma in Late Nineteenth Century Bengal', springer.com, 4 April 2017.

[53]Makarand Paranjape, 'Hindutva before Savarkar: Chandranath Basu's Contribution', DNA, 22 April 2017.

[54]Partha Mitter, *Art and Nationalism in Colonial India, 1850–1922: Occidental Orientations*, p. 222, Cambridge University Press, 1994.

Bankim was the doyen of Hindutva stream of thought. Writing on his nationalism, Sutapa Dutta says that it attracted the commoners. The notion of nation does not come from a political structure but from the common religious practices of the common man. That's why the nationalism of Bankim Chandra is attractive.[55] Bankim's *Ananda Math* and 'Vande Mataram' became the *Odyssey* of India's freedom struggle.

On Bankim's passing away in 1894, Sri Aurobindo said in *Indu Prakash* that what Bankim created was 'a language, a literature and a nation'.[56]

DESIGNERS OF HINDUTVA

Over many years, concepts like movement against caste-based discrimination, untouchability, temple entry, gender equality and the Indianization of education have been implemented for 'Bharat Gaurav' (glory of India) and Hindutva. The modern definition of Hindutva was presented before the world by Swami Vivekananda at the Chicago World Parliament of Religions on 11 September 1893. Swamiji learnt about Indian religious and spiritual practices from his master, Sri Ramakrishna Paramhansa, who had mastered his ego and had realized the ultimate truth—that the purpose of life was the realization of God. Revered as an extraordinary saint, he possessed childlike simplicity. He lived an austere life and became a spiritual magnet for worshippers, intellectual classes and people belonging to all religions.

A famous maxim of Sri Ramakrishna was '*Jata mat tata path*'—as there are many faiths, there are also many paths, but all lead to one. Swamiji took this message to the developed world and spread its effulgence through an invocation that has become

---

[55]S. Dutta, 'Identifying Mother India in Bankimchandra Chatterjee's Novels', *Women's History Magazine*, p.24, 2014.
[56]Sri Aurobindo, *Indu Prakash*, Compiled in the *Collected Work of Sri Aurobindo*, 1972.

immortal—'Sisters and Brothers of America.' Here was a young saffron-clad monk from India, who addressed people belonging to other nationalities as his brethren. The Chicago address of Swamiji was a high point of Hindutva and always will be.

Swami Dayanand Saraswati, a reformist leader, founded the Arya Samaj that sought to re-establish the Vedas as the earliest Hindu scriptures and helped to free Indian society from prevailing dogmas that enhanced the scientific and pragmatic elements of Hindu faith.

Swami Shraddhanand Saraswati promoted the movement for the education of girls. He started Vedic schools for the Indian masses and began the 'shuddhi' movement for the reconversion of Hindus who had converted to other faiths. In a way, this was the precursor of the present-day 'ghar wapsi' movement.

Famous revolutionary Veer Vinayak Damodar Savarkar viewed the tenets of Hindutva in the context of the nation. According to Savarkar, the essentials of Hindutva are common nation (rashtra), a common race (jati) and a common civilization (sanskriti).

Savarkar's spontaneity flourishes in his spirited appeal to Hindus. He said, 'The unique, natural and organic combination that exists in our land goes by the name of Hindu. None can sever it, regardless of their caste, creed or affiliations. It cannot be torn apart because it is not the result of any contract or historical exigencies.' Saying this, he emphatically pronounced that Hindus are bound together by ties of blood, birth and culture.[57] Savarkar wished to see the consolidation of Hindu society.

Gandhiji's political methods of satya (truth), ahimsa (non-violence), Satyagraha and his conception of an ideal state, or Ram Rajya, were all rooted in Hindutva principles and have entered the global dictionary of language, philosophy and political practice.

Hindutva scholars and practitioners undertook several exertions to end the evil of untouchability and other forms of caste-based

---

[57]bjplibrary.org

discriminations. Sree Narayana Guru (1856–1928) set a model of reform and social justice in Kerala, a state whose caste-related prejudices were severe and had appalled Swami Vivekananda.

The stoutest action against caste discrimination was taken by Dr Ambedkar. His actions rescued Hindu society of many ills and improved it. The entire society entrusted him with the framing of the Indian constitution. He was the chairman of the drafting committee of the constituent assembly. The whole country submits to him as the fountainhead of our constitutional values. For most countries, the introduction of the concept of equality in the law had to go through several waves and eras, but in India, this was accomplished at the first attempt. This was possible because equality is a core value of Hindutva.

The former president, A.P.J. Abdul Kalam, took the greatness of India to the youth of this country. In doing so, he merged Indian values with scientific progress.

Yoga and Ayurveda, two important cultural exports of India, were always famous but the real global scaffolding was done by Prime Minister Modi and celebrated yoga gurus. International Yoga Day is observed on 21 June by member states of the United Nations (UN). This began in 2015, at the initiative of PM Modi. The day was also suggested by him, as 21 June is the day of summer solstice, the longest day in the northern hemisphere, and is accorded a special place in many parts of the world. This observance is the acceptance of Patanjali Yogasutras. Hindutva's spiritual wisdom is being presented to the world in a contemporary style by spiritual leaders like Sadhguru Jaggi Vasudev, Baba Ramdev and Sri Sri Ravi Shankar. They have made many efforts to popularize Hindutva as a lifestyle.

HINDUTVA IS ONENESS

The principles of Hindutva predate the word and its applications. When other forms of organizing life like Christianity and Islam emerged, then for the sake of comparison, this oneness came to be notified as a Hindu way of life, interchangeably also known as Hindutva. Since it was India that birthed this way of life, Hindutva is Indian culture, where culture refers to an understanding of the network of relationships among people with different traditions, cultures, countries, and with nature, etc. as an extension of the common soul.

One who experiences oneness understands this culture of unity, comprehends the true nature of relationships and knows that differences are only apparent. The root is common and one. This commonality and unity in an expansive form is the idea of Vasudhaiva Kutumbakam, or 'the world is one family'. Hindutva is immersed in this philosophy, and therefore, it is beyond the small-mindedness of mine-thine. It encompasses the relationships between human beings and nature, between man and rivers, the mountains, the plains and vale, the verdant greenery and desert, and trees and animal life forms. From this compass of relationships arise care, concern and duty towards one and all. Nature worship grew out of the idea that nature is a living deity, worshipped in a myriad forms in India's tribal lands. The basil plant, tulsi, has an exalted place in Hindu households as do many other species of the plant kingdom.

Hindutva is this expansion of the duty of care from the kindred group to the village, from one village to a group of villages, from one's own country to the world, from one's own faith to all faiths, and so the concentric virtuous cycles are envisaged. Coexistence, therefore, becomes an organic outgrowth.

The world over, differences have led to conflicts. Differences of language, race, colour, geography, forms of worship and a host of other factors have been breeding grounds for divisiveness and bloodshed. India alone has shown that differences can coexist. That is why, for us, nationalism is not a conflict-laden concept but an arc of coexistence, whose basis is Hindutva—a pantheon of ideas and principles of oneness. For all other formulae, the existence of one is incumbent on the destruction of the other. The spirit of amalgamation and balance of all life forms and ideas is unique to the Hindutva experience. It is a vision of happiness (sukh) and prosperity (samridhi) for all humankind. This is at the core of Hindu ethics.

Hindu ethics led to the development of sciences like yoga, Ayurveda, material sciences, mathematics, astronomy, architectural marvels and fine arts like classical music and dance. Methods of wealth creation were developed with the same felicity as the modes for righteous conduct. This was the constant dharma of Hindutva. India's legacy of statecraft centred in the practice of dharma is 'Ram Rajya'.

The description of Ram Rajya, as conceptualized by Tulsidas, the author of the epic poem 'Ramcharitmanas'—the story and deeds of Rama—was a life of duty, living which, people were happy and free from fear, sorrow, and diseases.[58] In brief, Ram Rajya is an order of duty and morality under the stewardship of the Divine himself and Tulsidas provides a picture of an ideal commonwealth, where there is coordination between the people and the state and also between different local governments and the state for the common good. Mahatma Gandhi also believed in the same. He defined Ram Rajya as Divine Raj, the kingdom of God. And his God was the God of truth and righteousness.[59]

The Hindu way of life was developed through the austere practice, study and efforts of many, spanning thousands of years, and has nourished India since time immemorial. Examples abound: kings and maharajahs like Maharana Pratap, Shivaji and Sayaji Gaekwad, Rudrapratap's rule in Warangal and Krishnadevaraya's reign over the kingdom of Hampi at its zenith are representative of this ethical standard. Even war was subject to an ethical standard. The Hindu way of life raised universities like Nalanda

---

[58]Tulsidas, *Ramacharitmanas*.

[59]'Ramrajya', The Mind of Mahatma Gandhi, mkgandhi.org

and Takshashila so that these ideas could flourish and be studied by students in India and from overseas to benefit all of humanity. Acharya Mahapragya and Dr Kalam, in their book *The Family and Nation,*[60] have mentioned that the main premise of the Indian philosophy of economics was to take both individual and society towards peace and happiness. There was a doctrine in our culture that '*sukharthi samyto bhavet*', meaning a person during the period of happiness should be self-restrained.

In the modern context, Hindutva and Hindu Rashtra are the two terms that are most expressive of this way of life. This way of life and governance can lead to a happy life, so it is relevant and useful. Therefore, the RSS backs the usage of these terms and is working to give it greater currency. It believes that Hindutva's great reserves of knowledge are the source code of solutions for many sociopolitical, economic and environmental problems engulfing the world and verily the cure for many of the ills plaguing India. Driven by an essentially sattvic propensity, many saints and scholars have nurtured Hindutva, and in modern times this idea of Hindutva was incorporated and sculpted into the form and working of the Sangh started by Doctorji. The Hindutva of RSS is not for politics; it is for the well-being of all humanity.

Guruji, the second sarsanghchalak of RSS, in his book *Bunch of Thoughts* wrote, 'It is the forefathers of the Hindu people that have set up the traditions of love and devotion for the motherland. And they also prescribed the rights and duties with a view to keeping aglow in our mind, a living and complete picture of our motherland and devotion to it as a divine entity. And again, it is they who shed their blood in defence of its sanctity and integrity.'[61] He further expounded, 'We have a current of life, our sanskriti, which instils sublime qualities of purity, character, fortitude and self-sacrifice in

[60]A. Mahapragya A.P.J. Abdul Kalam. *The Family and the Nation*. Harper Collins Publishers, Uttar Pradesh, 2011.
[61]M.S. Golwalkar, *Bunch of Thoughts* (Third Edition), p. 122, Sahitya Sindhu Prakashana, Bengaluru, 2011.

the individual enabling him to attain the highest goal of human existence.[62] This sanskriti is bracketed as culture and Guruji said that the stamp of this culture is manifested in our daily lives.

Thus, we can see logically that Hindu nation is a result of thousands of years of experiential living and history. It is not an ism propelled by any political or economic motivation. It is a comprehensive conception of civilization developed through the observance of certain values and cultural ways of life.

INCLUSION EMBRACES DIFFERENCES

The forefathers of Muslim and Christian populations in India, too, lived by following the Hindu way of life. In our country, many forms of worship developed over several millennia, and so there was no discrimination on the basis of faith or the form and manner of worship. The germane question is: what is the vision of life, attitude towards the world, towards those who vary in beliefs and religion and orientation towards women. The Hindu, having answered this question several times, has demonstrated the breadth and depth of inclusion that those professing other faiths need to now propound.

The conduct of those who nurture separatist feelings—due to their modes of worship—and fashion methodologies against the unity and integrity of India or plot schemes for severance from the motherland is treasonous. It is also an act of treason against one's identity. Any activity of this sort is a dangerous portent and cannot be overlooked or neglected. To see through these realities and oppose such conduct is the duty of each Indian. To be born an Indian means to be a descendant of Indian culture; it is not just the physical act of being born, it is being mindful of a cultural ethos laid down by our progenitors. That's why Guruji said that culture counts.

The motherland is not just a territorial map; she is a great spiritual being. When a Hindu offers prayers through the rituals

---

[62]Ibid.

of sankalp, or resolution, he does so by stating his location and thus initials his prayers with an identity, address, anthology of his ancestry, date, time, and season. In today's world, this would be coterminous to a three-dimensional GPS location. This is how Hindu traditions developed through scientific methodology.

SEPARATISM SOWS CONFLICTS

When we fell from the Hindu way of life, we experienced problems in our society emanating from caste status, superstition, environmental degradation and the likes. If we recover the Hindu way of life, we will recuperate and find solutions to our problems. Therefore, the idea of Hindutva is most useful in the twenty-first century. It is a recipe for peace and prosperity along with a balanced and coordinated life.

Western secularism arose from the conflict between the church and the state. It was a time when scientific truths and those propounding it were condemned. Religious persecution was rampant. Kings chafed at the revenues the church exacted from their people. Funded by the revenues of the Christian world, the Pope and his cardinals lived in luxury. The church was so dominant and conservative in Europe that any liberal idea could only be brought forth in a deluge of blood, persecution and violence. Revenue extraction became the primary cause for some kings to support Martin Luther's revolt against the Catholic Church, which also led to the rise of Protestantism in Europe. None of this happened in India. Western secularism, which meant banishment of religion from temporal spaces and from much of social life, is inapplicable in India, and even unwise.

Indian religious sociopolitical lives are inextricably linked. Statecraft is linked to dharma, defined variously as virtue, including a range of moral precepts. Indian knowledge systems were open, encouraged enquiry, observation and experiments. The *Kathopanishad*, one of the most popular Upanishads, narrates how the young student Nachiketa did not hesitate to question his father, and even Yama, the Hindu God of Death. Accounts on Shankaracharya are filled with his debates and discussions with other reputed scholars.

Nothing was said with finality; everything could be probed and even amended if the evidence was compelling. Of course, this does not mean that everything was going fine.

Long centuries of foreign invasions begot exploitation. By the time European colonization planted itself on Indian soil and further exacerbated the loot of resources, poverty coupled with social ills took us away from the path of knowledge. Imperial renditions about India made these negative developments the attachments of Hindu culture. It is extremely foolish to blame Hindutva for the all present ill practices and to understand Indian culture without assessing the impact of colonial history and its effect on India. The consequences were debilitating.

ACHIEVING GREATNESS THROUGH HINDUTVA

When Doctorji began the Sangh, he outlined the project of Indian greatness to be achieved through the device of Hindutva. Hindutva, as revealed in his work and instructions, is the material and spiritual aspect of the Indian way of life; of organizing the work and life of an individual and that of the nation according to India's cultural values. Hindutva is the underlying unity that runs through the diverse, regional, linguistic and geographical forms of the Indian landmass and even beyond, to the shores touched by Hindu cultural impacts, of which Angkor Wat Complex in Cambodia and the Prambanam Shiva Temple in Indonesia are impressive examples.

Over the past few decades, owing to the consistent work of the Sangh in communities and also due to its interventions at multiple levels—intellectual, social, economic and political—Hindutva has become a vigorous movement. Gleaning the experiences of the past, learning from the pitfalls of history, correcting the vices that crept up along the way, Hindutva is the Sangh's vision of India for the future. Hindutva is New India. It is opposed to caste-based politics. It is the brotherhood and sisterhood of all Hindus. In fact, Guruji formed the Vishwa Hindu Parishad (VHP) to carry forth this message to every village, town and district, and to bring various sects and orders (sampradyas) under one umbrella. No one is high or low—all are equal. Every swayamsevak bears this as an immutable fact and carries onward the task of the regeneration of Hindu society.

Guruji's most commented-upon book, *Bunch of Thoughts*, deals candidly with hard questions: What about Hindu-Muslim unity? What about Muslims living in a Hindu Rashtra? Guruji and the Sangh were opposed to the politics of making the Hindu a perennial sacrificial lamb for the furtherance of so-called 'Hindu-Muslim unity.' Disallowance of 'Vande Mataram' in Congress sessions in October 1937[63] whetted aggravations of a similar nature, till it finally led to the unfortunate Partition of India. This was followed by a consistent undermining of all things that were Hindu in form and content. The Sangh never forgot the partition of the country and Guruji felt that unity and integrity of the country could not be fully secured unless Hindutva became the collective consciousness of our society—and this work is being done by the Sangh.

In economic matters, the ethics that is propounded is trusteeship, not ownership. All material goods are to be consumed with respect to the need of the others and not with the tendency of greedy acquisitiveness. Trusteeship emanated out of Hindutva's core idea of oneness. In this form of economic thinking, the law of abundance is operable, beautifully expounded by S.D. Buffington in a book by the same name. The book builds a case for how all material goods required in life can be available in plenty. Simultaneously, it also states that for this to happen, a non-self-aggrandizing work ethic is required. The non-essential goods can be priced freely. Market economy should be there but it is not only

---

[63]https://www.dailypioneer.com/2015/state-editions/tagore-aurobindo-on-vande-mataram-row.html

for production and profits, it has to be integrated with values of human welfare. Production should not become over-production and create environmental degradation and ruin fragile ecosystems. Hindutva is an environmental movement and the Sangh promotes sustainable development. Market economy has to grow out of the crucible of moral precepts.

High crime rates in the developed countries and frequent incidents of shootings in the US show that growth and development are not to be calculated only by infrastructure development and swanky products. Human beings are not only bodies; they are mind and spirit as well. External development or material well-being has to lead to a corresponding development in the ethical nature of man. This is the essence of the 'vyakti nirman' mission of the Sangh. It is about the development of body, mind, intellect and sprit. The same term was used by Swami Vivekananda as a call to action for all Indians. The whole world needs 'vyakti nirman', the guarantor for justice, equality, respect for women, welfare, and other values which make life a happy pursuit. Hindutva is always modern, flexible and adoptable for every generation.

RE-ESTABLISHING HINDU RASHTRA

Hindu Rashtra is a derivative of Hindutva. It is the imagination of a contemporary, non-violent nation where peace and prosperity prevail, which promotes freedom of worship and equality for women.

The Sangh works towards making the all-encompassing dimensions of Hindutva widely known, and is determined in its resolve for the establishment of Hindu Rashtra. The relation between Hindutva and Hindu Rashtra is the relation between ideas and action; both are inseparable.

Hindu Rashtra is not anti-Muslim. It never was. For instance, Chhatrapati Shivaji's naval chief, Darya Saran, was a Muslim. Shivaji's chief military officers were Ibrahim Khan and Daulat Khan. Shivaji's companion, during his fabled escape from the Mughal internment in Agra, was Madari Mehtar—a Muslim. Shivaji even extended courtesy to sworn enemies like Afzal Khan. After he slayed Afzal Khan, he ordered a tomb to be raised near Pratapgarh and arranged for its upkeep. There is not a single instance in the Hindu Rashtra of Shivaji, where the Quran, the holy book of the Muslims, was ever disrespected. These facts are omitted by history textbooks that misrepresent Shivaji as a communal king. India's sociopolitical kernel is that of Hindu Rashtra, hence different sects of Islam, Christianity and other religions still practise their faith and rituals openly and freely in India. Everyone participates in each other's festivals. Therefore, it is absolutely wrong to present Hindutva as a narrow idea to our future generations.

THREE SUTRAS

The Sangh opposes the series of devious stratagems that were implemented for denigrating Hindutva in the name of secularism. Sangh sarsanghchalak, Mohanji, in his three-day lecture series at Vigyan Bhawan in September, 2018, expounded on what is meant by Hindu Rashtra. He stated that the day it is said that Muslims are unwanted in India, the concept of Hindutva will cease to exist.

There are some motivated elements that ignore India's eternal values and present Hindutva in the image of a few draconian statements made in some old smritis or legal texts. This is absolutely wrong. Hindutva represents our constitutional values of equality, liberty and justice, and since most people in India live by Hindutva principles, freedom of worship for people belonging to other faiths is ensured. There is no place for exclusion on the basis of religious worship or practice in Hindu culture. 'Akashath Pathitham Thoyam Yatha Gachhati Sagaram, Sarvadeva Namaskaram Keshavam Prathi Gachati, is our message of religious harmony. This Sanskrit proverb means—just as rainwater falling from anywhere in the sky finally reaches the ocean, the worship of any divine aspect ultimately reaches the Supreme Being. A book by Prof. Bidyut

Chakrabarty[64] explains in detail the high compatibility between Hindutva and constitutional values.

Hindutva is the combination of three sutras—coordination, consent and coexistence. It is the twenty-first-century grammar of peace, democracy, a fulfilling life and a conflict-free world. The whole world is battling terrorism bred on jihadi philosophies, which believes in the survival of only one form of worship and violent destruction of all others. Hindutva believes in the coexistence of all forms of worship. On 11 September 1893, Swami Vivekananda, in his first speech in Chicago, addressed the World Parliament of Religions. He said, 'This convention should be a death knell of all fanaticism, of all persecutions with the sword or with the pen.' The Sangh reinforced this message throughout 2018 to mark the 125th anniversary of that legendary address. At the World Hindu Congress (WHC) held in Chicago on 7–9 September 2018, Vice-President M. Venkaiah Naidu, delivering the valedictory address, repeated Swamiji's words, 'We Hindus do not merely tolerate, we unite ourselves with every religion, praying in the mosque of the Mohammedan, worshipping before the fire of the Zoroastrian, and kneeling to the cross of the Christian.'

Hindutva is not a means for acquiring political power. If it had been so, Doctorji would have formed a political party and would not have created the RSS—a social organization. It is not all about spirituality either. For the RSS, Hindutva is a comprehensive theory and a range of life practices. Based on it, the Sangh envisages all-around reform and regeneration of the country with the full participation of society. The propagation of Hindutva is a foremost national service that all swayamsevaks engage in throughout their lives. Sustainability, organic, natural conservation, mindfulness, balance, self-awareness, meditation and holistic living are terms that have come into repetitive use the world over and they are becoming global movements, particularly among young people.

---

[64]Vidyut Chakrabarty, *Indian Constitution: Text, Context and Interpretation*, Sage Publication, New Delhi, 2017.

These concepts have been the permanent foci of Hindutva. There is a craving for such wellness in our digitally dependent world and they are adopting Hindutva practices to address this need. Yoga retreats and meditation camps dot all the continents. Apple sells the surya namaskar or sun salutation app on its app store for iOS devices. A few pages of Patanjali Yoga Sutras have been studied and they are re-pivoting the world to Hindutva. Many remarkable classics are yet to be brought before the world for the benefit of humanity.

RSS considers Hindutva to be the natural destination of the world. It will be India's greatest cultural export to the world, just as the *Ramayana* and *Mahabharata* epics which travelled to Southeast Asia in the age of antiquity and shaped the culture there, and just as Buddhism was geared to years later.

IMPORTANT HINDUTVA CONCERNS

The reconstruction of the Ram Temple, cow protection and the abrogation of Article 370 of the Indian constitution are important Hindutva concerns because it is linked to the identity and integrity of India.

The Ram Janmabhoomi Temple

Whenever we think of lofty ideals and virtues, the mental image is of Lord Ram. He is all that is good and noble in this world. India's identity is linked with Lord Ram. *'Bharat, Ram ki bhoomi'*, (India, the land of Lord Ram) is an oft repeated sentence among the masses. Lord Ram's temple at his birthplace in Ayodhya was desecrated by invading Mughal hordes. Archaeology proves it. Hence, a magnificent Ram temple at the Janmasthan, his birthplace in Ayodhya, is of paramount importance. Lord Ram's pure character, his many qualities of giving primacy to people's welfare, establishing respect for women, his unparalleled valour, his defence of dharma and his model conduct as a king, student, brother, son, husband and friend is a bedrock of values that is transmitted from generation to generation in India. So, Ram is the pre-eminent symbol of Hindutva.

The reawakening of India and the construction of the Ram Temple at the janmasthan is an important milestone of the Hindutva movement as it gives expression to a national cultural requirement. The RSS is committed to the construction of a Ram Temple at the janmasthan. It should be constructed within the constitutional framework; the contestation over land rights is being argued before the courts and the Hindu society has waited patiently.

The Sangh has publicly stated many times that the Muslims also draw their ancestry from Lord Ram. This is a historical fact.[65] It is historical forgetfulness, which has made them dissociate themselves from this lineage. The Ram Janmabhoomi issue has figured many times in deliberations of top decision-making bodies of the RSS like the Pratinidhi Sabha as well as in Karyakari Mandal. Several resolutions expressing the wishes of the people for constructing a Grand Ram Temple at the birthplace of Lord Ram have been passed—ABPS, Resolution-1 (1986), Resolution-4 (1987), ABKM, Resolution-2 (1989), ABKM, Resolution-2 (1990), ABPS Resolution-1 (1991), ABPS Resolution-2 (2001), ABKM (2002), ABKM (2003), and ABKM (2006). The Ram Temple will strengthen the unity of the country. The court and the government should pave the way for the construction of a grand Ram Temple at the janmabhoomi in Ayodhya.

Gau Raksha or Cow Protection

Cow protection is not a new concept. It is a symbol of nature worship, and an integral part of the Indian psyche. It is also the stuff of folklore in which the cow is venerated as mother and is the basis of the village economy. In rural India, for simple villagers, even time is referenced with cow; thus 'godhuli' is the word used for twilight—the time when cows return to their sheds after grazing.

---

[65]LiveMint

The Constitution of India recognized the centrality of the cow and the holiness attributed to it in the Indian mindscape. Article 48 of the directive principles of state policy prohibits cow slaughter. The directive principles are guidelines for the framing of laws by the government, and many Indian state governments and union territories have framed laws for cow protection. The RSS advocacy for cow protection is well known. Many ABPS and ABKM resolutions are there on this subject—ABPS (1952), ABPS (1958), KKM (1966), ABKM (1995), ABPS (2000), ABPS (2001) and ABPS (2010). Currently, as many as twenty states have laws on cow protection. These include Rajasthan, Andhra Pradesh, Telangana, Assam, Bihar, Chandigarh, Chhattisgarh, Delhi, Gujarat, Haryana, Himachal Pradesh, J&K, Jharkhand, Karnataka, Madhya Pradesh, Maharashtra, Odisha, Punjab, Tamil Nadu and Uttar Pradesh. These legislations have come as a result of a long struggle and awareness-raising activities that the Sangh undertook with elected representatives.

Guruji even said that if there were communities in some parts of the country who were beef eaters, dialogue would be established with them so that they abjured from such ways. However, those who engage in cow slaughter and beef eating as a brand of politics need to be opposed. Cattle smuggling is an organized crime. It starts with cattle theft and ends with cattle slaughtering. Cattle are the lifeline of the farmers. They are not only wealth but farmers also share a bond of affection with them. Therefore, villagers self-organize for protection and form vigil bands against cattle lifters and thieves. The love for cows and animals runs deep in Indian society. It is not only religious but attached to socio-cultural values.[66]

Though the VHP has been working in the field of cow protection since its inception, a formal department was established in 1986 under the guidance of Shrimant Vijayaraje Scindia.

---

[66]Swati Goel Sharma, 'Armed Smugglers are Killing Cattle Owners Across India. Here's A List of Cases', Scoopwhoop, 3 July 2017.

In 1996, Gau Vigyan Anusandhan Kendra was established for academic activities like seminars, conferences and workshops to spread awareness about cow protection. This centre also works to promote panchgavya, which includes cow dung, cow milk, buttermilk, curd and ghee. It also offers panchgavya ayurveda therapy.[67]

Several organizations, supported by the Sangh, are also working on how farmers can earn from non-milch cows, by harvesting cow urine and cow dung for use in medicinal products and as organic manure. The Sangh's programme of 'gram vikas', or village development, has actively involved farmers in spreading organic farming in sync with the belief that food should be natural and not chemical based.

POLITICIZATION OF SANSKRIT

The politicization of languages was done for conflict. The fact that languages in India have their roots in Sanskrit, the mother of all Indian languages, was wilfully obscured from public discourse and learning material. The emphasis was not on common origin but on separation. Language is the finest expression of the human mind and the most potent communication vehicle. For example, words like 'samay' (time) are the same in Bengali, Hindi, Marathi, etc., as Sanskrit is the root language. Sanskrit is a link language, with prayers in all temples, be it Guruvayur in Kerala or Kamakhya Temple in Assam, being offered in Sanskrit. Only when people appreciate these linkages will they be motivated to learn Indian languages other than their own, paving the way to linguistic unity. If these linkages of language are not formulated, there will be adverse sociological consequences of linguistic divisiveness.

The Sangh considers Sanskrit the great unifier and part of a grand heritage. There is no pyramid here. All Indian languages have their own literature, philosophy, grammar and syntax, and

---

[67]Cow Protection, Vishva Hindu Parishad.

together with Sanskrit, are a language family and giant pillars of the Indian knowledge system.

Yet, the politics over Sanskrit teaching has been unabashed. The SC, in a landmark judgement in 1994, rejected the charge that teaching of Sanskrit was against secularism. It said, 'Indeed our constitution requires giving fillip to Sanskrit because of what has been stated in Article 351, in which while dealing with the duty of the union to promote the spread of Hindi, it has been provided that, it would draw, whenever necessary or desirable for its vocabulary, primarily on Sanskrit.'[68] The same holds true for all other languages, which heavily enrich themselves with Sanskrit infusions.

Sanskrit is both the culture and civilization of India. Leaders of India, from Aurobindo to Ambedkar, considered it the genius of India. Western historians, linguists and scientists from Will Durant to Arthur Schopenhauer were bowled over by its wisdom, and forecast that this knowledge would blow over the Western world, producing a change in their knowing and thinking.

The Sangh believes that Sanskrit and all Indian languages should be promoted to make Bharat a Vishwa Guru. Samskrit Bharti is a social organization for the propagation of Sanskrit language, which fulfils the crucial role of Sanskrit language teaching and instruction. It runs short courses and has overseas activities in the USA, where it is headquartered in California. In British schools, Sanskrit is very appealing. At the St. James Junior School in London, the number of pupils wanting to learn Sanskrit has increased significantly. Linguists world over are saying that Sanskrit stimulates language development and phonetics. In Germany, fourteen top universities teach Sanskrit. Summer schools for spoken Sanskrit in Switzerland

---

[68]In The Supreme Court of India: Original Civil Jurisdiction: Writ Petition (Civil) No. 98 Of 2002, http://www.ncert.nic.in/html/pdf/schoolcurriculum/ncfsc/judge1_50.pdf

and Italy are seeing a flood of applications.[69]

Sanskrit teachers are in great demand. Those who were not exposed to learning Sanskrit are seeing it as a missed opportunity. Eminent personalities like former Chief Justices of India, M.N. Rao Venkatachaliah and R.C. Lahoti, former Chief Justice of Punjab High Court, Rama Jois, and former chief election commissioner of India, N. Gopalaswamy, have associated with Sanskrit scholars to propagate the language. The World Sanskrit Book Fair drew many youngsters and re-ignited investigations about India's intellectual wealth.[70] It is also exciting the scientific community. 'Sanskrit language is considered to be the only suitable natural language for computers. Software is being developed for the machine translation of Indian languages with Sanskrit as the intermediate language.'[71]

Hence, the Sangh's views on teaching Sanskrit are experiencing national and global endorsements.[72]

THE UNIFORM CIVIL CODE AND ARTICLE 370

All that augments Ekatmata must be promoted and all that whips up separatism must be done away with. Constitutions are not frozen in time; they are dynamic texts. If certain provisions like Article 370, granting autonomous status to the state of J&K, were brought in due to compulsions arising out of unprecedented situations, they ought to be reviewed with the changing times and in the light of new realities.

At the time this book was going to print, the Parliament of India

---

[69]Aditya Ghosh, 'Sanskrit Fever Grips Germany: 14 Universities Teaching India's Ancient Language Struggle to Meet Demand as Students Clamour for Courses', Mail Online India, 14 April 2015.

[70]It generated business of ₹3 crore in 2011.

[71]R.S. Lahoti, *Sanskrit: An Instrument for Promotion of India's Soft Power*, Second Deen Dayal Upadhyaya Memorial International Oration: ICCR, 21 May 2018.

[72]Samskrita Bharti also organized the Sanskrit Sambhashan programme. A total of 94 lakh participants attended 1,40,000 thousand camps.

abrogated Article 370, and with it, the discriminatory anti-women Article 35 A was also scrapped. The President of India signed the Jammu and Kashmir Reorganization Bill, 2019, passed by both the houses of the Parliament into an act and now there are two union territories—Jammu and Kashmir and Ladakh. In our understanding of the Sangh, Article 370 was a very painful experience for the Indian masses. Due to this special status, the conduct of the J&K state and the activities of the separatists continually stoked fires of disintegration in the Kashmir Valley. Political parties which formed the state government were discriminatory towards Jammu and Ladakh, depriving them of development. Social justice measures like reservations for the scheduled castes and tribes were inoperable in J&K.

Separatism got a foil of secularism and it snowballed. It peaked in January 1990. On communal lines, announcements blared over loudspeakers in mosques ordering the Kashmiri Pandit population in the valley to leave. Many faced slaughter and dishonour of women. So, in 1990, when the Pandit community was trooping out of the valley and becoming exiles in their own country, the RSS and all its inspired organizations swung into action. The present chief minister of Himachal Pradesh, Jairam Thakur, in those days was the ABVP organizing secretary for Jammu. Muralidhar Rao, presently the general secretary, BJP, was also the organizing secretary for Jammu and Kashmir in this phase. Ramesh Pappa, who is now an all-India level RSS functionary, worked as a local office-bearer. The Sangh set up the Jammu Kashmir Sahayata Samiti. Indresh Kumar was responsible for the Sangh work and Jyoti Swarup was the prant pracharak. Those were days of hard toil and all of them were leaders in this hyper-crisis situation.

The swyamsevaks and activist volunteers worked constantly to create logistics for refugee Kashmiri Pandits. Camps were set up in Geeta Bhawan near the parade ground in Jammu, Aknoor, Nagrota and Udhampur. A lot of pressure was mounted on the state administration for facilities.

Among the refugees were students from Kashmir University who were allocated to different Jammu colleges while maintaining their affiliation to Kashmir University. Classes held for them in Jammu colleges became known by the moniker 'Camp College'. In Maharashtra, the BJP-Sena which came to power made provisions for admissions of displaced Kashmiri Pandit students in the educational institutions of the state. ABVP started a Kashmir unit based out of Jammu. Rallies and rathyatras were organized. Kashmiri Pandit students traversed the country to raise awareness about the threats to India's unity that were unfolding due to terrorist activities in the valley.

Many conferences and seminars were held. In the 90s, swayamsevaks were participating in Ramjanmbhoomi movement and they were also part of a intense movement of 'Save Kashmir' by ABVP. ABVP organized 'Chalo Kashmir' rally on 11 September 1990 with slogans such as 'Jahan huye balidan Mukherji woh Kashmir hamara hai' (Kashmir, where Mukherji was martyred, is ours) and 'Jahan hua tiranga ka apman wahin karenge uska samaan' (We will restore the respect of our national Tricolour). These slogans defined the ethos of the common people of India. The Article 370 abrogation became a part of our nationalist consciousness during our college days.

A national seminar was also conducted on same topic in Jammu in 1991, which was addressed by Atal Behari Vajpayee and General J.F.R Jacob. In 1992, the seminar on 'Role of Centre and State in present J&K', was attended by Dr Jitender Singh, currently a minister in the Modi government. He is a medical doctor and this was his first step in public life.

In 2001, an important milestone was added. Students from Jammu were discriminated against and there was large-scale bungling for admissions in medical colleges. As a result of ABVP agitation, the bogus admission process was cancelled.

ABVP has had a long history of activism in Jammu and Kashmir. In 1952, the Student National Association (SNA) was formed. It merged in ABVP in 1954. Chaman Lal Gupta was an important figure in this generation of activists. ABVP has always drawn inspiration from the martyrdom of Shyama Prasad Mukherji for the Kashmir cause. In 2005, veteran SNA and ABVP activists were felicitated at a programme which I attended along with the RSS Sarsangchalak Mohanji.

The existence of a vibrant Hindu community in the districts of Kishtwar, Doda, Poonch and Rajouri is due to the sustained efforts of dedicated swayamsevaks. The Sangh worked continuously to prepare the society there to fight against terrorism and ensured that there was no flight of population from these areas on communal lines due to violence committed by terrorists. Therefore, the decision of removing Article 370, taken by Narendra Modi's government, is a historical act and completes the mission of Sardar Patel.

In the coming days, there are four major tasks. First, to restore the dignity and property of the displaced Pandit population in the valley. Second, to get back the portion of Kashmir occupied by Pakistan. Third, to make Kashmir free from terrorism. Fourth, Kashmir has several lost decades in terms of development because of the double disaster of terrorism and oligarchic family control over politics and resources. So, development has to proceed at a very fast pace. Now the people of the union territories of Jammu and Kashmir and Ladakh have all the rights that are enjoyed by the rest of the Indian citizens. All of Sangh Shakti will be deployed for achieving this roadmap.

Over the years, overall engagement with the Kashmiri student community has deepened. I myself have toured Srinagar, Badgaon, Pulwama and Anantnag, and have interacted with students in colleges, lecturers and professors. Conversations with Muslim students and teachers in the valley is an ongoing process. A vital finding is that most do not want separatism and are fed up with terror. They desire a life of dignity and see their future in India.

Similarly, we dialogue with Kashmiri students studying in

different parts of the country. On 19 December 2017, I addressed a big gathering of 400 such students studying engineering in Udaipur. Contrary to aspersions that were cast after the abrogation of Article 370, in all NITs and central universities, Kashmiri students are studying in a hassle-free environment. This demonstrates that the entire country is extending a warm clasp towards Kashmiris for them to script a new and successful future.

The issue of Article 370 and Kashmir is very close to the Sangh and has been taken up more than fifty times in its highest bodies in the form of resolutions. Notable among them are ABPS[73] (1953), ABPS (1965), ABPS (1986), ABPS (1990), ABKM[74] Resolution-4 (1990), ABKM Resolution-2 (1991), ABKM Resolution-3 (1993), ABKM Resolution-1 (1995), ABKM Resolution-1 (1996), ABPS Resolution-1 (1997), ABKM Resolution-1 (2000), ABPS Resolution-4 (2001), ABKM Resolution-1 (2002), ABPS Resolution-1 (2004), ABPS (2010) and ABKM (2010).

ABKM Resolution-3 (1995) is an important document on the issue of the Uniform Civil Code. The issue of Triple Talaq came into public debate after the Shah Bano judgement when the Congress government overruled the decision of the SC under pressure from certain sections of society. Since then, many organizations and women have continued the fight. The issue remained sub judice for a long time. In May 2017, the Constitution Bench ruled against the practice of Triple Talaq following which the government tried to introduce a law for the abolition of this practice. But as the opposition created hindrance in the Rajya Sabha, the government had to take the route of ordinance. The Triple Talaq debate and developments were steered mainly by Muslim women. Finally, The bill has been passed by both the houses of parliament on 30 July 2019.

Indresh Kumar,[75] national executive member of the Sangh,

---

[73] ABPS: Akhil Bharatiya Pratinidhi Sabha
[74] ABKM: Akhil Bharatiya Karyakari Mandal
[75] Indresh Kumar Nails SC Verdict, Says It Delivered Muslim Women From

hailed it as a significant move for the women's movement in the country. He said that eight to nine crore Indian women, who followed Islamic religion, were facing a huge social problem due to Triple Talaq. The SC has freed these women from torture and injustice. The practice of Triple Talaq goes against the basic principle of equality. The Sangh is against all kinds of discrimination against women. The Uniform Civil Code is not only a necessity for Ekatmata, but also a preventive against the exploitation that Muslim women have had to endure due to their religious laws.

Social justice, social harmony, self-reliant society, promotion of Hindu culture, promotion of Indian languages, pariwar prabodhan (awakening about the family system), resurgence of Indian knowledge system, popularization of Sanskrit studies, environment conservation and gram vikas (rural development) are the major ongoing Hindutva projects of the twenty-first century.

NATIONAL SECURITY ARMOUR

For India, Hindutva is the national security armour. Whenever Hindutva is strengthened, the unity and integrity of the country becomes impregnable and unassailable. The Muslim community has full freedom of worship and no one can foist divisive propaganda on them. One has only to study the living conditions of the Muslims during the rule of Shivaji and the Peshwas to understand their flourishing status. Their service to the state of the Marathas was based on an appreciation that their forefathers were Hindus and thus they shared common values. However, in subsequent decades, the forces of Hindutva were not well-organized; the Sangh had just started and a myth was spread that there are two peoples or nations in this country—the Hindus and the Muslims. The British implemented the 'divide- and- rule policy' and fanned Islamic fundamentalism. The leadership of the country

Bondage', Daily Hunt, 22 August.

at that point submitted to these imperial theories and logic. All talk of Hindu-Muslim unity shorn of Hindutva ideals was facile and could not stand. The Partition followed. Pakistan was created in lands that had followed Hindutva principles for thousands of years. When this new state scrubbed the historical slate of its Hinduness, the openness of its society was wiped out. History books of Pakistan consecrated the Arab commander Mohammad Bin Qasim, who invaded Sind in the eighth century, as the first Pakistani. The Bangladesh war of liberation, in 1971, showed to the world how flawed the two-nation theory was and these developments also taught Indian people the calamitous situations that could unfold when Hindutva was weakened. These are unforgettable lessons from India's freedom struggle that the Sangh learnt dearly and continues to teach in its shakhas, from generation to generation.

The nature, scope and progress of Hindutva is continually discussed in Sangh's 'shiksha vargas' (teaching camps). This is already accepted by the majority of the country's population. Merely a segment of the educated population who have little understanding about India whip up anti-Hindutva sentiments. Today, they are exposed and synonymous with the 'Break India' (Tukde Tukde) brigades. A lot of work by the Sangh and its affiliates devoted to building Hindutva epistemology for India has been able to unshackle the stranglehold of the Break India brigades in the institutions of higher learning and among the urban, English-speaking sections of Indian society. This has helped to correct the academic and cultural misrepresentations and distortions that have held sway in the past several decades since Independence.

The cause of Hindutva is therefore the cause of Ekatmata and Vasudhaiva Kutumbakam. Muslims and Christians can also subscribe to Hindutva because it is a matter of national identity. Many are accepting it through a process of self-awakening. Not much convincing is required once the shibboleths of false knowledge crumble.

In the realm of international relations, the Modi government has expanded and deepened its relations with Muslim countries in the Gulf region, both in terms of social and economic engagement. These nations see that a government inspired by Hindutva ethics is based on 'sabka saath, sabka vikas', or development and equal opportunity for all. They can clearly see that for the Muslim community, there is respect for their form of worship and religious observances.

In the twenty-first century, Hindutva is a bold vision for truth and oneness in a sea of sectarian isms and ideologies. It defines the Sangh. In the years and decades ahead, Hindutva will be India's greatest cultural export, the chief instruments of which will be the Sangh and its swayamsevaks.

6

CASTE AND SOCIAL JUSTICE

Social justice and caste are conjoined. There can be no meaningful dialogue on social justice without an honest deliberation on caste—about what it was intended to be and what it has become.

Varna vyavastha, the oldest system to bring social order and prosperity, was based on guna (qualities) and karma (deeds and efforts), not on birth. But over time, it was converted to jati (caste)—based on birth. The caste system has, unfortunately, become an instrument of polarization to wreck the unity of Hindu society to reap electoral benefits. Such an assessment does not mean living in denial about discriminative atrocities or glossing over certain practices that are decidedly inhuman. It reflects awareness that mitigation strategies are necessary, as caste has become a political sword. Our method for alleviation of caste injustices is 'samajik samrasta', or social harmony, where equality is envisaged on the basis of fraternity. Achieving this objective is a long process, and the sphere of action lies primarily in society, not in politics. To bring in samrasta, however, an understanding of the societal structure and the cause of deterioration of caste connotations is essential.

UNDERSTANDING THE STRUCTURE

It is virtually impossible to exactly ascertain when caste, which originally structured society based on people's aptitude or occupation, came to be determined by birth and became associated with discrimination and an iniquitous structure. This is not how it was intended to be. A pastoral, agricultural society needed division of labour and specialization of work. Caste was the answer; at least, that is how it was conceived.

The Bhagavadgita defines varna as *'catur-varnyam maya srstam guna-karma-vibhagasah tasya kartaram api mam viddhy akartaram avyayam'*, or 'according to the three modes of material nature and the work associated with them, the four divisions of human society are created by Me. And although I am the creator of this system, you should know that I am yet the non-doer, being unchangeable.' (BG 4.13) Lord Krishna, in the Bhagavadagita, clearly points out that these natural divisions in human society are created by Him, but these divisions are not based on birth but 'according to the three modes of material nature and the work associated with them.'

The emphasis is on guna and karma, or aptitude, action and capacity; birth finds no mention. Neither is there any segmentation into high, low or any segregationist postulate. And then Krishna says that though he is the creator of actions, he is the non-doer. The creator or the self of the Upanishads is beyond the concoction of any form of discrimination, high or low. The intended idea was only organization.

Every society all over the world needs to be structured to carry out its tasks. Some will take to army, politics and administration, some will take to business and agriculture, some will take to labour, and some will take to learning and higher spiritual pursuits. Broadly, these four categories are found in all societies.

Indian social attention, thus, was never on birth status but based on 'guna', 'karma' and 'swabhav'—qualities and aptitude of an individual. Vedic literature is full of examples of the change of varna. For instance, Valmiki, one of the greatest rishis and scholars of ancient India, was born to non-Brahmin parents.

The evil in this system began when it became hereditary, and was associated with power, privilege, domination by a few and denial of even basic human rights to vast sections of people.

CORROSION OF CASTE AS JATI

When caste corroded into jati-vyavastha, or caste system, it gave birth to a perverted oppressive system that became further divided into a hierarchy of about 3,000 castes and 25,000 sub-castes.

The modern understanding of caste is rooted in European social science methods. Anand Paliwal, professor and dean of law faculty at Mohanlal Sukhadiya University, Udaipur,[76] writes in his book, 'Vedas consider all varnas, including shudras, with respect. They do not contain any word that can be considered as synonym for "caste".'

Jaati, determined by birth, is different from caste. It refers to a classification based on the source of origin. As *Nyaya Sutra*—the first systematic work on the nyaya as a philosophical system that uses tarka or logic as epistemology to deal with subjects such as God, creation, knowledge and salvation—states that '*saamanap arasavatmika jattih*', or those who have a similar birth source form a jati. For instance, according to rishis, there are only four jatis— udbhija, who come out of the ground like plants; andaja, who come out of eggs, like birds and reptiles; pindaja, mammals or animals, human beings, etc., born out of physical bodies; and lastly, ushmaj, who reproduce due to temperature and ambient conditions like virus, bacteria, etc.

According to the Oxford English Dictionary, 'caste' is derived from the Portuguese word 'casta', meaning race, lineage or breed. There is no exact translation in Indian languages, but varna and jati are the two most proximate terms.

Over time, vested interests grew and birth began to play an increasingly important role in the determination of one's caste. During long centuries of foreign rule, Indian society became

---

[76]A. Paliwal, *Casteism*, Himanshu Publication, New Delhi.

stagnant and the same thing happened with the caste system. It became more and more rigid. Birth became the sole criteria to determine one's caste. Untouchability and taboos of various types also became prevalent.[77] Family lineage became a marker of social rank, which was further embossed as a result of foreign invasions and occupation.

As Sumit Guha,[78] professor of history in the University of Texas in Austin, US, notes, 'The Portuguese, who introduced later-coming Europeans to Indian society, were evolving a system of ethnic and social stratification by biological ancestry; it was for this reason that they immediately assumed that Indian jātis aimed exclusively at maintaining "purity of blood."'

Since British followed the Portuguese in India, they used the same classification to categorize and document the various social groups and thereby lost the critical component in our social stratification—mobility across the varna or 'castes'. This stagnation of our social system is the most significant deterioration that happened to our society and became the bedrock of most social and cultural conflicts.

Modern academics, such as Bernard Cohn,[79] have argued that the British, through their census and other works, effectively created the caste system as it exists today. From the outset in 1872, there was never a formal definition of the census categories for caste, race or tribe. For example, in 1891, the Jats and Rajputs were recorded as castes and tribes, respectively, although the category of tribe was not formally adopted until the 1901 census. The recorded details changed in every census from 1872 to 1941 as the administrators struggled to comprehend Indian culture. Reliance

---

[77]Balraj Madhok, *Indianisation*, Sultan Chand, New Delhi.

[78]Sumit Guha, *Beyond Caste. Identity and Power in South Asia, Past and Present*, Brill, Leiden/Boston, 2013.

[79]B. Singer, Cohn Milton, S. Bernard, *Structure and Change in Indian Society, Notes on the History of the Study of Indian Society and Culture*, pp. 24–25, Aldine Translation [A division of Transaction Publishers, New Brunswick (USA) and London (UK)], 1968.

on elites formed part of a colonial strategy to propel their idea of India to the masses. The Raj aimed to gain favour with the elites, whose position would then lead to the idea of Indian nationhood percolating through the rest of society. Yet, even the concept of Brahmanic elites is tricky—Indian statistician Prasanta Chandra Mahalanobis, who was instrumental in formulating India's strategy for industrialization in the second Five-Year Plan (1956–61), demonstrated that Bengali Brahmins were more similar to other castes in Bengal than to any Brahmin groups elsewhere.[80]

PERVASIVE DISCRIMINATION

The rigid framing of the caste structure for the purpose of analysis made it lose its flexibility. Thus, as a consequence of the identity liberalism and the mischief of the dominant Left historiography, caste transformed from a category of analysis to a category of practice.

Caste-based discrimination and oppression was neither episodic, nor in the nature of few, sporadic occurrences. It became an extensive system—a social structure. With time, there was an accumulation of these practices to such a degree that there was an overall culture of exploitation, ritually defined. Life was negative for large sections of society based on their caste status. Untouchability and caste-based decadent behaviour was pervasive.

There was a deep conventional belief in society that caste was determined by birth, and some so-called lower castes were untouchables. The exploited castes blamed it on themselves, and their bad karma, for which they would have to endure a life of suffering and humiliation. This situation was varied and not uniform. Such discrimination was nearly non-existent in areas inhabited by the janjati or tribal communities, while in some states,

---

[80]P.C. Mahalanobis, Article No. 24, N.S., XXIII, *Analysis of Race Mixture in Bengal, Journal of the Asiatic Society of the Bengal*, Proceedings of Indian Science Congress, Nagpur, 1931.

the scourge of untouchability was more or even extreme. There was no getting away from the fact that untouchability had become a feature of Hindu society.

ENTRY OF THE REFORMISTS

While the authors of the Upanishads would recoil from what became of caste when it was translated as untouchability, public-spirited reformist leaders in the Indian society worked for change. It was an uphill task. Even as gatherings and co-mingling of castes was promoted, those belonging to the so-called higher castes, after attending such meetings, would go home and have the ritual purity bath. Such practices were common.

Gandhiji created a major movement to fight untouchability, calling such castes Harijans, or people of the Lord. The most potent change factor in this sphere was Dr Ambedkar. In August 1923, the Bombay Legislative Council passed a legislation, which stated that the facilities maintained by the government should have open access for all castes. In January 1924, the Mahad Nagar Parishad located in Bombay Presidency adopted this law. But since considerable local 'savarna', or so-called higher castes, became restive, this law could not be implemented. This issue acquired mobilizational significance and was later taken up by Dr Ambedkar, when on 20 March 1927, he launched his famous satyagraha for allowing those who were considered untouchables to use water from a public tank in Mahad. This satyagraha is also known as 'mukti sangram', or liberation struggle. In those days, freedom fighter Veer Savarkar after his release from the cellular jail in Andaman settled in Ratnagiri in Maharashtra and stayed there from 1924 to 1937. Forbidden from undertaking political activity, Savarkar turned his attention to the burning social issues of the day. He was intent on temple entry for all. Drawing on the Vedas, Savarkar began mobilizing opinion through his writings. India needed rationalism and social reform. In his essay 'Abolition of Caste,' he writes on untouchability. It is impossible to justify this inhuman custom when we consider any aspect of dharma. So, this custom should be eradicated as a command of dharma.'[81] Even during his incarceration in the Andaman's, caste inequities of the Hindu society deeply troubled him. While in jail, he wrote in a letter, 'Just as I feel that I should rebel against the foreign rule over Hindustan, I feel I should rebel against caste discrimination and untouchability.' Both were equally reprehensible to him and he wanted liberation from both. He made it a precondition that he would address only those Ganesh Mahotsav meetings that would be open to all castes. In May 1933, Savarkar began a café—'The Pan-Hindu Café.' It had common dining rules, rare and path-breaking for its times.

This was the sociopolitical landscape when Doctorji came of age as a leader and it was in the backdrop of such movements and constructive social experiments that Doctorji established the Sangh and set some firm rules. Doctorji said caste discrimination had no place in Hindu society. He was a steadfast protagonist of social equality. He castigated the bad practices that had crept in and resolved to remove such discriminations. Doctorji was far ahead of his times. Untouchability and caste taboo were kept out of the Sangh and he started the Sangh based on equal relations among all castes. So, the Sangh, since its founding day, decided that caste will play no role in the functioning of its organization. No member is asked about caste identity in the Sangh and no special arrangement is made for food, sitting, sleeping or any other activity for different castes and religions.

The Sangh's faith lies in the Hindu nation. Everyone belongs to Bharat Mata and are sons and daughters of Bharat Mata. All are Hindus and so there cannot be any discrimination in relationships with each other. Swayamsevaks come from all castes and all are equal. Any swayamsevak can be given any task. He may be assigned the task of cleaning toilets one day and could next be assigned the

---

[81]'Religion, Religious Scriptures', savarkar.org

duty of preparing food or conducting a study session. Common dining, accommodation and intermingling have always been standard norms.

TRADITION AND REFORM

Since its inception, the RSS has been a reformist, forward-looking force. Equality among swayamsevaks was an established principle. Doctorji was deeply influenced by the Ramakrishna-Vivekananda tradition. Guruji, too, belonged to this tradition. His spiritual preceptor was Swami Akhandananda, who had undertaken many works for the downtrodden and was a brother-monk of Swami Vivekananda. Guruji was steeped in Vivekananda's man-making mission.

Much earlier, in 1897, assessing the social reality, Swami Vivekananda had stated that centuries of colonization had degraded our mind. These ideas stayed with Guruji and he immersed himself in the regeneration of Hindu society. Guruji felt it was not enough for the Sangh to only mirror samrasta. It was important for the entire society to possess this hue of social harmony. Scriptures were to be quoted not for perpetuating caste discrimination and untouchability but for establishing equality.

On the occasion of Guruji's 51st birthday in 1956, public functions were held all over the country to rouse the spirit of nationalism in the people and for offering shraddha nidhi, or contributions for social causes. At these public functions, he appealed to all Hindu brethren who had converted to other faiths to merge back into the Hindu mainstream. He also suggested that the respected Pejawar Swami, a living saint from the state of Karnataka, keen to establish social equality, work in this direction. Guruji said, 'The country was divided because of the disorganized state of Hindus. When Hindus stand organized and united again, time will not be far before Bharat becomes united once again.'

Guruji began meeting the heads of different religious faiths from Hindu society—all sampradyas, saints and shankacharyas—to make this a pervasive movement. This culminated in the formation of the VHP and a grand convention was held in 1969 in Udipi.

Guruji toiled hard for the success and effectiveness of the programme. He met a large number of people to convince them about the role that such a programme would fulfil. All the respected shankaracharyas came onto a single platform for a particular sankalp that stated, 'Na Hindu patito bhavet', which literally means that no Hindu can be impure. This assertion was important since caste discrimination was bound up with notions of ritual purity and impurity. What this meant in effect was that there is no place for untouchability in Hindutva. It was illegal. All Hindus come from the same womb—'Hindwa sahodara sarve'. Heroes who promoted these reforms and social justice like Dr Ambedkar, Mahatma Phule, Sant Ravidas and Narayana Guru are among the icons of the Sangh's Ekatmata stotra, or 'The Unity Verses'. Each and every swayamsevak is committed to this stotra. The 1969 Udupi convention of the VHP proved to be a historic occasion for the revitalization of the Hindu society and a call for action to reform.

The third sarsanghchalak of RSS, Balasaheb Deoras, in different speeches to various assemblies of RSS members across various locations, spoke of the need to build an efficient and exploitation-free Hindu society. In his Pune address on 8 May 1974, as part of his historic Spring Lecture Series (Vasant Vyakhyanmala), Deoras said, 'There is no greater sin than untouchability and it should go lock, stock and barrel.' During this phase, many resolutions to this effect were passed and several samrasta campaigns were started by swayamsevaks.

Seva, or service activities, for needy sections took on a grand scale from 1989 onwards, the birth centenary year of Doctorji. Voluntary service for the upliftment of scheduled castes and scheduled tribes became high-priority work. Seva Bharti forayed with activities in health and education in far-flung areas, which were extremely neglected by formal governance structures. The Sangh runs more than one lakh welfare service programmes, catalogued in detail on the Seva Bharti website. Seva Bharti is working through 973 organizations in all 602 districts of the country. It is running 11,670 projects in the field of education, 8,516 projects in the field of health, 9,416 in the social field and 5,813 projects to make people self-dependent. Rashtriya Seva Bharti has completed 35,560 seva projects till date. A total of 1,32,032 seva projects are run by the Sangh and Sangh-inspired organizations.

Sarkaryavaha Bhaiyaji Joshi (Suresh Joshiji) emphasizes the importance of seva work. He believes that seva work should touch all the communities and cross the boundaries of the nation as well.

THE PATH OF SOCIAL JUSTICE

Self-initiative, an organization principle in Sangh, is useful for work in social justice domains. When I was in college, in 1986–87, the ABVP started a campaign that in everyone's residence, a photograph of Dr Ambedkar would be installed. In those days this was not an easy task, as Ambedkar represented the so-called lower caste—and we, the so-called upper caste people, had to struggle to instal Ambedkar's photograph in our residences. This campaign was chosen in order to sprout reform first within the activists themselves. A key word used for the campaign was that the outreach work should become 'sarvasparshi', meaning that it should touch all. All the sections of society were to be included; none were excluded, not even those who were historically unfavourable to us. The Sangh boldly faces the truth and does not hide behind obfuscations.

While doing this work, I also experienced stereotypical caste discriminations. In my work, I have seen that layers of misconceptions have been spread about the Sangh, but these have lifted easily when people have seen our conduct. They have joined us in large numbers because they have seen that there is no dichotomy between what we profess and what we do. *Purank ki Aur* (Towards Completeness), a book on ABVP's redoubtable leader, Yashwantrao Kelkar, records the impressions of many student-activists belonging to the so-called lower castes who tested him on his teachings. Kelkar lived by what he taught. When these activists would visit Kelkar at his home, he would jovially tell them that if they wanted water for themselves, they should go to the kitchen and get it, and bring a glass of water for him as well. This is a small daily-life incident which demonstrates that Kelkar complied with what he said, and it also shows what we were up against at that time as a society.

Those belonging to scheduled castes (SCs) and other backward castes (OBCs) have headed ABVP work in the Osmania University and Telangana region. As Sangh work expands, SCs and OBCs will be seen in prominent positions in all tiers of Sangh activity. When the Rohit Vemula incident (suicide of a scholar of Hyderabad University) happened, a bitter discourse of caste identity was foisted on us about the discrimination of Mala-Madigas. Such nefarious tactics fell flat because most of the ABVP student leaders of the region came from these two castes. When they went for television debates, they exposed the canards. Due to this reality, even though opponents repeated their lies on national television channels, this issue had no impact in Andhra Pradesh and Telangana.

When the Sangh began the Ram Janmabhoomi movement, the shilanayas, or the foundation stone-laying ceremony, for the Ram Temple was done on 9 November 1989 by Kameshwar Chaupalji, who belonged to the scheduled caste community of Bihar.

Crucial work on freedom from a corrupt caste system is being done at multiple levels. Firstly, an all-round development and equitable distribution of public goods and services will deter perverted identity politics. Development will consolidate people, not caste politics. Secondly, Marxist distortions will be countered and a correct narrative of the Hindu society will be presented through proper historical and philosophical investigations.

Thirdly, our people have to be educated that the 'caste system' is an open and dynamic form of social stratification and is not based on birth. Personalities and events that highlight activities unbounded by caste sentiments will be presented in popular-culture formats. For instance, recently, a Bengaluru-based couple of Sangh persuasions, advocate Kshama Nargund and her industrialist husband, Vyvaswatha, conducted the upanayana, or sacred thread ceremony, for their twins—Samvith Banavaty, a boy, and Asmitha Banavaty, a girl, at their residence in the city. Kshama's father, M.B. Naragund, a senior advocate, and working president of Adivakta Parishad, an RSS-inspired body for advocates, said, 'This practice was prevalent as mentioned in our Vedas and Upanishad. But over a period of time, the practice stopped for many reasons. All are equal before God.' The couple faced questions about their decision but there was great excitement too. Many attended the ceremony and it received media coverage. This emerging reality must also be acknowledged.

Fourthly, the basic tenets of Hinduism are tolerance and spirituality—this is highly popularized to promote solidarity and a sense of belonging.

FREEING POLITICS FROM CASTE

The Sangh is not influenced by the political drama that unfolds each day. It is advancing with its beliefs on social justice and wants that the new leadership should emanate from different castes and communities that have lagged behind. This leadership should be nationalist in temperament and constructive in action. Such leadership is necessary for we have seen all too often that social justice struggles coalesce around select cliques. An expansion in leadership numbers is required and this can happen through the methods of the Sangh to bring about social change—clarity of thought without prejudice and vested interest, and seva and affection for each other. The idea is to challenge divisive propaganda—to be conscious reconcilers. The so-called upper castes also have to be mindful of the wrongs and atone. The Sangh is working on this pattern of social structure and social leadership. Only then we will have true social justice. These dialogues and efforts are being carried out regardless of the political atmosphere in the country. It is being done at the basic tier of the village and town, and is bearing fruit.

In April 1999, Bihar was full of caste violence. This was the age of caste senas and caste enclaves. People belonging to one caste did not venture into the hamlets of other castes for fear of life. Jehanabad was the epicentre of such inter-caste clashes and goonda-ism. In such circumstances, the state executive of ABVP, which comprised members of all castes, resolved to go on a padayatra in Jehanabad district to restore relations. The times were dreadful and tense, at many places, random firing was the order of the day. The padayatra took place despite such adversities in the field and helped to change the environment. The Sangh never claims to be the only harbinger of change, but in preparing the ground for positive change, the Sangh always makes a significant contribution. While there are groups which keep on belabouring about problems due to vote politics, the Sangh focuses on solutions.

Often, so-called social justice forces use weaker sections as a camouflage to feed their politics; they even turn it into a bogey while portraying that they are working to bring about social equality. But what they actually do is promote caste rivalry; they use attractive packaging for garnering the support of weaker sections and use antithetical idioms to ensure disharmony. For reaping electoral dividends, they institutionalize inter-caste hatred. They create an illusion that the cause of social justice is being served, but in reality, they farm personal political gains. The marginalized sections remain marginalized. Politically, benefits are accrued only to a few families and their cronies who are as oppressive as the system they initially set out to fight. This is a destructive and negative design.

The Sangh's work is constructive and its people-centric activities in all fields are related to progress and unity. It works to fashion and rebuild Hindu society on the principles of equality and to shear off the ill practices that have crept in through the ages. This is what distinguishes the Sangh from other organizations.

RE-INTERPRETING CULTURE FOR CHANGE

The practice of a convoluted caste system based on birth led to distortions in our society and the deepening of social cleavages due to the misidentification of caste as the master key to understand India. For example, can we understand the society and culture of Assam using the lens of caste? No. Hence, we need to seriously reflect on the way knowledge is produced and disseminated in our country. Fundamentally, our system does not discriminate against any social group. There are many examples of this. In the famous Sri Ranganatha temple at Jiyaguda in Hyderabad, there is a 2,700-year-old ritual, wherein the priest carries a person belonging to the Dalit community on his shoulder to the sanctum sanctorum. Within Hindu society, anyone can become a Brahmin through the process of upanayana and thereby access the Vedas. The idea that Vedas are only for Brahmins is a wrong notion. Reformers like Chattampi Swamikal, through his work *Vedadikara Nirupanam* (1918), established that Vedas are for all Hindus irrespective of their birth status. Students from all castes could learn the Vedas. Thus, by training, Dalits, too, have become priests, thereby breaking the barrier of only Brahmins becoming priests.

There are multiple instances of non-Brahmins becoming priests and learning Vedas after Independence. T.T. Kesavan Sastri, president of the All Travancore Pulaya Mahasabha, from the Pulaya community, now notified as scheduled caste, was supported as a student by Mannathu Padmanabhan (1878–1970), founder of the

Nair Service Society. He was initially taught Sanskrit by Brahma Vidya Pushan P.K. Pannikar, a Nair, and later his studies in the Vedas was taken over by none other than Sri Narayana Guru, a Sanskrit scholar, who admitted him in the Sanskrit school at Aluva. In 1983, during the centenary year of Sri Narayana Guru, a Vishal Hindu Sammelan, or a global Hindu conference, was organized by the RSS in Ernakulam. The chief priest of the main puja who conducted the sammelan was an Ezhava, and his assistant was a Namboodri, a Malayali Brahmin caste. The same year saw the founding of the Thanthra Vidya Peedham (TVP) by senior pracharak (lifetime worker) of the RSS, Madhavanji, along with eminent Vedic scholars.

The votaries of identity liberalism and Marxist-Macaulayist historians have painted the picture of a dark past. Due to political manipulations since Independence, social groups were crafted into vote banks on the basis of caste. These two phenomena— intellectual and political—created unwanted tension in Hindu society. Nowadays, it is fashionable to dismiss Hindu beliefs based on its negative aspects. This is a tragedy and reform is required.

Therefore, in terms of developing a theory of social justice, the Sangh is working to challenge the convoluted interpretations of Hindu texts and scriptures that have become the dominant narrative in academics and popular culture. The Purusa Sukta hymn of *Rig Veda* is often cited to show that shudras have a lowly origin because they emerged from the feet of the creator-God Brahma and certain other castes have a higher position because of their physiological location. Who has created this regimentation of superiority and inferiority? In Indian tradition and culture, the worship of the feet is important and is considered pious. Many hymns and shlokas are expressive of this sentiment. So, such hypothesis, divorced from cultural mores, is to be severely countered because it is not in sync with the principles of Hindu conduct.

In 1989, Maharashtra was on the boil over the renaming of the Marathwada University after Dr Ambedkar. ABVP held a conference in Aurangabad where the Marathwada University is located and carried out a massive mass-contact programme to build public opinion for the renaming of the university as Dr Babasaheb Ambedkar Marathwada University. This campaign was carried out even among those caste groups that opposed this move. Leaflets, pamphlets and fliers that were published stated the conference address as Dr Babasaheb Ambedkar Marathwada University campus. This was an influential campaign. Finally, when the change in the name took place in 1994, we distributed sweets and celebrated. Due to the social movement of ABVP, the name change of the university was happily accepted by society.

Many swayamsevaks have studied the phenomenon of caste. Swayamsevak and author Ramesh Patange's book, *Manu, Sangh & I*, is a descriptive account. Patange writes about his life experiences, and why in Sangh, the caste of swayamsevak is inconsequential. Earlier legal texts like smritis are redundant and irrelevant. While we may learn some didactic elements from their passages on statecraft, citizenship and righteous conduct, they are not applicable texts for present times. Talking of smritis, Dr Krishna Gopal, sah sarkaryavah says that the only relevant smriti for the country in the present context is the Constitution of India.

The basic tenets of Hinduism are in the Vedas and Upanishads and these preach oneness and equality. There are other texts authored by people who delineated conditions according to their situations. In Hindu tradition, there is no place for rigid dogmas. Today's reality is that we are governed by a constitution which was framed under the chairmanship of Dr Ambedkar. Yet, there are certain people who are peace disrupters and they persist with selectively quoting statements from certain bygone smriti texts which are not even read today. They do so with the intent of fanning animosity between castes.

In the Indian tradition, there is no book which is not open to review or which cannot be amended or discarded. We have robustness of thought and everything is debatable.

For the Sangh, there is no place for discrimination and the annihilation of massive distortions in our society is a project of monumental proportions. Samajik samrasta, or social harmony, is a Sangh samskara. Samskara, a word of Sanskrit origin, refers to mental attitudes, thoughts, actions and intents that are inheritable from generation to generation. The Sangh wants to see the inculcation of this samajik samrasta samskara in society. For the past nine decades, samrasta has shone forth in the Sangh's daily conduct as well as in many mega events and programmes.

When Dr Ambedkar visited the Sangh camps, he praised its samrasta in action. The RSS stalwart leader and thinker for workers' rights, Dattopant Thengadi was a young swayamsevak during Dr Ambedkar's embrace of Buddhism through 'dhamma parivartan'. Converting to the religious faith of Buddha is called 'dhamma'. Thengadi was given the task of attending on Dr Ambedkar. In his book, *Dr Ambedkar and Samajik Samrasta*, Thengadi writes:

> Dr Ambedkar stayed in Shyam Hotel located in the Sitabuldi area of Nagpur from where he proceeded for his dhamma parivartan. The Sangh functionaries present during this journey asked Dr Ambedkar why he was undertaking this path. They said the Sangh was working in the field of social equality. To this, Dr Ambedkar responded, Sangh work is good work, but in view of my health, I am in a hurry as are the members of my caste. Sangh work will take time. There are many challenges before the country because of which I am taking this step.

Definitely, Sangh work is time-consuming but it is a secure path through which the social conditions of complete samrasta can be achieved. Samrasta is the Sangh's vision of social relations. Samajik Samrasta is a high-priority task for the Sangh. Improvements have to be effected in Hindu society. Weeding out ritualistic malpractices and discrimination is a necessity. Answers to questions like 'When did caste become a social formation?' and 'Why it came into existence?' are difficult to look for. Hardly anyone can respond to this authentically. Additionally, even though many may debate about the positive and negative dimensions of caste, one issue which is not debatable is that today, caste has become a bad system and cannot be the basis of harmonious relations. Therefore, it is necessary for Hindu society to think and ideate a new society. A person's station in life will not be determined by birth. Neither will heredity determine his occupation. Every occupation is important and equal. There can be no hierarchies in work and it cannot be ritualistically defined and confined. Based on these egalitarian principles, the samajik samrasta vyavastha will be constructed by all members of the society. The politics of caste and the undue importance of caste in politics must cease. Politics must express the unity of Hindu society; such is the perspective and striving of the Sangh. Hindu society should not look at representation through the prism of caste but through the prism of Hindutva. Only then can casteism end. Politicization of caste will not yield any solutions of equality. Instead, it will lead to a spiral of problems and complications.

Samajik samrasta has to be implemented first in individual lives and only then progression can proceed to collectives. The swayamsevak begins the practice with the self. The swayamsevak busies himself with three tasks—one is expanding the shakha system, second is seva, which entails work for the vast underprivileged sections of society and the third is agitational activities to end exploitation and rights deprivation. The latter is the sphere of all mass organizations of the Sangh. The Bharatiya Mazdoor Sangh (BMS) agitates for workers' rights and better conditions for agricultural labourers or those working in the unorganized sector, like the anganwadi workers. ABVP works for students, SC/ST scholarships and hostel facilities. These agitations happen irrespective of which government is in power. ABVP activists are working on an enormous outreach programme, going from hostel to hostel. Sometimes, they face pent-up anger due to misconceptions and stereotyping on caste lines. But still undeterred, they work for creating an environment of respect and dignity for all.

Due to such an orientation, Sangh work is reaching every caste and community. The necessary tools of organization and leadership are being given to the hitherto downtrodden and exploited castes. The Sangh does not aspire to the leadership of these castes. It becomes the enabler, offering a do-it-yourself toolkit. Members of the downtrodden communities can harness the support to become community leaders. This is a vital component of the Sangh's man-making mission.

SAMRASTA PLATFORMS

It is just not enough to merely raise questions; one must bear the responsibility of providing answers. There are many who present temporary, impractical and isolated responses, but the Sangh provides sustainable, responsible, practical and integrated solutions. It is observed in the course of activities that there is a scarcity of forums where members belonging to all castes can come together and conduct dialogues. This is not possible on political platforms. The forums organized by media generally do not promote dialogue; rather, sometimes, they magnify the disputes.

The Sangh is working to create samrasta platforms. On 1 October 2015, a conference of tribal leaders was organized by the ABVP. It was an extraordinary sight. A youth and students' parliament were organized in 2015 by ABVP in Delhi to deliberate on the developmental priorities of our tribal people.[82] In the session on education, employment and skill development in the tribal areas and how it could be promoted in accordance with their cultural practices, participants demanded that the government should take

---

[82]Manash Pratim Gohain, '300 Students From 18 States Are Participated in the Tribal Parliament', *The Times of India*, 1 October 2015.

steps to conserve as well as promote tribal culture, languages and traditional knowledge.

The Northeast Parliament of Students and Youth Leaders was organized on 3 October 2015.[83] Various issues like the overall development of the Northeast, education of the Northeast, and development and security were discussed. The Sangh wants temples to become samrasta forums and it is in continuous discussions with members of temple committees to involve them in this task.

I was part of the Students' Experience in Interstate Living (SEIL) tour over the years. This is one of the most beautiful initiatives of ABVP which was started in 1965. This initiative is about an interaction programme between Northeastern students and people of other regions.

Under this programme, students from the Northeast come to other states where they stay in the houses of the students belonging to that region. They get to experience the cultural diversity of the country, and do the same when welcoming other students to their homes in the Northeast. This interaction has been one of the key features of ABVP since 1965.

The Sangh has absolute clarity that samajik samrasta is above sectional interests; it will be crafted by the wisdom of the entire society and by the actions of revitalized social institutions, which truly reflect Hindu dharma. The creation of this ecosystem is the task of the Sangh.

THE NEW ORDER OF EQUALITY

At the heart of caste inequity and discrimination is the grading of occupations into high and low. It is necessary to establish all occupations on the same footing. Rabindra Sharma, a social worker with the dispenzation of a rishi and aligned with Sangh thought, spent long years in Adilabad, a district in Telangana,

---

[83]'ABVP to Organise Tribal Northeast Students' Parliament', Northeasttoday. in, 3 November 2019.

studying varied occupations in the region and their contributions in society.[84] He has founded an organization named Kala Ashram. Though he was not a swayamsevak, RSS has acknowledged his work. Some swayamsevaks have joined his organization and are keen to carry his legacy and work forward.

In the emerging times, the main challenge is how to accord dignity to those occupations which were ostracized and the people who are engaged in these professions. No task should bear ritual stigma. All occupations have to be placed on an equal footing. Dignity of work has to be established in our conduct and social behaviour. New protocols are required. For example, whenever a Sangh facility is constructed, all those workers who toil to build it are publicly felicitated. This may seem small but it is symptomatic of a new social order that is being seeded. The Swach Bharat Abhiyan of Prime Minister Modi signals this new social order by shedding light on the sanitation worker. When the prime minister of the country washes the feet of the sanitation workers or picks up a broom to partake in a cleanliness drive, it is a lesson about their importance for the entire society. It is also a civic cue that this is a vital task to be performed by all, irrespective of their station in life. In any case, this is a task that is performed by all swayamsevaks in Sangh camps from the highest functionary to the ordinary volunteer.

Rigidity of caste rules have to be overturned. There has to be flexibility in the choice of occupations. Technical education and skill development are very necessary for such flexibility to develop in a practical form. Cutting jokes about 'chaiwala' or 'pakodawala' in politics are strongly redolent of a discriminatory temperament. Pakodawalas work hard and earn money, fulfil family duties, make their homes and people eat their cuisine. They cannot be referred to dismissively. When a washerman from a village sets up a laundromat in a city, the social optics change. There has to be scaling of occupations and change in mindsets. A flexibility of

---

[84]"A Glimpse of Ravindra Sharma's World and Work", www.ncra.tifr.res.in

choice of work is there in white-collar professions. A doctor's son or daughter can become a lawyer, an engineer's child can become an administrator, but in blue-collar, labour-intensive occupations, such mobility is rare. Even rarer is for such a profession to become a choice. For example, the agriculture sector hardly sees anyone from privileged backgrounds opting to become a farmer. Many swayamsevaks are now making this decision after receiving good education. In the days to come, innovative trends will be set in motion in which all occupations will be considered honourable. We will have to collectively accept our flaws and deficiencies and responsibly correct them. Simultaneously, there has to be justice for all. There can be no victimization on the basis of reverse caste prejudices for those belonging to upper castes.

The new social order has to reflect maturity and dialogue. This is not an easy task and the Sangh knows this. There are many forces that want to vitiate this atmosphere of social dialogue. There are some who want to stoke violent agitations or want to carry out religious conversions. There are many prejudices, misconceptions and social gaps spanning several years. Fully aware of these pitfalls, the Sangh is working in a sustained manner to develop a conducive atmosphere for social harmony. Those who spread disharmony should have no place in the leadership of our country. For such forces, the expansion of Sangh work is a cause of discomfort, and naturally, they mount a vilification campaign.

Sarsanghchalak Mohanji has given a clarion call for ending all kinds of discrimination prevalent in society. Every village should have a common temple, a common source of water, and a common cremation ground. The Sangh is trying to reach out to every village to establish this idea.

Dialogue, participation, new leadership and new platforms are the watchwords. The guiding principles are a resolve to solve issues and stand for the rights of exploited sections. At the same time, conspiracies will be exposed so that people know who the true social justice warriors are. The Maoist-Naxalite designs of feeding disaffection on the basis of caste identity will be smashed. Perverted interpretations of the Hindu pantheon, like the depiction of Mahishasura as a scheduled-caste hero and the denigration of Goddess Durga as an upper-caste entity, will be fought with the ferocity that it deserves. We are committed to removing hardship for the deprived sections and ensuring their quality of life. We will not allow anti-India forces to poach and profit from the problems of Hindu society. Detractors raise a hue and cry on the expansion of Sangh's social justice works. It is understandable but we will not stop.

'Hindu Utthan' means upliftment of each and every section of society. Away from publicity campaigns and glittering statements, the Sangh works quietly and diligently for social harmony in Hindu society at all levels. The Sangh wants temples to become samrasta forums and it is in continuous discussions with members of temple committees to involve them in this task. As the efforts are sincere, the Sangh has grown despite adverse comments and negative campaigns against it.

7

THE SANGH PARIVAR

Doctorji believed that national work required a good number of quality human beings. Sangh shakhas became incubators for vyakti-nirman. He used to say, 'Sangh means Shakha and Shakha means programmes for personality development.' Many would ask what the Sangh would do with this people power. But Doctorji was clear that for the swayamsevaks, the larger sphere of activity lay beyond the Sangh shakhas. He wanted swayamsevaks to regularly remember that their lives were consecrated for securing the well-being of Hindu lands.

The pledge of the swayamsevak is important as he signs up for some key duties for life. Every swayamsevak takes the oath to work for *'Hindu Rashtra ki sarvangin unnati.'* Underlying the basic Sangh programme is the vow for the comprehensive development of Hindu Rashtra, the protection of Hindu dharma, Hindu culture and Hindu society. In pre-independent India, this pledge included fighting for freedom from the British. Swayamsevaks forged in Sangh shakhas worked in all fields. This led to a constellation of organizations in different fields, within the ambit of Sangh ideas that are known as 'Sangh Vividh Kshetra Sangathan'. Media calls this the 'Sangh Parivar'.

Various Sangh bodies, such as the ABVP, BMS, Bharatiya Kisan Sangh (BKS), Vanavasi Kalyan Ashram (VKA), VHP, Swadeshi Jagaran Manch (SJM) and Vidya Bharati, are among the most well-known. But there is an entire gamut of Parivar organizations. There is no sphere that is left untouched. For the armed forces, there is an organization for ex-servicemen named Purva Sainik Parishad; for the welfare of those living near the border areas, there is Seema Jagran Manch; the lawyers' body is known as Adhivakta Parishad; for sports there is Krida Bharti; in medicine, there is National Medicos Organization; and the Aarogya Bharati that promotes Indian systems of healing. Saksham works for rights of the differently abled and is a respected name in the field of disability services. During the Kumbh, it organized Netra Kumbh, the basic aim of which was to screen vision and distribute free spectacles. A total of 2,02,020 patients were screened and a total of 1,55,210 spectacles were distributed between 12 January and 4 March 2019. The growth of Sangh and Parivar organizations has made the intra-relationships a subject of great interest and study.

THE PARIVAR STRUCTURE

The ground for organizations in the Sangh fold was prepared during Doctorji's lifetime itself. They are called Parivar because they share the same genealogy of ideas. But they are all autonomous and independent in structure and function. A large number of activists, or karyakartas, in these organizations are not swayamsevaks. However, there are some swayamsevaks among them, who move from the RSS to work in Parivar organizations, while some new karyakartas over time become swayamsevaks. If any coordination is required, Sangh communicates through swayamsevaks working in these organizations, by giving advice whenever demanded.

Individual initiative is encouraged as a creative process for national reconstruction. ABVP stalwart, Prof. Yashwantrao Kelkar, on his sixtieth birthday, at a felicitation programme, thus said, 'The ambition of ABVP is to provide leaders in all walks of life with high national spirit, a commitment to nation and society and improved quality of leadership.' This is true of all Sangh-inspired organizations. Each organization evaluates the capacities, constraints and problems of its sphere of action.

Deploying the techniques learnt in Sangh shakhas, it draws on people's participation and formulates its onward journey. These organizations work 24x7, stay abreast with issues, are conscious of not only the present but are also able to anticipate and plan for future requirements with the objective that everyone in society should experience hassle-free lives and if problems occur, there should be sufficient capacity for mitigation within the system. Such systems are designed with popular participation and people's consent by Parivar organizations. They are focused on their domains, but not isolated. The Sangh imagination is always integrated, constructive and long-term. It is a self-sustaining process. So, different sectors—farmers, workers, students—may be discrete units, but they are not separate silos. There are inherent linkages and mutual coordination which results in a nation-building vision. This is known as 'Sangh Samanvay', or coordination, essential in society. As Swami Vivekanand said in his speech at Madurai, 'There are three stages necessary for the future of India. The whole secret lies in organization, accumulation of power and co-ordination of wills.' In the Sangh's life, the first two stages are already true. We are in the third stage and the Sangh is working on the coordination of wills.

If there are issues of an economic nature, where different stakeholder views permeate, even those issues are resolvable through a coordination process. Sangh organizations confer among themselves regarding prevalent situations, programmes and new findings. At every tier, people's participation is added and new ideas and models incorporated. The objective of 'samagra parivartan', or comprehensive change, is attained. Through the Sangh Parivar organizations, an effective model of participatory democracy has been developed.

All Parivar organizations have certain common threads and functional autonomy. They arrive at decisions independently, have their own aims, objectives and make their own timetables. For instance, all training camps of ABVP, or Abhyas Varg, are driven solely by ABVP; the study module and subjects chosen reflect the priorities of ABVP. The slogans reveal the focus and domain—*Gyan sheel ekta* (knowledge, character and unity); *Aaj ka vidyarthi, aaj ka nagrik* (today's student is a citizen of today); and *Chatrashakti, Rashtrashakti* (student power, nation's power). ABVP's work is beyond party politics; it is constructive work among students in colleges and universities. Agitations are launched with demands on one hand and propositions for problem-solving on another. This is a common approach of all Parivar organizations.

Every Parivar organization is a domain expert. They can represent effectively with the administration and the political establishment. The government also takes the work of Parivar organizations seriously because they are a data mine of people, experiences and empirical methods. People, too, find Parivar organizations valuable because through them they can organize themselves better for the fulfilment of their existential issues and negotiate with greater bargaining power. Thus, they perform a dual function—finding solutions and creating of new systems for society. This entails reform and systemic change.

Reforms are solving problems here and now, while systemic changes are engagements in fundamentals, a long-term evolutionary process of sorting what is to be retained and what is to be changed, and whether everything has to be cast away or a new system has to be heralded.

Yet, another commonality is an all-India perspective and democratic processes. There are no orders given out. Regular meetings are held and views of even the smallest unit are considered. Programmes are determined after factoring varied viewpoints.

The principle of collective decision-making is adhered to deeply. Inculcation of this practice among members is given primacy for it is a belief that consultative temperaments sustain organizations and make them durable. Also, any Parivar organization can hold consultation with RSS leaders but decisions are not taken in Sangh meetings. They are decided by the organizations themselves in the light of their precedents and assessments.

Fund-raising is self-generative. For instance, in ABVP, whenever any programme is decided, activists constitute reception committees and do an outreach for financial support. All organizations raise voluntary contributions from society to run their activities.

Membership drives are individualized. In ABVP, we meet scores of students to enrol them as members; several among them, after attending programmes, decide to become activists. When any new organization is seeded, Sangh pracharaks are sent to develop that organization, but as it grows into maturity, the expectation is for that organization to have its own raising of volunteers, activists, full-timers and leaders. There are many examples in ABVP of activists for whom becoming ABVP activists was a first-generation experience of Sangh thought. They went on to become swayamsevaks and seeing their contribution of time and talent, some full-timers were later declared as pracharaks by the Sangh. This is the working style of the Parivar. They draw their intellectual and behavioural templates from Sangh ideas, but are complete in themselves and firmly grounded in society.

Every organization has a micro focus and forays into newer areas. The BMS has taken up the concerns of anganwadi workers, farm labour, fishermen, forest labourers and the unorganized sector.

BMS has forty-four federations covering all components of organized and unorganized sectors with 5,300 unions. It has delved deep into twenty-first-century labour situations and the scope of labour rights. A Pune-based research centre, Bharatiya Shram Shodh Mandali, founded by BMS has taken up emerging occupations like business process outsourcing and others in the developing service sectors for study. Other research organizations under the BMS, like Samdarshi Research Institute (SRI) Delhi; and Labour Research Centre, Ernakulam are playing an important role in the formation of future labour policies of BMS. These organizations also give suggestions to ministries and other government bodies on labour policy-related issues. Pune-based Sewawardhini, a service organization for the empowerment of grass-roots workers and organizations, run by Pramod Kulkarni, provides consultancy services from formation to funding requirements for service-oriented organizations. No organization is static; all of them are always in action.

ABVP is reaching out to all layers of the student community. It has begun work among students who want to take up sports as a vocation. ABVP also sensitizes authorities regarding the requirement for student facilities other than the classroom, laboratory and library to promote the interests of students in different activities.

ABVP tends to reach out to students from different academic streams and tries to involve them in activities with specialized forums and initiatives. The idea is that all faculties should be included. Many streams and sub-units, initiated by ABVP, are flowering. Some of these focus on the state of medical education and are forums for allopathy, medical and dental students in bachelors and masters study programmes; pharmavision, a forum for pharmacy students buttresses this by propagation of the values of honesty and the hazards of over-medication. Molecular research is another area of interest. As India has a strong agriculture sector, agrivision has been set up as a network of students in agricultural universities for improvement of agri-education and farming practices, etc. Work encompasses reaching out to students of all educational streams and social combinations among hostels, city-bred and hinterland populations, and it is inclusive of all castes and tribes. The Sangh and all its organizations ensure that no dimension is left unattended. A common emphasis of all organizations is that, as their activities are service-oriented, they should touch all.

Sangh and Parivar organizations are engaged in various programmes and activities related to the environment as well. Tree plantation, cleaning of village ponds and waterbodies, and conservation of the mountain ecosystem—green initiatives are plentiful. ABVP's Students for Development (SFD) and Vigyan Bharati, do important environment-related works that is well known and effective.

SFD's activism for Clean Narmada received extensive media coverage. It so happened that the local unit of ABVP had observed the pollution and deteriorating condition of the Narmada River. They shared their concerns with the state's ABVP office-bearers. A team was constituted for the study of Narmada River under the banner of SFD. The team embarked on a Narmada yatra on 7 February 2013 from Amarkantak, the source of the Narmada river in the state of Madhya Pradesh. The yatra ended on 21 February 2013 at Bharuch in Gujarat where the Narmada drains into the sea. The aim of this river expedition was to check the actual state of the river along its journey into the sea. Suggestions and feedback were taken from the people, following which a report was prepared.

The report identified twenty-eight factors as causes for pollution. The SFD unit began work on two fronts. Firstly, they took up a public awareness campaign to stop the people from polluting the river and began a tree-plantation drive on the river banks. Secondly, they filed a petition in 2014 before the National Green Tribunal (NGT) to make Narmada pollution-free. The NGT acted on the findings of the SFD team and passed an order[85] in November 2017 for installation of water-treatment plants and stoppage of plastic use within a 100-m radius of the river. The menace of illegal mining near the riverbank was also taken care

---

[85]'Before the National Green Tribunal Central Zone Bench, Bhopal', indiaenvironmentportal.org

of. Though the entire movement was initiated by the SFD team, with time, it became a people's movement. The Narmada River is central to the ritual consciousness of the people of Madhya Pradesh and they came in large numbers to protect it. Sachin Dave, the SFD convenor along with the ABVP state unit of MP successfully converted it into a mass programme. Parivar organizations have converzational skill, an immense emotional connectedness with society and a social competence to coordinate multifarious views. These are the characteristics that make them effective twenty-first-century instruments.

DIALOGUE BEFORE AGITATION

The Sangh Parivar organizations are people-centric. They have to engage with the establishment, which is chiefly the government, political system and the administrative setup. The relationship of these organizations with the establishment is one of samvad and sangarsh, or dialogue and agitation. This is applicable to all regimes, even governments led by the BJP. The intensity of dialogue and agitation may, more or less, depend on the responsiveness of the establishment. A higher incidence of dialogue and a lesser frequency of agitation flows from greater responsiveness while the reverse is the situation if the establishment is not amenable to voices from the ground or does not implement what it promises.

Generally, Parivar organizations have an impartial attitude towards power structures. But if there is a favourable government, like a BJP government, the Parivar organizations use their relationships to peruse people's issues with maximum impact. As these organizations command a large following, they can weigh in on any power structure. No government led by any political party can ignore them.

As an ABVP activist, I have met up with leaders of almost all political parties, be it the governments of Lalu Prasad Yadav, Mulayam Singh, or the Congress government. Dialogues were held and some of them were constructive experiences. Barring some outstanding political questions on which there was absolute and opposition, for issues that were non-political in nature, a convergence was found.

The constructive work of Parivar organizations is supported by all. For instance, DIPEX (Diploma Exhibition), an annual science expo conducted by students and organized by ABVP in Maharashtra, has been held for the past thirty years. Education ministers, whether belonging to BJP-Sena or Congress-NCP, have visited the expo to see the models being demonstrated by college students. Often, students with the best exhibits are invited to the residence of ministers, where officers are also called to discuss how such work can be promoted. The Sangh never hesitates to garner support from an eclectic range. This is its mindset.

Such a mental attitude of dialogue with everybody is possible because Parivar organizations feel that as they are all Indian citizens, there may be differences on the plane of ideas, but there is no animosity.

Except for a handful of leaders, who, due to their peculiar nature, are antithetical, we have largely encountered a good response from most of the leaders whenever we have gone to meet them. Therefore, Sangh Parivar organizations are dialogue assets of society. They can engage with the establishment for solutions. They do not speak the language of destructive and reckless unionism. The slogan of BMS is *'Desh ke hit mein karenge kaam, kaam ke lenge poore daam'*, meaning 'We will work in national interest; for our work we will secure full wages'. ABVP's slogan is 'Students' power, nation's power'. We do not indulge in demonstrating mobilization of power for muscle-flexing. Restrained use of power is a characteristic seen in all Parivar organizations and this is used to serve constituent interest and national interest at the same time. Due to mass participation, the work of Parivar organizations strengthens the democratic means for justice. For example, in ABVP, before any students' cause is taken up, there are several rounds of discussions that happen. Surveys are conducted to understand the nuts and bolts of the issue. It is an in-depth consultative process. Last year, a nationwide survey on the issue of women's education, involving 40,000 respondents, was conducted. Another expansive survey on women's issues was done by the coordinating body of all women-related issues—the Akhil Bharatiya Mahila Samanvay. This report is under preparation. Issues are studied as they are and there are no prefixed quality judgements; raw data is allowed to emerge. The output is, therefore, genuine. Based on these survey findings, programmes are firmed up.

All democratic tools, social research, memorandum, delegations, dharnas, demonstrations and social media are used by Sangh Parivar organizations. For instance, when parliament is in session, VHP activists meet all the members of the parliament (MPs) to press for the construction of Ram Janmabhoomi temple and also to hear the views of the parliamentarians on this issue. In the past two years, VHP activists have met up with more than 500 MPs of Lok Sabha and Rajya Sabha, cutting across party lines.

Dialogue with different sections, stakeholder bodies and societal notables is a continuous process. Due to such converzations happening all the time, a big catchment of issues emerges, and localized solutions are made possible, largely through dialogue. However, sometimes, the degree of agitation increases to truly reflect the cause of the people. This is what happened, when in J&K, there was a crisis over land belonging to the Amarnath Shrine.

The Amarnath Shrine Board was constituted by the J&K assembly through a unanimous legislation in 2000. As the number of pilgrims for the Amarnath Yatra was on the rise, the Shrine Board decided to expand the facilities on the Baltal route. The board placed a request before the state government for allocation of land for the purpose of providing amenities to the pilgrims on this new route. Following the directive of the J&K High Court, the state cabinet took a decision on 26 May 2008 to allocate forty hectares of land to the Shrine Board for only two months in a year for temporary arrangements.

But the decision was revoked on 2 July 2008 by the newly-appointed governor of J&K, presumably under pressure from extremist forces in the valley. The entire episode was witnessed by the nation and people were agitated. A movement was started by the people of J&K and support emerged from all quarters of society.

As part of the agitation, the Jammu region observed an unprecedented 'bandh', or a general strike. Initially, it lasted for nine days from 30 June to 8 July 2008 and again for 39 days from 23 July to 30 August 2008. The bandh was successful because it had the support of the entire nation. The local support was huge. The movement was supported by dignitaries from diverse fields and across the political-ideological spectrum. Under pressure from multiple corners, the central government had to yield and land was restored to the Shrine Board, as were other rights on 31 August 2008.

Repeatedly, Parivar organizations and swayamsevaks have led successful mass movements. But they do not look upon themselves as only instruments of agitation. Their objective is the resolution of problems and birthing of systems that benefit society. To what level an agitation may swell reflects the people's cause and is a judgement call that each organization takes. Their decisions are respected, even if they are made against the BJP government. This surprises many but that is where the beauty lies. Parivar organizations are not tied up with any political party; they are tied to people's interest. They are not dependent on political patronage for their strength or expansion but on their credentials of public service. This ensures their high credibility.

LINKAGES AND RELATIONSHIPS

What is the working relationship of these organizations with the RSS? This question is frequently asked. Mohanji gave an exact description when he said that Sangh Vividh Kshetra organizations are independent and autonomous. They are Sangh-inspired and bear a firm commitment to the sphere they profess to serve. Autonomy generates positivity, confidence and passion among activists. In all these organizations, the non-swayamsevak component is high. In other words, most activists in Parivar organizations are from outside the shakha system. The traffic is not only from the shakha to Parivar organizations but the other way around too. During the course of their work, activists become attached to the Sangh ideas and enter the shakhas. The Parivar organizations are, thus, a conveyor belt of Sangh ideas in society.

In structural terms, there are interlinkages. Sangh pracharaks are sent to Parivar organizations and non-swayamsevak activists are also connected to the shakha network. The trajectories of full-timers in Parivar and Sangh pracharaks are similar. Both categories leave their homes to work for society. All of them are bachelors in ABVP and in other organizations as well. They are not in the ring to earn their livelihood. They work on the task that is assigned to them. Many full-timers in Parivar organizations are even notified as Sangh pracharaks. It is a natural and continuous flow and happens regularly. There are a few full-timers with families in some organizations like VHP, VKA and Seva Bharati who work with minimum-required honorarium as well.

When emergent issues arise, the leadership can be vested even in someone unrelated. The only condition is that he should enjoy the confidence of different sections of society. This happened during the J&K crisis relating to land allocated to the Shrine Board for the Amarnath Yatra. When the Amarnath Yatra Sangharsh Samiti, an umbrella body, was founded, it included the common people and all the organizations of the Sangh Parivar. But it was Leela Karan Sharma, then a practising lawyer in J&K and protest leader, who became the convenor of this committee. Parivar organizations and swayamsevaks have no cravings for prominence and prestige. They guard themselves against arrogance.

While describing the intra-relations of Parivar organizations, the word 'samanvay', or coordination, is repeatedly heard. For this, there are formal as well as informal mechanisms. Sangh shivir, or camps, and Sangh baithaks, or meetings, belong to the first category. Structured coordination on matters of negotiation with the government is common. Parivar organizations take up issues on their own and also in unison to eke out the maximum possible for their constituents from the government. Then there are certain programmes that are implemented cohesively by several organizations together. For instance, the Ekal Vidyalaya is run by several organizations including VHP and Ekal Vidyalaya Samiti, and so, they all come together. This kind of coordination is particularly seen in the planning and rollout of seva works to achieve geographical dispersal of activities. Also, it ensures that there is no needless replication of programmes.

Parivar functionaries interact informally during nationwide tours, travel to and stay at each other's office-cum-residence facilities. Many times, activists shift from one organization to another, according to their propensities. In such instances, the Sangh becomes the nodal coordinator for such transfers. Sometimes, an organization may ask for a certain activist belonging to another Parivar organization to be sent to it. The Sangh facilitates all these combinations.

On issues of struggle, like the Ram Janmabhoomi temple construction, despite a very public coordination process, differences do emerge between the government and the Parivar organizations regarding the handling of the issue. In ABVP, we have been struggling for the stoppage of commercialization of education and have demanded that the government bring a comprehensive bill on this matter. But the government has taken a stand of non-interference where government grants are not involved. The court rulings are also on similar lines. We disagree with this and our struggle continues. In recent times, we succeeded in bringing NEET, a single national entrance exam for medical courses extending to private unaided institutions. In the time of NDA-I, too, several issues cropped up when it seemed that the government and the Parivar organizations were arraigned against each other. But with time, the coordination system was expanded, and it was made sure that the issues were not diluted. There were also no climb-downs on the government side and resolutions were arrived at.

So, on certain matters, there are disagreements despite coordination but there is an underlying consensus that we love our motherland and all of us work for its glory.

In the language of political science, Parivar organizations may seem like pressure groups or special interest groups of farmers, students, workers, small businesses and Hindu cultural aggregates. They are not. They are juggernauts of social pressure organized in a formation to bear upon the government with their mass power to ensure that the government acts in public interest. The tremendous presence of Parivar organizations will influence the formation of future governments and if there are more swayamsevaks in such governments, then more work in social interest can be done by these organizations. Even if non-swayamsevak governments are there at the helm, Parivar organizations will engage just as actively. Therefore, they are most relevant and useful in our democratic setup.

Coordination springs from dialogue not only in intra-relation networks but also with those who are not related to the Sangh network because dialogue is a Sangh temperament. This has several manifestations. Nanaji, a towering swayamsevak in the Jana Sangh, had friends across the political spectrum in different political parties. He partnered with them to lead the struggle for the restoration of democracy in the aftermath of the Emergency. This continued later into his life when he branched into non-political social work with Deendayal Research Institute (DRI).

Similarly, Dattopant Thengadi conferred with all hues of workers' unions. BMS interacts with communist workers' organizations, and whenever a coordinated move is made on advancing workers' issues, BMS plays a crucial role.

Ashok Singhal, the tall VHP leader who became an icon of the Ram Janmabhoomi movement, reached out to all sampradayas and developed a network of relationships. His leading role in Ekatmata Yatra in 1983 made him one of the most acceptable figure among all Hindu sects and sadhus, extending to many bhantes (buddhist monks), Jain acharyas and sadhvis, and sikh spiritual leaders.

In fact, if the origins of the Ram Janmabhoomi Temple movement are to be traced, it was everyone's issue, not only that of the Sangh Parivar. Dau Dayal Khanna, a leader of the UP Congress at a public meeting, organized by the Hindu Jagran Manch in Muzaffarnagar in 1983, spoke about the reconstruction of not only the Ram Temple, but also the other two sites that were desecrated—Kashi and Mathura.[86] Reconstruction of holy shrines vandalized by Muslim invaders is nothing new. The Somnath Temple on the western coast of Gujarat was rebuilt at the initiative of Sardar Patel with the involvement of the Hindu society. Patel did not live to see the revival of Somnath. It was inaugurated by India's first President Dr Rajendra Prasad in 1951. Nehruvians opposed it but leaders like K.M. Munshi within the Congress were the main protagonists. They were contemptuously referred to as 'Hindu revivalists.'[87]

Such experiences also came to the fore during the Ram Janmabhoomi Movement. In 1984, The Ram Janmabhoomi Mukti Yagna Samiti was formed. The general secretary of this committee was Dau Dayal Khanna, a serving minister in the cabinet of the three-term Uttar Pradesh chief minister, Chandra Bhanu Gupta. Whenever the Hinduness of India is assaulted, the Sangh and the Parivar are the go-to organizations and an extraordinary

---

[86]Sumit Pande, 'Such a Long Journey', News18.com, 5 December 2017.
[87]Manish Maheshwari, 'When Nehru Opposed Restoration of Somnath Temple', Swarajya, 12 May 2017.

coordination is witnessed.

In 1981, when the Meenakshipuram incident of mass conversions happened, a sense of sudden shock engulfed Hindu society. At that time, the Sangh initiated a massive awareness campaign with, 'Virat Hindu Samaj.' 'Virat' is a sublime description of that which is vast. Senior Congressman Dr Karan Singh was the president of this formation.[88] Hansraj Gupta, who later became sanghchalak in Delhi, was the vice president. Ashok Singhal became its organizing secretary. In those days, Singhal was carrying out the Sangh work in Delhi.

Swayamsevaks, when they become ministers, expand the arc of cooperation. A recent example is that of the late swayamsevak-minister Anil Dave in the Modi government. Dave, in a short time as minister of environment and forests, fixed intractable issues involving multiple stakeholders—forest, land, revenue, NGT—that were at loggerheads. The perennial tussle that forests should not be felled for development and development should not be stalled in the name of forests was suitably resolved and many projects were given the go-ahead.

Looking back on my own experience, I recall an in-depth coordination meeting with top ministers in the Indian government in 2003. I was 36 then and the youngest in that setup. Pramod Mahajan attended this meeting and I was very impressed with his conduct. He had a candid attitude. What I observed then was that there were no egoistic tantrums. Flaws and weaknesses were owned up, there was introspection leading to realistic thinking and new suggestions were accepted amicably. Such is the culture of 'samanvay.'

During situations of natural calamities like the tsunami in Tamil Nadu, and the earthquakes in Gujarat, Uttarakhand and even in neighbouring Nepal, this samanvay worked with super efficiency. Sangh swayamsevaks have a special talent for seva

---

[88]Sumit Mitra, 'Virat Hindu Samaj Holds Massive Rally to Protest Against Conversion of Harijans to Islam', *India Today*, 28 October 2013.

activities and this is recognized by the entire society wherever rescue and rehabilitation work is done. In normal times, Parivar organizations habitually coordinate with other seva bodies of temples and religious heads like Sri Sri Ravi Shankar, Baba Ramdev, Chinmaya Mission, etc.

DEMOCRATIC DUTY OF THE PARIVAR

Elections are colossal democratic events and there is a lot of curiosity regarding the work that Parivar organizations do during them. However, as a matter of principle, Parivar organizations do not engage in pure-play political campaigns or politicking. No senior functionary of any Parivar organization takes part in electioneering. There is absolute clarity about this aspect, although at the local level, activists may participate.

While it is true that Parivar organizations do not take up any specific election campaign work, elections do excite many kinds of awareness campaigns that are undertaken throughout the year on issues of national import, through which public opinion emerges. For example, in 2011, ABVP set up the forum, Youth Against Corruption (YAC), against the corrupt practices of the UPA-II government. YAC, in turn, was partnered by some renowned citizens and other anti-corruption movements, which were agitating for transparency and corruption-free governments. During the 2014 elections, many town halls and mass contact programmes were held by YAC. So, directly, there was no electoral role but indirectly there were massive awareness campaigns during election time, which is a democratic duty of Parivar organizations.

Another instance of Parivar organizations helping to raise awareness was when those plotting the break-up of India ganged up in JNU. On 16 February 2016, these inimical elements raised anti-national and fissiparous slogans. ABVP exposed this before the whole country and nationalism became a litmus test for all debates—

academic, political and media. People felt that our universities cannot be turned into safe havens for anti-national mongering in the name of freedom of speech and expression. Elements engaging in such activities were called the 'Tukde Tukde Gang' by mainstream media. Such was the resonance of this issue in society that ABVP's slogans became the nation's cry. Large sections also felt that those availing the benefits of state subsidy and the rights that citizenship entitles one to, cannot be let off when they spew incendiary anti-national rhetoric in a top university of the national capital. Obviously, this resistance against anti-nationals in universities creates political awakening and influences voting patterns.

Undoubtedly, the work of Parivar organizations impacts politics, and electoral politics at that. The party that is responsive to their campaigns will be benefitted in the power race. The Sangh's umbrella idea of Hindutva has effectively challenged several parameters of politics and this has deep significance in the political discourse of the country. Casteist mobilizations, though not halted, cannot be unbridled. The use of pseudo-secularism and minority appeasement have been exposed to the bare bones.

ROADMAP FOR THE FUTURE

The Sangh is a network of networks. There is no limit on the number of organizations that can be seeded to support the multiple issues in society that necessitate intervention. Thus, a large number of front organizations can be created with Sangh inspiration. What becomes redundant will be phased out. As of now, no redundancy is detected but there is an inbuilt flexibility should the need arise. There are no rigid lists. Due to this nature, sometimes, Parivar organizations are referred to as Sangh srishti—or—creation but the fact is that these are India's creations born out of Indian visions. The Sangh mantra is the synergy of constructive energies in national interest.

GRAM VIKAS

An important future focus prevalent across all Parivar organizations is Gram Vikas, or sustainable village development. India has over six lakh villages, which are our basic geographical units. Farm cultures predominate and yet rural distress seems to be a permanent fixture. How to raise farm incomes, develop rural occupations, utilize livestock wealth and build ideal villages is a big imperative.

Gram Vikas will work when it comes to creating villages with civic amenities, education facilities, healthcare centres and economic occupations. Many swayamsevaks took up the task of Gram Vikas after seeing social activist Nanaji's work in Chitrakoot.

After leaving active politics in 1978, Nanaji created a model for the development of rural areas on the basis of RSS thinker and leader Deen Dayal Upadhyaya's philosophy of integral humanism and decentralization for the development of the village.

He started this project from Gonda (U.P.) and Beed (Maharashtra). He finally developed an integrated programme for the development of villages, which covers many areas related to health, hygiene, education, agriculture, income generation, conservation of resources and social conscience. The basic foundation of the project is people's initiative and participation.

Nanaji made Chitrakoot in the hardship-ridden Bundelkhand region in central India the pivot of his village development work. Presently, it serves 500 villages and works on the model of sustainability and basic needs.

The centre runs several programmes for rural development. Krishi Vigyan Kendras are engaged in converting non-economic holdings into economic holdings, thereby raising agricultural production in the villages. Small and marginal farmers face a major problem in crop yield due to their inability to purchase good-quality seeds. To meet the demand and to make the villages self-reliant in seed requirement, seed production programmes were introduced through selected villages. Some projects were also working on Rishi

Aurobindo's idea of a cluster of villages.

Gaushala works to conserve and propagate superior genetic germplasm for milk production. The issue of water scarcity is big in the Bundelkhand region, which is being resolved through sustainable watershed management, a programme developed by scientists at the Krishi Vigyan Kendra.

Apart from economic programmes, work conducted in Chitrakoot has focused on the creation of a conflict-free society and litigation-free villages.

Many eminent organizations have lauded Chitrakoot and the work of DRI. Notable among these are several government bodies like ICAR and Khadi and Village Industries Commission (KVIC) and welfare trusts of respected business groups like the Tatas, Apeejay and the Wadia group. Nanaji was posthumously awarded Bharat Ratna for his village development work and service to the nation.

GAU SEVA

For centuries, there has been a notion that a cow-based economy contributes to the financial stability of village people and farmers. Therefore, gau seva is important for the Sangh and will be developed further. For the last twenty-five years, cow-based products are being researched in a laboratory in a place called Deolapar near Nagpur, which is maintained by VHP. Gaushala or cow shelter operations and maintenance are also linked with gau seva efforts.

MICROFINANCE

There is a strong self-help group tradition in the Sangh. Sahakar Bharati works in the cooperative sector, chiefly providing credit for the tiny and small sector. It believes that banks should not only serve big depositors and big businesses but provide credit access to rural occupations. The urban co-operative infrastructure in the states of Maharashtra, Gujarat and Karnataka bear the imprint of Sangh inspiration. The Nagpur Nagrik Sahakari Bank, Thane Janata Sahakari Bank, and the tehsil-level Chikhli Urban Co-operative bank or Rajkot Nagarik Sahakari bank in Gujarat are some sterling examples of 'social responsibility' banks created purely through social initiatives that are seeding first-generation small enterprises.

Understanding and responding to present requirements, learning from discrete experiences and anticipating future needs are common behavioural threads of Parivar organizations.

FEEDBACK MECHANISM

There is an extensive feedback-gathering mechanism. There are times when opinions differ as well. The conservation of Western Ghats and BT Cotton trials are examples where opinions clashed and more scientific evidence is awaited. Growth with employment creation, too, needs to be tackled.

In conclusion, it may be said that all future work of Parivar organizations will promote total development of India and is directed towards building a capable and confident society. The objective is to provide good leaders for all walks of life. This is a major task and if one were to account for capacity building, we have an astonishingly rich kitty. The Sangh does not have a remote control for Parivar organizations but provides the skill wherewithal and the thought process with which they ought to be run, thereby fulfilling the ethical-manpower needs of the country.

Many swayamsevaks have also begun individual initiatives, which represent this ethical-manpower dimension. Ashish Gautam whose Divya Prem Mission in Haridwar serves leprosy patients and their children is one such fine example. My good childhood friend, Sunil Deshpande from Nagpur, and his wife Nirupama, presently work with tribals of Melghat in Maharashtra on the making and marketing of bamboo products. Prasad Deodhar, an ABVP old-timer working for rural development in Maharashtra's Sindhudurga district along the Konkan belt, is another such person. Several swayamsevaks, inspired by the Vidya Bharti model, are running their own educational institutions. The first such school was started in Gorakhpur, UP, in 1952. A state-level Shishu Shiksha Prabandh Samiti was formed in 1958 for their proper guidance and planned development. Shishu Mandirs started spreading to other states, and within a few years, many schools were established. Currently, a total of 13,067 schools are being run by Vidya Bharti, in which 34,75,757 students are receiving education.

As time passes, there will be a multiplicity of such Sangh-inspired forums in all fields. There are no full stops for Sangh activities. It is an early respondent to changing needs and stays ahead of the curve in all fields. Swayamsevaks and Parivar organizations are laborious, disciplined and unstinted in their efforts. They are on firm ground to meet the twenty-first-century challenges. We welcome the task of preparing the vritti, or mental attitudes, of society for change. This will be no airy-fairy utopian stuff. The outcomes will be demonstrable and verifiable. Thus enabled, society itself will create the instruments that it requires for its service, thereby rendering the saying, 'Sangh samaj banega', true.

There will no duality between Sangh and society. Thus infused, New India will be developed, strong and rooted in its life values. It will be a welfare force for the whole world. We will speak our language, and not the idiom of the colonizers. It is the spirit of hope, trust and upliftment for the future.

8

IN THE GLOBALIZED WORLD

'Communicate, connect and collaborate' is the all-encompassing pattern of today's technologically advanced world. The whole focus of the communications sector is to leverage science to make the world as integrated as possible, irrespective of geographical spread and time zones. The advent of World Wide Web brought the global village phenomena within the grasp of the common man. This is the reality of our physical world.

SPIRIT OF VASUDHAIVA KUTUMBAKAM

In India, several millennia ago, a verse from the Taittraya Upanishad was realized at the philosophical-spiritual level: *'Ayam Nijah Paroveti Gananalaghu-chetasam, Udara Charitanantu Vasudhaiva Kutumbhakam',* meaning 'This is my own and strange is the way of the narrow-minded; for the noble-minded the world is a family.' This idea denotes the quality of relations among all life forms on Earth. This verse, belonging to the Samaveda tradition, is also sung and often used as a defining motto. It is reiterated so that every individual may behave with everyone living anywhere in the world in the same manner as one would with their own family. So, the Hindu thinking on world affairs is not governed by politics and diplomacy. Global welfare, constructive attitude, cooperative relations and familial etiquette are the main ideas on which India's relations with the world are conceived.

Even in earlier times, when monarchy was the form of government in India, the mightiest of kings with the greatest armies followed this Hindu approach when they dealt with rulers and people of other world nations.

INDIA AND SOUTHEAST ASIA: CULTURAL COUSINS

Relations with southeast Asian countries were developed over a millennium by kingdoms of India, and especially those from south India. There are many references to voyages between Indian ports and 'Suvarna-Bhumi' or 'Suvarna-dwipa' in the Sanskrit works based upon the Brihat-Katha, as well as in the Buddhist *Jatakas*, Jain *Samaraichcha-kaha* and other texts.[89] The Mauryan King Ashok is believed to have sent Buddhist Bhikshus to different parts of Southeast Asia. The oldest Sanskrit inscription in Southeast Asia was found in the Khánh Hóa province of Vietnam, which dates to the first or second century AD.[90] Two inscriptions of Rajendra Chola, dated 1017–18 AD and 1022–23 AD, gives an account of the victory of Chola forces over thirteen kingdoms of Southeast Asia, which included the kingdoms of Sri-Vijaya and Kadaram. The Indian kingdoms of Pallavas, Cholas and later the Vijaynagar empire are known to have trade and diplomatic relations with the kingdoms of Java, Sumatra, Champa, Yava-dwipa and Khamer empire of Kambuja (modern Cambodia). Even after Islam was introduced in Indonesia, the Hindu cultural traditions of the epics were cherished there. The Indonesian embassy sculpture in Washington D.C. is that of Ma Saraswati,[91] the Hindu Goddess of learning. Buddhism dots the landscape of Thailand, Cambodia, Japan, Sri Lanka and Bhutan. Our epics are part of their drama

---

[89]R.C. Mazumdar, *Ancient Indian Colonization in South-East Asia*. p.13, 1955.
[90]Ibid, p.15.
[91]'A Little Help From Saraswati', Uncategorized News, Embassy of the Republic of Indonesia, Washington D.C., Source: *The Huffington Post*, www. embassyofindonesia.org

recitals and monuments. India's two greatest cultural exports, the Buddha and the Bhagavadagita, are a source of great solace and peace to the world. The English-speaking world became aware of this much later. Sir Edwin Arnold called The Buddha, 'The Light of Asia', and celebrated the Bhagavadagita in English verse as 'The Song Celestial.' So, when Prime Minister Narendra Modi visited Japan, his gift for the Japanese premier was the Bhagavadagita. As Prime Minister Modi had stated then, this was the best gift he could give, and it was the best gift the world could receive as well.

Thus, Hindu cultural traditions are an important binding factor not only for southeast Asia, South Asia, East Asia but also for many other parts of the world. These have stayed alive and vibrant not only in Bali, the Hindu-majority province of Indonesia, but in the overall historic memory of that country, which is also home to the largest Muslim population in the world. We see the benefits of these linkages in our present-day relations. India and Southeast Asia are cultural cousins. Many geopolitical subterfuges are thwarted due to this inheritance.

However, there was a long hiatus because of colonialism due to which we could not decide the nature of our relations with the world. We were a subject nation at a low ebb, firstly under the rule of various Muslim kings, and then under the British. The rulers of these colonial regimes called the shots when it came to our relationship with different countries. The folly has been to look at our engagements from a prism of this limited interface even though our relationships predate these phases. If we can reignite the past of thousands of years, we will inaugurate immense possibilities.

THE CHINESE CONUNDRUM

Conflicts and border skirmishes define our relations with China but only when we look at this relationship since the time China was under Mao-Zedong and communist rule. Beyond this, India and China have had 2,000 years of cultural relations. Lord Buddha is at the centre of this edifice. Many in China still connect to India through The Buddha. Accounts of India, and her political, economic and social life were carried to China by visiting Chinese Buddhist monk-scholars and travellers.[92] Fa Hien, who came to India in the fourth century, during the Gupta period, recorded his observations about India in his work *Fo-Kwao-Ki*. Hiuen Tsang, another Chinese pilgrim who visited India in the seventh century during Harshvardhan's rule, penned down *Hsi-yu-Chi* (Record of the Western Countries). These works brought the details of Indian life to Chinese rulers and also become popular among their people. T'ang dynasty (681–907) ruler, T'ai Tsung (626–649), who was in power in China when Hiuen Tsang had returned, welcomed him and provided him with all the facilities needed to put his newly acquired knowledge into script.[93] Are we cognizant of this long cultural dialogue that existed between India and China? If we are, we can process a friendship, but if we continue to be embedded in the diplomatic record of the past seventy years, several deficits will gnaw at the relationship. While we cannot wish away the realities of today by getting lost in a golden past, the past is pertinent because it provides a ground for negotiation. Hence, it is necessary to refresh the historical memory of cultural exchanges between India and China. It shows our communication intent and attitudes. It leads to a realization on both sides that the stresses of present complexities can be swerved towards a constructive path. We should never lose sight of the fact that both our countries are old Asiatic civilizations with much to offer to the world.

The Sangh neither views international relations as politics among nations, nor in terms of any hegemony formula, but only as sociocultural relations. At whatever level we study it, the relations of India with members of the world community are always going

---

[92]Sanidhya Jain, Meenakshi, *The India they saw: Foreign Accounts*, Ocean Books, New Delhi, 2011.
[93]Samuel Beal, Hiuen Tsang, *Si-Yu-Ki: Buddhist Records of the Western World*, 1884.

to resemble the relations between individuals of a family in the spirit of Vasudhaiva Kutumbakam.

GLOBAL REACH

For centuries, Indian traders plodded through overland and maritime routes, on caravans and naval ships, carrying their goods and wares to distant lands. The cotton route was synonymous with Indians.

India's trade histories are unique. Unlike many sea-faring nations where trade became the vehicle for imperial structures, territorial capture and aggrandizements, Indian traders soared commercial heights without militaristic designs or running down local populations. Commerce and culture were parallel and complimentary tracks, with the latter seen as a spiritual mission richly supported with endowments. They popularized the Indian value systems of life, and its philosophy of happiness, welfare and peace. These footprints are sturdy in many countries of the Silk Road route and in the Indian-Ocean Rim countries. This heritage is being excavated through Indian foreign policy research undertaken by scholars. How our food, values, luxury items, art and culture travelled the world through our seafaring legacy, or how our merchant guilds ruled the sea lanes, have been produced in books with elaborate cartographic material by the Kolkata-based Institute of Social and Cultural Studies (ISCS)—*The Indian Ocean Civilization* by Arindam Mukherjee and *Mapping the Indian Ocean*, edited by Babul Dey.

A much earlier work of Benoy Kumar Sarkar states that Hindu thinkers who analysed India's sovereignty realized that 'sovereignty is not complete unless it is external as well as internal, that is, a state must be able to exercise its internal authority unobstructed by, and independently of, other states.' This concept is one of the key doctrines of the Hindu theory of sovereignty and world affairs.

The Sangh believes that every country should develop economically and politically, but not at the cost of other countries. The relation should not be based on fear. India's stand has given confidence to many countries that have concerns regarding the Belt and Road Initiative (BRI) of China. BRI is a programme to connect Asia with Africa and Europe via land and maritime networks to stimulate trade and economic growth. India's principle opposition is that BRI initiatives should respect the territorial integrity of the countries. RSS views on BRI are similar to the government's. Equally, it advocates good connectivity with neighbouring countries and deems improvements in road and sea connectivity with countries essential in today's world. Prime Minister Modi has proposed that India should reinvent its spice route which goes back over two millennia.[94] Connectivity is important in contemporary times, and that's why India is working on connecting neighbouring countries. Some efforts have been made to connect SAARC. A memorandum was signed for a free movement between Bangladesh, Bhutan, India and Nepal (BBIN).[95] The government is also trying to make the same provisions for ASEAN countries. India has also signed The International North-South Transport Corridor agreement, which is going to connect the entire Eurasia. India and Russia are trying to connect the Eurasia region with the Indian Ocean region.[96]

Indians have a global footprint. Due to trade, occupation and the indentured labour system being under the British, a vast community of Indians grew in strength on foreign lands. Called variously—NRIs (non-resident Indians), People of Indian Origin (PIOs) or the Indian diaspora—they are today widely known as Pravasis.

---

[94]K.M. Seethi, 'A 2014 Project to Revive India's Historical 'Spice Route' Remains a Non-starter', www.epw.in
[95]Press Information Bureau
[96]Dipanjan Roy Chaudhury, 'India Signs MoU with Russia to Fast-track North-South Corridor, *The Economic Times*, 5 February 2019.

The term 'Pravasi' gained currency after the Pokhran II nuclear tests were conducted on May 1998, following which India became a full-fledged nuclear state. The most powerful nations of the world reacted with sanctions and declared embargoes against India. It was at this juncture that the Pravasi community played a crucial role. An 'upbeat' Pravasi community overwhelmingly subscribed to the Resurgent India Bonds (RIBs), which, at a very difficult time in India's economy, contributed to maintaining India's forex reserve adequacy. Foreign currency-denominated bonds were issued by the State Bank of India (SBI) and M.S. Verma, then chairman of SBI, was effusive in his praise: 'The NRIs are upbeat, they want to make India a strong nation.'[97] This was the maiden attempt by any Indian government to tap into the mass of overseas Indians for India's national construction. The Pravasis took it upon themselves and went to great lengths to explain to the world why India had conducted the tests. Prime Minister Vajpayee expressed the nation's gratitude by instituting the PBD, which also commemorated the return of India's most famous Pravasi, Mohandas Karamchand Gandhi, to his motherland. This annual grandiose Ministry of External Affairs (MEA) event has now completed its fifteenth edition and the engagement with Pravasis has peaked under Prime Minister Narendra Modi. The government made special efforts to connect with the third and fourth generation of Pravasis through youth PBDs. The Pravasi community has deep cultural bonds with India and they are respected members of the countries whose citizens they are.

The Sangh has an attitude of reverence for the Pravasis. There is hardly a country today where Pravasi Bharatiyas are not present. In several countries like Suriname, Trinidad and Tobago, their present status of fortune and well-being have been preceded by long eras of struggle and back-breaking work. The first generation

---

[97] *India Today*, 24 June 1998.

of Indians in these countries were indentured farm labour on white plantations who worked from dawn to dusk. From such a hard life, they hewed a livelihood for their families and moved up the social and economic ladder. While doing so, they held on to Indian customs, values and traditions. Therefore, the Sangh holds Pravasis in high esteem.

When India won its freedom, Shambhunath Kapil Dev, who had retired as Chief Justice of Trinidad in 1961, thought that assistance and instructional help to keep alive Hindu traditions should be forthcoming for the Pravasis. So expectantly, he came to meet Pt. Nehru, the first prime minister of independent India. But Pt. Nehru declined, saying nothing could be done for those Indians who had left Indian shores prior to 1947. This was policy and Nehru refused to 'interfere'.[98] Extremely dejected, Shambhunath went to Lala Hansraj who was the sanghchalak of Delhi. Lala Hansraj advised him that as the issue was international in scope, he should meet Guruji Golwalkar. Shambhunath explained to Guruji the need for linking Hindus scattered all over the world with India. This culminated in the formation of VHP. Branches of the VHP were subsequently opened in all the countries. This shows that Pravasis needed a platform to keep their cultural coding intact. These are not geopolitical penetrations but spiritual relationships. Different countries experience the values of India through the Pravasi communities.

Inspired by the RSS, many Hindus living in different parts of the world have created various Hindu organizations. Foremost among them is the Hindu Swayamsevak Sangh (HSS), a sociocultural organization that is registered in many countries with Indian diaspora. It has a dual purpose—maintenance of Indian culture while being exemplary and law-abiding citizens of the countries in which they live. As Indian traditions are the centrepiece of their objective, they are connected to the RSS. HSS, UK, as part of its golden jubilee celebrations, organized a big three-day retreat,

---

[98] Vishva Hindu Parishad, 11 July 2019.

or 'mahashivir', on 29–31 July, 2016, and invited Sarsanghchalak Mohanji as the chief guest.[99] This witnessed a participation of more than 2,000 swayamsevaks in the UK. The theme of the retreat was samskar (values), seva (voluntary service) and sangathan (organization). Hindu Sevika Samiti also works in the UK as an organization for Hindu women. In the US, HSS began its activities in 1989. After every five years, HSS volunteers and other Hindu organizations working globally, congregate at some place in India for a Vishwa Sangh Shivir, an international volunteer camp of the Sangh, where many sessions are held on topical subjects. The last such shivir took place from 29 December 2015 till 3 January 2016[100] at Indore.

The temple network and prayers offered in the domestic altars of residences keep Indian traditions alive and are sought by Hindu families raising children. Social media is harnessed and there are many online groups networking with Pravasi communities.

The WHC is a global platform for Hindus to connect, share ideas, inspire one another and impact the common good. It is held once in every four years. Its conferences showcase how the values, creativity and entrepreneurial spirit of the global Hindu community find expression in a variety of spheres—economic, education, media, voluntary organizations, politics as well as the unique leadership and contributions of Hindu women and youth. Its philosophy is *'yato dharmas tato jaya'*, which means 'where there is Dharma, there is victory'. The latest WHC was held in 2018 in Chicago and it commemorated the 125th year of historic address of Swami Vivekananda to the World Parliament of Religions. WHC 2018 was attended by 2,500 Hindus from sixty countries. There were 220 speakers, experts from the spheres of economy, politics, social work and media. Several religious heads

---

[99]https://www.indiatoday.in/pti-feed/story/rss-chief-to-address-mahashibir-in-uk-674824-2016-07-28
[100]Aditi Khanna, 'RSS Chief to Address Mahashibir in UK', *India Today*, 28 July 2016.

also made their addresses. The WHC is mentored by Swami Vigyananand. There are few other notable organizations like the Kenyan Swayamsevak Sangh which promotes yoga; the Kenyan anthem is their organizational prayer and the Kenyan national flag is their flag. Individuals and organizations, too, have contributed in seeding and growing the international work of the Sangh, including the growth of VIIP overseas.

Antar Rashtriya Sahyog Parishad (ARSP) based in India was begun in 1978 and was devoted to working among the Pravasis. It continues to do a lot of work in countries where the third or fourth generations of Indians live, like Trinidad, Tobago, Mauritius, Suriname, Fiji, Reunion Islands, South Africa and Guyana. Sangh pracharaks like Devidas Apte and Baleshwar Agarwal ploughed this field well and worked across party lines. Shyam Parande presently leads ARSP.

Seva International is another reputed Sangh-inspired body working in the field of international relations with a specific focus on voluntary work during distress situations like natural calamities. It has a vibrant presence in the UK, the US, Kenya, Trinidad and Sri Lanka. For its contribution to relief work in flood-hit Houston, Seva International, US, got a grant of $5 lakh from Red Cross. Such endowments attest the high credibility of the organization among the local populace.

Apart from being a cultural fulcrum for Pravasis, Indian spiritual traditions and philosophical systems draw global audiences. The recently concluded Kumbh Mela in Prayagraj was an occasion for such commingling. A raised site was created on the banks of River Ganga, where the national flags of many attendee countries were unfurled and they stood there during the entire duration of the Kumbh, from January to March in 2019. Ambassadors from seventy-two countries visited the Kumbh.[101] The number of foreign

---

[101]'Kumbh 2019: 72 Diplomats From Various Countries to Visit Sangam', United News of India, 14 December 2018.

tourists was 35 per cent higher than the last year[102] due to Kumbh. Globally, the Sangh sees the Kumbh as a grand religious-cultural fest to expand the continuing interest about India and connect the world with the wisdom of this great land, especially now, when not a single day passes without a terrorist strike headline from somewhere in the world.

THE SCOURGE OF TERRORISM

The deadly terrorist attacks India has suffered—the 1993 Mumbai blasts at thirteen locations on a single day, the attack on the Parliament in 2001, the 26/11 Mumbai attacks, and the most recent one in Pulwama—indicate a certain sequence of the destruction of the identity of India. All these attacks, carried out in the name of jihad, are assaults on humanity and dangerous for the whole world. Globally, analyses are being produced and methods are being sharpened to stall these dark forces. However, in India, some so-called secular interpreters present terrorism as a Hindu-Muslim issue, blame the Hinduness of India as a causative factor and classify legal actions against any terrorist as anti-Islam. Such falsehoods must be run to the ground. All anti-terror laws, Terrorist and Disruptive Activities Prevention (TADA) Act (1987), Prevention of Terrorism Act (POTA) (2002), and other anti-terror laws of different Indian states have been targets of calumny. The mastermind of the Parliament attack is valorized, and midnight vigils are kept for the convict of Mumbai blasts to appear liberal and humane.

Islamic terrorism is threatening the entire world—9/11 in the US, multiple strikes in France and Russia; not even China's Xinjiang area is tension-free. The response of the Chinese government

---

[102]Garima Singh, 'Thanks to Easy Visa Facility, 'Ardh Kumbh Sees 35% Jump in Foreign Tourist Arrivals', National News, *Business Line*, *The Hindu*, 5 February 2019.

became a matter of Islamic State video propaganda.[103] This terrorism is prefixed 'Islamic' because innocents were massacred in the name of jihad. Let's not say it in a different way. Denying it would be estranging the truth.

Muslim-majority countries definitely are not a monolith. They have differences in texture. Five are declared Islamic states: Pakistan, Afghanistan, Saudi Arabia, Yemen and Iran. There are seventeen countries where Islam is the state religion and there are many secular states too. We do not say that terrorism thrives in Islamic states but what we do say on the basis of irrefutable evidence, is that Pakistan enables and sponsors terrorism. It is important to understand this fact.

Grounded in Hindu thought, the Sangh considers all faiths as equally true and respects all roads to the divine. In our times, there can be no peace on earth without respect and coexistence of all religions. But zero tolerance of terrorism is the need of the hour. The striking power against terrorists has to be in mission mode.

CHALLENGES BEFORE THE WORLD

The top global challenges before the world are namely two: violence that flows from terrorism and environmental degradation for which the trigger is lifestyle and resource exploitation that spirals greed, creates haves and have-nots, and mounts physical fatigue and deprivation for the masses so that a few islets of privilege can pamper themselves.

A life devoid of spirituality will surely make the world go to pieces. The Sangh believes that in modern times, India bears the responsibility to uphold the philosophy of life. If we have all the materialistic development that we can dream of but possess no traits of character, we live on nothing. The world is in great need of India's spiritual life for it is the tested road to peace, prosperity and balanced development. The Sangh sees itself as an instrument

---

[103]Carrie Gracie, "'All-out Offensive"..' *BBC News*, 2 March 2017.

to fulfil this role in world affairs. It thus works with the oldest spiritual traditions of the world to curate global harmony.

PROMOTION OF INDIGENOUS CULTURES

Throughout the world, there was a deliberate move to wipe out indigenous cultures. The Bible described them in judgemental and pejorative terms such as pagan and these terms are largely used in Western discourse. The Sangh calls them the Elders. Their civilization is gone but they have retained their culture. After immense depradations, the Elders have been reduced to sparse populations in Australia, European countries and in Muslim-majority countries. In contrast, in India, even the oldest tradition is alive, vibrant and kicking. So, in the global sphere, the Sangh began building relations with all Elder cultures.

In 1994, an organization called International Centre for Cultural Studies (ICCS) was formed by Yashwant Pathak and today, it connects sixty different Elder cultures. Every three years, they assemble for a conference. The first conference was held in 2003 in Mumbai and the theme was 'Mitakuye Oyasin', meaning 'we are all related'. There were attendees from thirty countries. The second conference was held in Jaipur in 2006. The theme was 'Spirituality beyond Religions' and was attended by delegates from forty countries. The third conference in 2009 was held in Nagpur and the theme was 'Renaissance of Ancient Traditions', which focused on challenges and solutions. The fourth conference in Haridwar, held in March 2012, was themed, 'Nourishing the Balance in the Universe.'[104] The keynote address was delivered by Mohanji, wherein he stressed the priceless treasures of Indian thought. He said that the maxims of 'live and let live', 'unity in diversity', 'the world is one family' and 'let us ennoble the world' have major

---

[104]'Report of the 4th International Conference Gathering of the Elders of Ancient Traditions and Cultures', Samvada, samvada.org, 14 March 2012, https://samvada.org/?p=8852

relevance today. A universal outlook is the hallmark of Indian thought. Happiness and well-being of everyone is always sought. Only through an integral view and not a compartmentalized view can attitudinal changes be brought about. In these conferences, the Elders of Maya, Māori, Druid, Navajo, Cham, Romuva, the European Congress of Ethnic Religions, Children of Mother Earth, etc. were represented. The commonality is nature worship and veneration of the five elements—earth, air, water, fire and sky—similar to the pancha mahabhuta of Hindu practices. There is a lot of openness and free thinking in the Elder traditions and Hindutva.

The so-called liberal space is completely silent on the intolerant ways in which alternate ways of life and thinking were snuffed out by those who wanted total submission of all non-adherents to their modes. Ethnocultural studies of diverse cultures decimated either by Islamic invasions or European colonialism do not form a part of mainstream discourse. The Sangh wants to correct this and is assiduously building Elder narratives globally.

STRANDS OF REALISM AND IDEALISM

The Sangh's message in a globalized world is simply this—the prosperous countries must unfurl their constructive energies for the benefit of humanity. It should not just be mere talk but tangible actions so that nations that are poverty stricken can come out of destitution and move towards progress. If we have to build a stable road to the future, we must remember the words of Swami Vivekananda's 1893 Chicago address to the World Parliament of Religions: 'Help and not fight, assimilation and not destruction, harmony and peace and not dissension.' These words are as valid today in the era of globalization as when first uttered during the heyday of colonialism. We feel these truths in the marrow of our bones and the Sangh will propagate these great values of humanism in the global arena. The Sangh believes that fundamentalism and rigidity shuts us to other ways in the world and the origin of terrorism is politico-religious.

It is a hard reality that the Partition was a result of fundamentalism, so we can't ignore either the separatist activities in Kashmir or organizations like Students Islamic Movement of India (SIMI) or PFI (Popular Front of India).

Left Wing Extremism (LWE) was a product of twentieth-century communist theory and practice. A destructive ism or political ideology with the slogan 'Political power grows out of the barrel of the gun' ravaged many Afro-Asian and Latin American countries. It has petered out even among the countries officially notified as communists, which in any case are few. The five communist countries, People's Republic of China, Democratic People's Republic of Korea or North Korea, Socialist Republic of Vietnam, Lao People's Democratic Republic or Laos, and the Republic of Cuba, are not anti-capitalism. These nations use their communism to serve their nationalism, and in the case of China, to nourish their expansionist plans. In India, however, LWE forces are anti-nationals. Very active in the forest belt of India, they have created an overground network of urban Maoists who exploit democratic means like Right to Information (RTI), human rights and modern professions like media, legal establishment, film-making and academia to justify and carry on their urge for plunder and violence. They have deep roots and are pernicious. Urban Maoists are in nexus with jihadi Islamists and are their most vocal supporters.

In Sangh's agenda, these fundamentalisms have no place in independent India. The Sangh wants to remove the cobwebs of closed thinking. India has done this before. We know from the past that the graduates of Nalanda and Takshashila were all over Asiatic lands, spreading the Indian knowledge system for peace, and the inner and outer development of man. The Sangh wants to re-establish this Indian university system for the betterment of the world. In the age of source codes, patents and proprietary standards, India wants to give open access of these knowledge systems to the whole world.

The world must globalize. But how? That is the question. It should not be centred only on trade and geopolitics. The Sangh's globalization is not merely for business, power and money, but a programme to take care of each other, to grow together and seek everyone's welfare. Sustainability, respectable incomes and care for natural resources will be the new rules of globalization. We should learn to grow together. If a good technological innovation happens even in a least developed country, it should be taken on board. Likewise, in the field of medicine, all disciplines should be evaluated on the basis of merit. Just because a system is traditional, it must not be typified as charlatan stuff. They should neither be discarded for not being mainstream nor patented for exclusivity. Technology and healthcare should be affordable for all.

The accumulation of economic power led to many conflicts, inhumane systems and environmental degradation. This was the basic malady of colonial and neo-colonial behaviour. It did not end when colonies became free. Former colonies still mimic colonial language and biases. Decolonization of the mind is therefore necessary for development and progress. All over the world, deliberations of this nature are underway. Ecuador and Bolivia have even made constitutional changes to reflect these realities. Decolonization researches are investigating such trends.

We also see Bhutan's gross national happiness challenging the GDP concept. There are renewed assertions of going back to native traditions for reorganizing and rebalancing national life, and India, due to her historical background, is at the centre of decolonized thinking.

In the environmental domain, new combinations and forums are required. There can be environmental politics on emission rates, but there can be no solutions without dialogue that is mindful of local conditions and values. Crimes like drug cartels and human trafficking cannot be stopped without the world coming together.

The Sangh feels that the UN should be more democratic. The world cannot be run by a single forum. Multiple channels are required. The world cannot be unipolar, or even bipolar. It will always be multipolar. Every country possesses its circumference of influence. The main issue is that of relationships and the whole world should feel interconnected. There can be no matrix of superiority and inferiority. This is the Sangh's imagination of global peace.

ABVP had also demanded in its resolutions that India must have a nuclear arsenal. Peace can be secured only by the strong and by those who have the power to deter and the power to punish. The Sangh supports India's missile programme and feels that India's defence capabilities have brought balance of power in the world. We are a country of Durga worshippers and we believe in using our strength for protecting what is good and destroying what is wicked and harmful. Our strength is sattvic as global welfare is the core value of Hindutva.

So, the Sangh theory and practice of international relations is well organized. It teaches Indian values in its Pravasi shakhas, global social summits and religious conferences. It has strands of both realism and idealism. But above all, it is underwritten by humanism.

9

FAMILY AND EMERGING MODERN RELATIONSHIPS

The gift of family can hold humanity together. A resolution was passed at a meeting of ABPS in March 2019, which talks about the importance of the family system, its present challenges and possible ways to secure a happy and fulfilling family life.

There were many who questioned why such a resolution came about. While some felt that the Sangh was overthinking such issues, most felt that the family is the basic functional unit in society and the ultimate social institution that needs attention.

In modern times, converzations pertaining to interrelations within families are required to address the inadequacies which have emerged in imparting value education to the next generation, especially small children—the social and national duties of families and their daily-life schedules. Such a resolution is the need of the hour. The Indian family system covers everyone and there is no need to categorize it into Hindu, Muslim, Christian and so forth. A happy family life is everyone's desire and a well-known Indian tradition.

Of the five main activities of the RSS, the first one is Kutumb Prabodhan while the other four are Gram Vikas, Gau-Vikas (developing cow-based economy), Dharam Jagran and Samrasta (social harmony). A new activity called Paryavaran vikas (environmental development) was added to this collective. Kutumb Prabodhan is public awareness combined with dialogue activity. It answers the question of what ingredients are needed for a happy and successful family life in the present context. It is an expectation that all swayamsevaks will lead by example, and pay attention to whatever changes are required in their families while maintaining traditional strengths. This shows that Sangh gives primacy to the individual and family, for it is their qualities that reflect upon society and influence national life. Indian values owe their existence to our sturdy and resilient family system. In the thousands of years of our history, Indian families have given birth to great sons and daughters, educated them and given them the right ethics with which they have served the country.

SOCIAL CHALLENGES

Over time, certain flaws that have emerged within our families are showing up in our society. For example, the rate of divorce and separation between couples is rising, though the overall number is still small. Crimes committed by men against women due to certain mindsets are on the rise, both in rural and urban areas. This number is small compared to worldwide trends, but society is gravely concerned about the rising instances of crimes against women, especially in the backdrop of Indian cultural values. Other social issues, too, have cropped up, like abandoned, illegitimate children, sending elderly parents to old-age homes, live-in relationships and dysfunctional marriages. Though these instances are few, they show the weaknesses and abdication of responsibility in our families, which gives momentum to other decadent behaviours.

The Sangh views this very seriously. In the twenty-first century, with modernization, economic growth, urbanization, internal migration for work and work-life balance, there is a deep thinking about the nature of family life and how its idyllic pattern can be maintained. The family is the centre of romantic sentimentalism, but it is also the fundamental instrument for social good. The Sangh believes that given her traditional Indian values and a rich, caring cultural history, India should be able to present the example of a sound family system to the whole world.

AN IDYLLIC FAMILY

In the traditional Indian context, 'grihastha', or householder life, is sacrosanct. It is a coming-of-age requirement that is enjoined upon everyone as it bears the responsibility for bringing up the next generation. Only in special circumstances, where people give themselves up for a social or spiritual purpose, can they step outside this life. When householders fulfil their duties, society is crafted and sustained.

The husband and wife living happily together, bringing up their child with equal involvement, caring for their parents—these features are symbolic of a civilized society. The upbringing of children is a joint responsibility. The father has to work as much as the mother does in bringing up the child. Childcare responsibilities have to be shared. The Hindu ideal is the Shiva-Parvati marriage and their mutual relationship on an equal footing as they move forward towards completeness. There is no man-woman super-ordination or subordination. There is equality and the promise of a life together. The Ardhanarishvara[105] form of Shiva-Parvati represents the state of complete compatibility in marriage and the synthesis of man and woman in holy matrimony. This idea, as old as Indian civilization, captures the imagination of people to this

---

[105]The Sanskrit terms Ardhanarishvara or ardhanari mean half-woman, half-man. One of the most important forms of Shiva, showing the male and female aspects in a single form, Ardhanarishvara symbolizes gender harmony and the fusion of all extremes and opposites—Prakriti and Purusa, the object and the subject, the microcosm and the macrocosm, body and spirit, the real and unreal. The essence of the Ardhanarishvara concept is that the male and female aspects always exist together and are inseparable from each other.

day and is the bedrock of our family system.

In India, marriage traditionally means the coming together of two families and not just two individuals becoming a married couple. Everyone, including the couple, needs to work to ensure that relations within families are harmonious. Families are not meant to stay in isolation. They should maintain harmonious relations with relatives, neighbours and the community, for society is a network of relationships.

Due to work-related compulsions and greater movement to cities with smaller houses, there is a spurt in the growth of nuclear families. But even these nuclear families have maintained their relations with the larger families.

Householders traditionally perform several key roles. They care not only for their own children but are also concerned about those in need. They educate the next generation, maintain religious festivals and instructions and instil the mentality of national service among family members. Our country has functioned in this manner for centuries. In old times, making meal arrangements for students was considered a pious act. Even today, a large number of families gladly bear this duty. Pracharaks being hosted by families or activists on tour staying as house guests with families are a usual occurrence in Sangh Parivar[106] circles. Thousands of families, spread across the length and breadth of our country, feel blessed to look after pracharaks and activists in their homes. It is seen that children raised in such families develop deep empathy and a social conscience. They are eager and sensitive volunteers who help to ameliorate the sufferings of others in their surroundings.

INDIAN FAMILY VALUES

Families in India generally enjoy a blissful life. Intra-family and inter-family relations are important highlights of our social life. Even the smallest occasion in a family becomes a reason for a

---

[106]Sangh Family

get-together. Indian marriages become an exercise in consensus building, from the consent of the bride and groom and common vision of families to a host of discussions about dresses and feast menus that make wedding rituals vibrant and colourful. They are occasions of fun and festivity, of song and dance, and of coming together of different generations and diverse sections of society in an affectionate embrace. There is much charity done during such occasions.

Social work in India has always been dependent on the piety of families. Even a family with the most modest means will set apart some portion of its resources for donations during religious observances practised regularly. The mother of the house will never allow visitors to her hearth to depart without serving them a meal. A dutiful mother is a formidable force on earth and the centrepiece of the Indian family system. I know of well-established ABVP activists who have adopted children from orphanages just to provide them parental care, even when they had a biological child. There have been instances of natural calamities and earthquakes when children were orphaned and the Sangh organized campaigns to have good, well-off families adopt such children instead of sending them to government orphanages. Our families are our most precious assets and a bulwark against all social and emotional disturbances.

The family is also the basis of physical, emotional and financial security. It is a blanket of care and protection. It is simultaneously spiritual and material. It creates awareness about our rights but also teaches us our duties. It nurtures our capacities so that we can live our lives freely and ably. People tide over difficult times with family support. Indian families have an important economic dimension as Indian households have a zeal for saving. When generations in a family stay together, they can cut costs in terms of home expenses, not to mention benefit from the supervision. Our socioeconomic model is family-centric.

In contrast, in the West, a large chunk of the costs have to be shouldered by the welfare state because families abdicate their role. The state bears the responsibilities of the elderly and children. Family life in such countries is nationalized. It is not private anymore. They need professional counsellors because there is no family from whom to seek advice or in-front of whom one can give vent to their feelings. It is a pretty high-strung situation and young people are often seen falling off the cliff, with an increase in the number of school shootings, drug abuse, depression, mental health issues and a directionless life.

DIVISIVE FORCES AND FAMILY BREAK-UPS

In Western societies, there is aching loneliness due to the breakage of the family system. In this age of the Internet, endless information is just a click away, yet some content can wrongly engage youths as well. In this context, it is necessary to study and investigate the issues cropping up worldwide, anticipate problems and be precautious.

Family-related statistics from some developed countries, especially the Crude Marriage Rate (CMR)—a ratio that gives the annual number of marriages during the year per 1,000 people—showed a decline among rich countries. In the US, it is 7, in OECD countries, mostly European, it is 4.5 to 5. The dips are sharp when compared to different time bands of the twentieth century.[107] For example, in Portugal, this rate was 6.6 in 1995 and dropped by more than 50 per cent in 20 years, to 3.1 in 2016. Other facts, too, deserve mention here, like late marriages and a record of first marriages only. Correspondingly, divorce rates are increasing. Luxembourg has a hyper divorce rate, being the highest at 87 per cent, Spain is at 65 per cent, France 55 per cent, Russia 51 per cent, and the US

---

[107]OECD Family Database, OECD: Social Policy Division, Directorate of Employment, Labour and Social Affairs: Marriage and divorce rates, https://www.oecd.org/els/family/SF_3_1_Marriage_and_divorce_rates.pdf

46 per cent.[108] These statistics reveal that more than 50 per cent of marriages in the developed world are broken.

In the western hemisphere, only some Latin American countries like Chile and Columbia report single-digit divorce rates at 3 per cent and 9 per cent, respectively. Others like Mexico and Turkey, also considered in the lower band, report double-digit figures at 15 and 22 per cent. Divorce and separation between couples impact children too.

A book titled *The Fatherless America: Confronting Our Most Urgent Social Problem*, authored by David Blankenhorn and published in 1995, describes how after the Industrial Revolution, work-home balance began to affect family life. Blankenhorn writes:

> First industrialization and then the modern economy led to the physical separation of home and work. Yet, the overall trend of the 19th century was clearly towards the shrinking of fatherhood. Paternal neglect, as warned a pastor of New England in 1842, was causing 'the ruin of many families'. By 1900, another worried observer would describe 'the suburban husband and father' as 'almost entirely a Sunday institution.'[109]

In its 1991 survey of children in the US, the National Commission on Children described the spreading phenomena of the father-child relationship as frequently 'tenuous and all too often non-existent'.

We can therefore surmise that in the US, fall in marriage rates and increase in divorce rates have led to severe consequences. The number of children born to unwed parents more than doubled from 18.4 per cent in 1980s to 39.8 per cent by 2016.[110] Another startling statistic pertains to the percentage of American children living with their biological fathers, which is on the decline while

---

[108]'India Has the Lowest Divorce Rate in the World: Countries With Lowest and Highest Divorce Rates', *India Today*, 20 November 2018.

[109]David Blankenhorn, *Fatherless America*, pp. 13–15, Harper Perennial, New York, 1996.

[110]Riley Griffin, 'Almost Half of U.S. Births Happen Outside Marriage, Signaling Cultural Shift', Bloomberg, 17 October 2018.

the reverse statistic of children (12–17 years) not staying with their fathers doubled from 17.5 per cent in 1960 to 43.1 in 2017.[111]

The beginning of this disturbing trend is now being witnessed in India as well. Those who call themselves 'modern' often present family as a structure of bondage, or as a leash that encumbers freedom. Not surprisingly then, some problems have arisen in India.

Although the divorce rate is still less than 1 per cent, big cities steeped in Westernization are reporting a spike. For instance, in Mumbai, the total number of divorce cases filed in 2010 stood at 5,245, but in a span of four years in 2014, this had shot up to 11,667. Same is the trend in Kolkata. In 2003, the number of cases filed was 2,388; in 2014, this had risen to 8,347. Statistics that emerged from Lucknow are worth mentioning here. In 2014, the number of divorce cases filed were 2,000, of which, 900 cases involved young couples who had been married for less than a year. Three new family courts had to be started in India's IT hub, Bengaluru.[112] These trends are dangerous and a cause for alarm.

One cannot be complacent just because India's overall average is low. An upward curve in the number of divorce cases in developed countries is being reflected in our cities as well, particularly among the educated classes, which are exposed to Western concepts in a big measure. The major reasons identified for the breakdown of marriage and divorce seem to be ego clashes, perceptions about marriage and family, and thought processes about life objectives.

ACKNOWLEDGING REALITIES

The failure of the family system is also linked to juvenile crimes. Deplorably heinous crimes against women being committed

---

[111]'Children Under 18 Living With One Parent', www.census.govt
[112]Apoorva Dutt, 'How and Why Number of Young Indian Couples Getting Divorced Has Risen Sharply', *Hindustan Times*, 4 January 2015.

by juveniles are on the rise in our country. There are screaming headlines of child abuse almost every single day.

Global media even labelled Delhi as the rape capital of the world. However, statistics do not support this claim. The UK's crime rate against women is 36.44/lakh and the US's is 35.85/lakh while India is at 5.7/lakh, according to data sourced from United Nations Office on Drugs and Crime (UNODC). In the US and UK, crimes against girls and young women in schools, colleges and universities are serious. Thus, these counter-stats debunk the falsehoods generated against India. The rates in India are low, but this is no solace to us. We are concerned about these shocking trends in our country, which are occurring despite a strong family tradition.

In the twenty-first century, society needs to acknowledge these barbaric realities and work towards a remedy. India has to demonstrate high levels of virtue. There is no space for offenders. Families have to perform their role of guardianship efficiently. The Sangh calls upon society to strengthen the family system through inculcation of proper values to prevent crimes. This alone is the long-term solution. Only a close-knit family can discipline the hormonal surges and the vagaries of the minds of young people and give them a certain direction. No state machinery in the world is fully equipped to do this. Once the family system is strong, the small residue of wicked people outside the protection of a family system can then be suitably handled by the law and policing apparatus.

FAMILY: THE BASIC UNIT FOR ONENESS

Overall, marriage and family are our two successful and longstanding institutions that mostly live up to the ideals set by our forefathers. This has been possible because our families intrinsically have a wide latitude for conciliations, and inter-personal differences can be ironed out.

Therefore, the basis of the Sangh network is the family. The Sangh reaches out to people and expands through the family. All the members of each swayamsevak family and their neighbourhood become a part of the Sangh topography. How to strengthen the family in modern times is a major preoccupation of the Sangh.

The guideline to the swayamsevaks is stated in the ABPS resolution:[113]

> It is the firm opinion of the Pratinidhi Sabha that wide-reaching multifarious activities are required to keep the family system thriving. Our daily conduct and living should nourish our family values and set an example for society. Our attitudes should strengthen mutual relations. Families are urged to come together for their prayers, festivals and pilgrimages. Speaking in [one's] mother-tongue, [and] use of swadeshi products ought to be encouraged. Those who uphold family values and social traditions shall know happiness in their lives. Family and society are complimentary. Our families should nurture tendencies of social responsibility and develop mindsets to donate resources for social, educational and religious purposes. To help the needy should be an ingrained habit of our families.

Activists deployed in Parivar Prabodhan, or family awakening, work get in touch with families to spread this message. Given the scheduling complexities of urban life, families are urged to adjust a day in the week to have their meals together. During such occasions, it is impressed upon families to converse about their lives—concerns and experiences—rather than cricket, films and politics, which are over-discussed.

MEET, GREET AND LEARN

The Godbole family of Jabalpur and Deodhar family of Pandharpur are good examples. These families regularly organize

---

[113]'Bharatiya Family System: A Unique Contribution to Humanity', ABPS Resolution, http://rss.org//Encyc/2019/3/9/ABPS-Resolution.html

get-togethers where they invite both the maternal and the paternal sides of the family. It is like a conclave with the fourth and fifth generation of family members in the age group between 8 and 92 years attending the event with enthusiasm. Family members living in different cities in India and even overseas assemble for the event. Great bonding takes place in which family members, particularly the younger lot, learn about cooperation and team spirit. They illustrate the abiding values of oneness and love that inculcates a sense of security, the defining factor of Indian families.

We feel this is a model worthy of emulation and in the coming days, we need to promote such type of gathering in metro cities on a weekly, monthly and annual basis to keep the feeling of family and kinship in every family member intact.

Men and women from stable family environments enjoy emotional well-being. To be brought up in a sound environment that cultivates the good in us is important. If we want a good cricket team, it is only possible if the game is commonly played across diverse locations. Similarly, if we want honesty and national character as a country, every family has to practise good behaviour.

The Sangh Shivir that takes place for youngsters within the age group of 15–18 years includes a programme called 'Matru Hast Bhojan.' Herein, families prepare and bring meals for the camp attendees. Each family is assigned two to three children with whom they share a family meal. It is a wondrous sight to behold and has a qualitative impact on society. Any large Sangh programme involves many families for provisioning, lodging and other logistics. This can be seen in the BJP as well. The All-India BJP Mahila Morcha conclave was held during 21–22 December 2018 in Ahmedabad. While the media reported Prime Minister Modi's address to the conclave and other political speeches, what is not known is how the lodgings of the women delegates were organized. Swayamsevaks in charge of arrangements took the decision to involve families in different apartment blocks. They gave each apartment block the responsibility of hosting a certain number of women delegates. All participating families were not swayamsevak families, but they happily accepted this duty. These families would arrange for the drop-off of the delegates to the conclave venue, their morning breakfast, their pick-up from the venue, and dinner. It was carnival time for the Ahmedabad society. Those with a solely political orientation cannot think like this; only those who believe in connecting society will think and act in this manner.

EQUALITY: SHARING IS CARING

Admittedly, twenty-first-century life has brought about mass-scale changes in the patterns of the division of work between men and women. Rural areas are still accustomed to structurally segregating work roles; the domestic sphere belongs to women and breadwinning is the task of men. This is despite the fact that many women from underprivileged backgrounds do back-breaking work in the fields. In urban areas where the nature of occupations is different and most families are nuclear, there can be no sharp division of labour. The Sangh position is that domestic work is shared responsibility. In mofussil areas and villages, where girls are being educated and getting employment-ready, this acculturation has to take place. One cannot live perennially with past conditioning. Systems have to be in sync with emerging needs. If women are working and contributing to family incomes, then men, too, have to participate in household chores. In Sangh meetings, the swayamsevaks are often asked whether they do household work or not. When Sangh functionaries go on tours and visit families of the swayamsevaks, they make it a point to speak to the women of the family; when they detect that something is amiss, they ensure that any imbalances in these families are corrected.

LIVE-IN RELATIONSHIPS AND INTER-CASTE MARRIAGES

Live-in relationships are much discussed these days. What is the purpose of such an arrangement? The rationale behind this is that couples want to stay together to know each other before deciding to get married. This has led to huge social questions. What about the children who are begotten out of wedlock? What happens when these relationships fall apart owing to disputes and attendant complications? There are no answers. Evidence shows that live-in relationships do not culminate in marriage, but lead to separation, and the sexual relationship has physical and psychological ramifications. In conclusion, live-in relationships are a negative role model for society.

In countries where strong family systems are absent, this arrangement is still understandable but, in our society, where there is a fully functional family system, such social compositions are not needed. In the case of love marriages, too, the boy and the girl know each other before marriage. So, there is no requirement for them to stay together.

The Sangh also feels that inter-caste marriages should not become a flashpoint. If a girl and boy are intent upon getting married, their parents should bless their union. In case of arranged marriages, mutual consent is vital. In the Sangh, swayamsevaks are asked before the wedding takes place, whether the consent of both the boy and girl have been sought. If households are to run successfully, there has to be mutual consent.

ELDERLY CARE

The number of old-age homes is growing in our country. We often receive complaints that elderly parents suffer utter neglect. With improvements in life expectancy, the senior-citizen population is growing and there are forecasts that it will touch 143 million by 2021,[114] and many among them would be dependents. In our culture, serving old parents is a sacred duty. This is always reiterated by swayamsevaks and Sangh leaders. Caring for ailing parents is encouraged and appreciated.

For senior citizens, the Sangh conducts prabhat, or morning, shakhas. It is also known as 'praudh' or elderly shakha. There is an age-appropriate physical fitness programme. Those who attend these shakhas are also engaged in relationship-building with families. It is a win-win proposition. The benefits of having grandparents while growing up are not experienced by children in the nuclear settings of cities. So, nuclear swayamsevak families enjoy hosting seniors. Small children flock around them and their counsel is respected. The elderly, too, enjoy social relevance.

As per Sangh initiatives, many elders spend their time in seva, like teaching those who need tutoring, conducting hospital visits to lend moral support for patient care and related public service. Only when absolutely necessary, old-age homes are developed through Sangh-inspired institutions. Sometimes, old-age homes are paired with student hostels to create a family atmosphere. In urban areas, the Sangh appeals to young people to devote some time on weekends in care homes.

DOMESTIC VIOLENCE AND FEMALE FOETICIDE

In our society, we see ugly forms of domestic violence against women arising mostly out of dowry demands and as a result of troublesome marriages. Many families have gotten rid of the evil practice of dowry. However, it is a slow process. The Sangh has conducted a sustained campaign against dowry. In a Parivar Prabodhan resolution, it has described dowry as a social ill that must be removed from society.[115]

---

[114]Nikita Doval, '20% of Population to Be Elderly By 2050: HelpAge India Report', LiveMint, 21 February 2015.

[115]'Bharatiya Family System: A Unique Contribution to Humanity', rss.org

Female foeticide is another social curse that has stuck, mutating from female infanticide. Government machinery and laws alone cannot end it. It emanates from how women are viewed in society and the mental frame of each family. Women are also participants in families where such sick and criminal acts take place. Due to laws and social awareness, this disease is receding. However, even in a small measure, such inclinations cannot be allowed to exist. In 2012, ABVP organized a big campaign against female foeticide all over India, particularly in the most affected states of Haryana, Punjab, Rajasthan and parts of Madhya Pradesh. We came up with a conscience-provoking slogan, 'Ma ke pet mein hi ma ki hatya', meaning 'In a mother's womb, a mother is being killed'. On 12 December 2012, public programmes were organized at the Gateway of India to create awareness. Many students ventured into society to spread social awareness. These practices and the Hindu conception regarding women are at complete variance. In the twenty-first century, billed as India's century and the era of Hindu Rashtra, these reprehensible acts must perish. The Sangh strongly believes that the Hindu society has to get rid of these ills.

HOMOSEXUALITY

On 6 September 2018, the SC delivered its judgement, decriminalizing homosexuality. Speaking at the *India Today* Conclave, on 17 March 2016, as an answer to a question, the sah sarkarvyah of RSS, Dattatreya Hosabale,[116] had said, 'I don't think homosexuality should be considered a criminal offense, as long as it does not affect the lives of others in society. Sexual preferences are private and personal.' He further said that the RSS does not express its views on public forums and neither does it discuss such issues in its meetings. Lest these words be over-interpreted, the very next

---

[116]RSS, 'RSS Supports Reservation till Discrimination in Society Exists-Dattatreya Hosabale Ji at *India Today* Conclave', rss.org. 19 April 2016.

day, he added, 'Gay marriages should not be institutionalized for it will institutionalize homosexuality. So, it should be prohibited.'

However, inclusion is a key concern. Mohanji made this pitch while addressing intellectuals and mediapersons as part of his lecture series in Delhi on 18 September 2018. Mohanji said that everyone was part of society. 'Society is changing, we need to accommodate everyone so that they do not feel isolated,'[117] he elaborated.

TRANSGENDER RIGHTS

There are several references to transgender people from the earliest times in our religious texts and epics. In the *Ramayana*, there is a heartwarming narration. When Lord Rama was leaving Ayodhya and proceeding for his banishment towards the forests, he instructed the sorrowful men and women of his kingdom to turn back and not to follow him any further. All acceded and left. When Lord Rama returned after his fourteen-year banishment, he found that the transgender community was transfixed at that very spot because the Lord had not specifically instructed them. He was overwhelmed by their devotion and blessed them with special powers to work for the benefit of others.

From this stems the social belief that it is auspicious for newborn children to be blessed by transgender people. However, though endowed with a ritualistic significance, they have been a neglected lot—treated badly and jeered at severely. Confronting this big gap in our society, this community started living outside the society and began following deviant practices. Due to their isolation, they face livelihood issues and are often seen begging at the crossroads of streets and traffic signals. The Sangh has a respectful attitude towards transgender people and wants them to have a dignified life.

---

[117]RSS, 'Future of Bharat: An RSS's Perspective', Press Statements, rss.org, 27 August 2018.

For the first time, the Kinnar Akhara was formed and allowed to take out its peshwai or ceremonial procession in the Prayagraj Kumbh, 2019. This was welcomed in Hindu society. The Juna Akhara, the largest order of sadhus in India, recognized the Kinnar Akhara in Hindu spiritual traditions. The Juna Akhara must be lauded for this gesture. They also ordain the 'Mahamandaleshwar' title the head of the Kinnar Akhada, the position of spiritual guardianship accorded to this order of sadhus or monks. Pavitra, secretary of Kinnar Akhara, spoke of Kumbh 2019, 'The public and all the devotees who are here have supported and shown us lot of respect. We are happy that people here have accepted us.'[118]

The Sangh views such developments as constructive. Acharya Lakshmi Narayanan Tripathi,[119] Mumbai-based head of Kinnar Akhara, is working to remove prejudices against transgender people and to improve their conditions.

In politics, too, people from the transgender community are assuming positions. They have voting rights, which were secured after a fair amount of struggle. In Lucknow, ABVP organized a conference on 19 April 2019,[120] for the transgender community, on their suffrage rights and voter awareness, with the slogan, 'Nation first, Voting must'. Ramesh Garia, the regional organizing secretary of ABVP, addressed this meet. The Sangh banks on the innate capacity of the Hindu society for acceptance to bring reform and inclusion. Laws are definitely required, but more than laws, reliance is placed on changing the mindset of society. Social dialogue, processes and laws is the Sangh way of facing change and challenge.

---

[118]"Akhand Beyond Sexuality": Transgender Akhada Participates in Kumbh Mela For the First Time Ever', organiser.org, 15 January 2019.
[119]'Kinnar Akhara Expansion Make Two New Mahamandaleshwar', *Navbharat*, 7 February 2019.
[120]'Democracy For All: ABVP Reaches Out to Transgenders in Lucknow to Enable Participation in Elections', Swarajya, 25 April 2019.

The Sangh believes that modernity of the twenty-first century should not result in the withering away of interpersonal relationships. The family is and always will be the common unity denominator. From Kashmir to Kanyakumari, the arrival of a guest in the house is heralded like that of God himself—'Athithi Devo Bhava.'

The family is our future and we are obligated to preserve and protect it. The example of the superficiality of the West is before us, with tremendous shallowness beneath its external glitter. Economic developments should not lead to the impairment of our family system. The Sangh is focused on this fact. Therefore, it is concentrating on the dialogue on family matters in society. In modern times, how can we secure an ideal family life that will reflect our traditions and values? This is a deep engagement. Whatever issues are as yet unaddressed or need resolution will be evaluated as they are, with an open mind and a compassionate heart—'with the intellect of Shankara and the heart of the Buddha,' in the words of Swami Vivekananda.

The RSS is basically a sociocultural organization. It will not dither in the face of difficult social questions. It will plunge headlong. Swayamsevaks will join the ranks of Indian reformers, philosophers, leaders and scholars to defend and expand India's worthiest values.

Now Kutumb Pramodhan, or family awakening, has become one of the key activities of the RSS and its influence is spreading in society. People are sharing their views and family practices. They are finding Sangh's suggestions useful and valuable. So, 'the family is our strength' has become a mantra for the twenty-first century.

10

WOMEN'S MOVEMENT

A decade after the founding of the Sangh, a nearly identical women-only organization was started; it was named Rashtra Sevika Samiti. In a way, its origins were bound up with the personal experiences of its founder, Laxmibai Kelkar, referred also as Mausi (aunt) Kelkar. Born on 6 July 1905, Mausi Kelkar was given to nationalist stirrings and was a contemporary of Guruji Golwalkar.

Widowed young at the age of 27, she was a mother to a small girl and often brooded over where to educate her daughter. So impelled was she, as a guardian, in her commitment to the role of education that Mausi Kelkar started a girl's school, by the name of Kesarimal Kanya Vidyalaya, in Wardha, which survives even today. Having met Doctorji and after several rounds of discussions with him, she set up the Sevika Samiti work in 1936. At that time, Mausi Kelkar was only 31. She was the pramukh sanchalika, or head, of the samiti till she passed away at the age of 73, in 1978.

The fact that during an age of rampant social conservatism riddled with normative assumptions, Doctorji was a firm believer in the intellectual capabilities of women, shows his open-mindedness. At that time, to hold several rounds of converzations with a widowed woman about starting a parallel women-only organization was out of the ordinary. Doctorji explained the Sangh's beliefs, methods, objectives and other technical details to Mausi Kelkar. As a result, the Sevika Samiti was formed after adopting the form and content of the Sangh for women. The Sevika Samiti also has a ganavesh, or uniform, like the Sangh. Just like the Sangh, the Sevika Samiti, too, has its first-year, second-year and third-year training camps for a duration of fifteen days usually in the months of May and June each year. Self-defence training is imparted as part of the curriculum. These training camps are held in Nagpur and other places. Every year, more than 10,000 women attend these camps. The Sevika Samiti was started in 1936. Barely three years later, in 1939, the training camps began. Such was the influence of Samiti work.

ALL-INDIA FOOTPRINT

Contrary to the belief that there is an absence of women in shakhas, the Sangh's ideas and its founder's methods have always focused on the contribution of women in public affairs and civic duty. Very early, it was realized that without creating awareness among women, these perspectives would neither be understood nor appreciated. As Mausi Kelkar on numerous occasions said, 'Woman is the inspiring force for the family and the nation. So long as this force is not awakened, society cannot progress.'[121]

Presently, Sevika Samiti has an all-India footprint and this expansion is according to Sangh expectations. Just as the Sangh has pracharaks, the Samiti has pracharikas. As of now, there are forty-eight pracharikas. Nearly thirteen pracharikas are devoted to the Northeast. Sunitaji Haldekar has been a pracharika for more than thirty years, standing for Assam and other Northeastern states. She is a heroic pracharika and has faced hardships—just like a male pracharak—doing Samiti work under hostile circumstances.

There are short-term full-timers called vistaraks, who devote themselves full-time to Samiti work for two years. Sevika Samiti has a big turnover of service projects. In the year 2018–2019, this number was 870. All positions in the Samiti are controlled

---

[121]'Matrushakti and RSS: The Inspiring Saga of Rashtra Sevika Samiti', Organiser, 26 October 2018.

by women and all responsibilities are carried out by them, for example, running and maintaining the Samiti offices, logistics for camps and service projects. Annaman Seethakka from Telengana is the Sevika Samiti's pramukh karyavahika, or general secretary. There are four sahkaryavahikas, or joint general secretaries. They are householders as well as pracharikas. Shantakkaa is the pramukh sanchalika.

The work of Sevika Samiti is too big and no one can ignore it. It has a big presence in almost every sub-division of the country. Each state has a pracharika and there are 4,900 shakhas of the Sevika Samitis across India.[122] The Sevika Samiti runs fifteen education projects and has 385 service initiatives. Globally, the Sevika Samiti has its network in twenty-two countries across the world.

The Samiti headquarters is in Dhantoli, Nagpur, commonly known as Ahilya Mandir. Apart from the office premises, it also has a residence for pracharikas and activist visitors. The smaller offices in different locations also have similar dual arrangements.

The eightieth year of Samiti celebrations in 2016 was marked with a camp in Nagpur of 3,000 district-level women activists, or sevikas. A special camp in Delhi, named 'Prerna', or inspiration, was also organized. In 2005, during the centenary celebrations of Mausi Kelkar, the Sevika Samiti organized a camp of 10,000 women activists, belonging to all age groups drawn from different parts of India.

SAMITI WORK

The Samiti has taken up many issues that will be relevant in the times to come. Certain feminine responsibilities are enjoined upon women by nature, as mothers and guardians. Women are also stepping out of their domestic spheres to assume professional roles, striking a balance between family and work-life, which is a cause of concern in the twenty-first century. Maintaining this

---

[122]Rashtrasevikasamiti.org

balance between family and work-life is one of the top most issues of contemporary times. Much thought is devoted to this.

City safety and security evaluations are dependent, to a large measure, on female insights and experiences. Thus, the question of how safe our cities are for women frequently pops up. Women have a vested interest in municipal systems of roads, parks and garbage collection working efficiently so that they can ensure the health and wellness of their families. Simultaneously, women are also concerned about value education in their families. The Samiti runs a religious instruction forum for women, as most of our values have a religious origin. Also, a major engagement of Indian women is religious observances—singing devotional hymns, or kirtans. Most homes have a domestic altar and a family deity. Samiti work has expanded the initiatives of women in temple management.

As part of a process to develop an outlook for women in the twenty-first century, women achievers like officers, scientists, professors, doctors and journalists are regularly invited to Samiti meetings for interactions.

BIKE RALLY CELEBRATIONS

The Sangh's thinking on women's place in society is reflected in how social customs are approached. More than ten years ago, in 2007, the Sangh formed an all-women committee and deputed Anil Sambre to work on the celebrations for the Hindu New Year, called Varsh Pratipada. On its eve, a women's bike rally was organized in Nagpur. The tradition continued over the years and what had started out as only one bike rally expanded to thirteen bike rallies on 5 April 2019. More than 5,000 young girls and women participated, turning up in their traditional finery. The residents of the city came out in big numbers to cheer for them. There are no barriers in terms of economic status, education or caste. It is a fully integrated setup and all women participate unfettered in this celebration.

Shradha Pathak, a very able ABVP activist in her student days, is the organizer of this event and has been doing so for the past ten years. Reflecting on the overwhelming response to this rally the first time it was held, she said that one rally which covered a 5 km-stretch was accorded a ceremonial welcome at twenty-six places. About 850 girls and women participated in this particular rally. Shradha runs her own social organization, 'Kushalta', or excellence, which she deploys for conducting women-related programmes. She is whole-heartedly supported by the Sangh and Parivar organizations. There are many like her, working in different locations. The Sangh is well-grounded and has ample talent to take up twenty-first-century women's issues and to ensure just and fair systems in public and private domains.

ABVP ACTIVISTS

After Independence, ABVP was established in 1948 with the objective of working among students. Boys and girls became activists to serve the students' cause. ABVP was the first Parivar organization to be started. Initially, all the girls who became activists belonged to swayamsevak families. Thus, the swayamsevaks first started bringing up the issue of women's participation in their families. This was the pattern followed in other Parivar organizations, like BMS, which were founded subsequently. The percentage of women in the Parivar organizations has grown and is ever-increasing.

In 1990, due to separatist violence, there was turmoil in the valley. In those days, Kashmiri Hindus were being driven out in droves from the valley. ABVP began a nationwide stir against this. This involved going to colleges and universities to mobilize opinions against the ethnic cleansing of the Kashmiri Pandit population from the valley. In all the programmes that ABVP conducted during this phase, it was seen that the participation of girls was in equal proportion to boys. When the appeal went out for 'Chalo Kashmir' on 11 September 1990, female students volunteered enthusiastically despite terrorist threats and menacing vitriol. While some of these girls were easily permitted by their families, many others had to struggle to convince theirs. ABVP office-bearers took extra care of logistical support for female students and the Sangh was very supportive.

In ABVP, participation of girls in agitations for national and public interest is very high. During 1980s, the infiltration of the Bangladeshi Muslim community was at its peak in Assam. It had altered, to a great extent, the demography of Assam and resulted in land alienation of the Hindu community and the indigenous tribes. All of Assam was pulsating with the anti-infiltration movement and ABVP supported this agitation. After a nationwide campaign, ABVP organized a mass demonstration in Guwahati on 2 October 1983. I have recollections of listening to my seniors, female activists who had travelled to Assam in the heyday of the trouble in 1983, braved lathi charges and arrests but stood resolute. None of them were unhappy or discouraged. They were in high spirits.

When I was a B.Sc. student in 1985 and 1988, our organizational chief of Nagpur—Mahanagar organizing secretary—was Manisha Bakshi (now Kothekar). She was an Ayurveda doctor, and instead of practising, had become a full-timer, devoting most of her time to the organization. Thus, my initiation in ABVP work happened under a woman organizational head. We followed her instructions, and she worked in the same manner that any male organizing secretary would have worked. She was invited in Sangh coordination meetings as well.

PROMINENT WOMEN AT THE FOREFRONT

This principle of equal participation in public life, considered a modern conviction, has been an accepted fact in ABVP since its very beginning. ABVP founders like Dattaji Didolkar and its architect, Yashwantrao Kelkar, who were swayamsevaks, worked for establishing this work ethic. As a result, many female activists went on to become active workers and even handled the responsibilities of positions like state and national secretaries.

A very well-known and respected name in ABVP circles is that of Geetatai Gunde. She became an activist as a student, and after the completion of her MSc., began to work for Glaxo in Mumbai. In 1984, when she was in her 30s, she resigned from Glaxo and became a full-time worker of ABVP. She was very active during the anti-Emergency movement and worked with quite a number of human rights and women's rights organizations. Geetatai has worked with several generations of female activists in ABVP. She was the national vice-president as well as the all-India head of all activism related to woman's issues or undertaken by girls. She crisscrossed the length and breadth of the country in order to expand and augment the role of female activists. Aged 65, this has been the singular purpose of her life. Tremendously gifted, she could have had a lucrative corporate career but such was the potency of her calling for public service that she gave it all up and embraced the humble life of a full-timer. In a month, Geetatai would tour different states in around twenty days, grooming female students, counselling them and preparing them for leadership roles. She is deeply revered by the Sangh. I have known Geetatai since I was a higher secondary student. She has truly been a lady at the wheel, always on the go with her extensive work.

Several female activists went on to start their own enterprises— foundations and non-profit institutions in the social sector. In Tamil Nadu, Sumathi Venkatesh, who runs a cotton mill and other allied units, had put in long years of work in skill development. Vanathi Srinivas is widely acknowledged as a powerful BJP leader in Tamil Nadu. Asha Lakra, from a tribal family of Gumla, is a first-generation educated woman. Such was the impact of ABVP work in the area of personality development that she turned out to be a powerful speaker and went on to become the national secretary of ABVP. She also had a good innings in the BJP Mahila Morcha.

A short while after her marriage, her husband was tragically killed by Naxalites. It was difficult for her to come out of this trauma but she showed rare fortitude. She did not lock herself up in despair, but became active in public life once again. She is a successful mayor, having been elected to the Ranchi Municipal Corporation consecutively for two terms.

Meera Kadbe in Nagpur does counselling for women who face legal issues, ranging from criminal to marital problems. Her work takes her to police stations. Viney Kapoor Mehra, an advocate by profession, is now the vice-chancellor of the new Dr B.R. Ambedkar National Law University, Haryana. There are examples from earlier phases as well. Smita Kolhe (Manjre) was a practising Ayurveda doctor in the 1980s, when I was a student in Nagpur. Women in professional roles in the field of Ayurveda were uncommon in those days. She had worked in ABVP for a long time. After her marriage to Ravi Kolhe, she left her practice in Nagpur and started working for tribal people in the forest areas of Melghat in Amaravati district of Maharashtra for a long time. The Kolhes have transformed the lives of the tribal populace in these areas by adapting their ways to the tribal culture. Both were honoured with Padmashree Awards in 2019.

Tejaswani Ananth Kumar was an ABVP activist in her college days. She is the wife of the late Ananth Kumar, who was a senior union minister and a famous BJP politician from south India. After her marriage, she continued with her social work. Tejaswini runs 'Adamya Chetna', a society under which the Annapoorna Midday Meal Program serves meals to more than two lakh schoolchildren. Even grief could not impede this great lady's sense of duty. The day after her husband's demise, food was distributed as usual to the children.[123]

Madhuri Sahasrabudhe, a teacher by vocation, is a feisty activist-mother. She drove a sixty-day car rally with three other mothers and visited twenty-two countries. The voyage, tellingly

---

[123]www.adamyachetana.org

titled, 'Mothers on Wheels' began from Delhi and terminated at London. The mothers visited forty-seven cities, driving 23,657 km, with the objective to understand the changing family structures around the world and the role of mothers in these households. Madhuri has a treasure trove of experiences and real-life mother-child stories from across varied cultures to share. Her pursuit is noble—to find solutions for the large-scale family disruptions that will occur in the coming generations.[124]

Women from ABVP's student batches are professionals of high standing and continue to contribute to public life. One of them is Dr Rashmi Das, who was the elected general secretary of JNU Students Union in 1996, a time when ABVP was the target of extremely hostile behaviour on campus. She went on to become a financial journalist and presently runs two successful sectoral magazines in telecommunications and infrastructure. Simultaneously, she is active in public life as well.

I have known a number of such activists who began as spirited girls in their student days. They remained committed and robustly served the national cause. Such personality development is possible because Parivar organizations provide an equal, safe, free and secure environment. In the future, too, Parivar organizations will be important vehicles through which women will move forward and make positive contributions towards society's development.

TACKLING CHALLENGES

For women, education is a game changer. One of the main challenges in higher education is hostel facilities and admission in institutions of excellence located far from one's residence. In 2008, ABVP undertook an all-India survey of hostels—boys, girls and hostels for the SC/ST community. It was found that the state of the girls' hostels was pathetic. Their safety was a concern, the

---

[124]"Four Mothers Take Road Trip Across 22 Countries to Understand Motherhood', Mid-day.com, 23 May 2019.

toilets were dilapidated, and overall, the lodgings were miserable. Reports were submitted to all the state governments irrespective of who was in power. Finally, ABVP filed a petition in the SC. There were several hearings and all parties—state governments, union territories and the union of India—filed their affidavits. To show themselves in proper light, many governments started constructing hostels. For instance, the Maharashtra government built 100 new hostels, including many for girls. The issue of more hostels for girls is constantly raised by ABVP in the top institutions, of our country, like the Indian Institutes of Technology (IITs) and National Institute of Technology (NITs), which, over the last five years, have seen a spike in the admission of girls—and the number is only growing.

Similarly, access needs to be extended. In 2016, ABVP went on an agitation in Mumbai University for the twenty-four-hour availability of library facilities for the girls' hostel on campus. A comprehensive survey in 2017–18 on the state of education for girls was conducted. It had a vast coverage—257 districts in twenty-two states. There were 21,245 respondents who answered a long questionnaire that included several parameters. The responses were collected by 5,040 volunteers who were also female. Several issues for follow-up action were collated. These issues included security and safety in campuses and hostels, need for more skill development programmes, future career guidance and more opportunities for personality development. These are being addressed by local and state units.

MAHILA SAMANVAY: CO-ORDINATION IN THE PARIVAR

For the last twenty-five years, special attention has been given to women working in Parivar organizations. The Sangh is a great votary of intra-organization coordination among women and for propelling leadership stakes. When the system of Mahila Samanvay, or women's coordination, was formed, Geetatai was relieved from ABVP in 2009 to head this body. Her mandate is to ensure procedural competence in Parivar organizations to encourage women's participation. Of course, this was preceded by consultations with the Sangh. She advises heads of different Parivar organizations, conducts workshops for students, directs an annual retreat of prime women activists of the Parivar, gathers feedback, steers identification of major issues and sets the agenda for women's movement of the Sangh.

A whole team of women activists work with Geetatai in Mahila Samanvay. Prominent among them are Mamata Yadav from ABVP, Gita Gokhale from BMS, Srimati Meenakshi from VHP and Ranjana Khare from VKA. When initiations for Mahila Samanvay began in 1990 in Maharashtra and it was rolled out at an all-India level in 1993, Geetatai was the one who led it. Drishti, a research-based women's studies organization based out of Pune, was also started in 2000 to support initiatives of women by the Sangh. Presently, it is headed by Anjali Deshpande.

The impact of such intensive work is felt across Parivar organizations. The lawyers' body, Adhivakta Parishad, organizes conferences to spread awareness about legal rights of women at state and national levels. The attendees are both men and women. Krida Bharti has turned its lens on campaigns for building facilities for women athletes and players. Itihas Sankalan Samiti is working on presenting the history of Indian women and conducts conferences of women historians. In 2017, BMS organized a massive march in Delhi with two lakh people, and one lakh of this activist force were women. Vigyan Bharati started Shakti, a conclave of women scientists. VKA and Samskar Bharti have many women full-timers.

In 2010, the Sangh held an important meet on Mahila Vimarsh, or women's discourse, which was attended by the sarsanghchalak. A two-day meet on 23 and 24 March 2019, in New Delhi, was held under the aegis of Mahila Samanvay. It was titled 'Bharatiya Stree Vimarsh' (Discourse on Indian Women). It deliberated chiefly on how the issues and challenges of present times can be resolved on the basis of Hindu thought and the family system. This is an ongoing and constructive dialogue within the Sangh.

With Sangh inspiration, many women associations have been formed—Bharatiya Stree Shakti Jagran in Pune and Maitreyi in Nagpur, and finally, these culminated in the formation of the All India Women's Organization as a public platform. It was named 'Stree Shakti', or 'women power'. Based in Mumbai, it was started by Nirmala alias Urmila Apte and has several localized variants committed to a range of activities.

One programme is interestingly called 'vivah ki pathshala', meant for college and university students. It stems from the practical consideration that marriage should be a well-thought- out decision, so that future vulnerabilities that girls often find themselves in can be avoided. This is a good preventive against domestic violence, divorce and other fragilities. Value inculcation is done for men too; that they should be civil, not domineering, they should abjure violence in thought, speech and action. Stree Shakti has addressed the squeamishness around sex education. It has made mature arguments on the syllabi and called for the involvement of medical experts. Stree Shakti is empanelled by the Ministry of Women and Child Development and is consulted on issues of women's dignity and safety in the realm of the Vishaka guidelines[125] and Nirbhaya Fund.[126] Presently, K.S. Jayashree from Kerala is the president of Stree Shakti, Kumudini Bhargava is its general secretary and Manisha Kothekar, from Maharashtra, is the organizing secretary.

CONTEMPORARY CONVERZATIONS

Contrary to a stereotypical perception that the Sangh is a conservative organization that is unfavourable to women, it is a

---

[125]Handbook on Sexual Harassment of Women at Workplace, https://wcd.nic.in/sites/default/files/Handbook%20on%20Sexual%20Harassment%20of%20Women%20at%20Workplace.pdf
[126]Nirbhaya Fund Guidelines, Ministry of Women and Child Development

space of free-flowing converzations. For example, ABVP took up a campaign to fight social taboos associated with the menstrual cycle. As secretary of the Delhi University Students Union (DUSU) 2017–18, Mahamedha Nagar led this and included boys in the social campaign as well. College principles were contacted and class-to-class campaigns were conducted for popularizing the usage of sanitary napkins. She talked about availability, affordability and for prices to be as low as ₹5. An awareness run was organized on 22 January 2018. At this event, boys, too, could be seen distributing sanitary napkins. Nearly 5,000 sanitary pads were given away.[127] Thus, the social conditioning of shame associated with menstrual cycle was broken and the consciousness of this physical process as something natural was publicized. This awareness-raising was much appreciated by all in the Sangh and Parivar organizations as a timely action.

For the Sangh, the issue of women's rights is not just material for seminars but ground-level work with practical ramifications. Article 35A in the context of J&K places a disability on women by virtue of them being women. Their property rights are severed if they decide to marry someone outside their state.* No such restriction is placed on men. In a modern democracy, this is a medieval notion of law, interdicting equality between sexes. 35A was anti-women and when the Sangh talks of its removal, it should not be seen through a communal lenses. The struggle of Muslim women against Triple Talaq and the Sangh support for it has to be viewed in the sequence of reformation and women's empowerment. Just as the Sangh launches movements to end all discriminatory practices against women and to purge Hindu society of social ills is also supports the struggles of women belonging to other faiths. Much ado is made about temple entry by women even when they have full rights of entry (barring one or two temples because of the special nature of

[127]Riya Sharma, '"Padman" Akshay Kumar Comes to Support DU's Run for Tax-free Sanitary Pads', TNN, Entertainment Times, *The Times of India*, 24 January 2018.

the deity). Here also for changes to be peaceably implemented and to have lasting value, the ideal route is deliberations within Hindu society and with devotees about the need for change.

Women's empowerment needs a big tent approach. It encompasses all castes, faiths languages, regions, economic and educational statuses. It is just not enough to say that all are equal. Equality has to be seen and experienced. Such is the method of the Sangh.

WHO IS A FEMINIST?

The Sangh believes in equality for women and works hard to establish it. True, there have been many grave problems and attacks that women have had to suffer. When feminism was imported as a diagnostic tool to assess the situation in the Indian context, it failed badly, although certain questions worth considering were raised and did stimulate law-making which eventually helped women. Its basic flaw was its fault-line approach and a fundamental alteration in the idea of Indian womanhood. They defined women's empowerment in terms of 'sexual politics' and 'philosophy of power relationships.'[128]

For them, the nature-defined role of women as mothers and carers was a model of femininity based on a patriarchal past, like cages associated with a gendered identity. Feminism is the language of male oppression and class struggle and it shows no flexibility to account for diverse experiences. Improvements in economic condition and education are not considered transformative enough. All contestations are about the woman's body. The hippie culture of the West in the 60s and 70s became the coda of this stream of thought.

It is, therefore, natural for most women to be uneasy with Western feminist thinkers and their tropes, which have come to

---

[128]K. Millete, *Sexual Politics. Theory of Sexual Politics* (Third Edition), p. 26, University of Illinois Press, Chicago, 2000.

inhabit the social science space in India. In any case, whatever pretensions it had as an academic discipline soon degenerated into a fad and reckless lifestyle choices. Unfortunately, this has taken hold among certain sections of our society and university campuses, where feminist paraphernalia of Woodstock symbolisms are considered as rites of passage for being considered progressive.

It can be safely stated that the march of women's empowerment in India has no traces of Western feminist thinking. It follows the Indian trajectory of integration, where women and men work together to remove social ills that are incapacitating to women. In Russia, they have coined a new concept—they say, they do not need harmful feminism but a good family life. I also heard their preferred word 'familyism', while on a tour to Russia during their presidential elections in March 2018, as an 'international observer'. The Sangh, on the other hand, does not believe in the dictates of straitjackets and isms. It is a comprehensive mission of society to empower women, to remove restrictions of purdah, which came about as a result of a long history of invasions, and to raise educational levels and economic ability. The Sangh has supported enabling laws and policies. However, the moot point is change in social mindsets where each family takes the decision to bring about a qualitative change in the status of women. Therefore, the Sangh is reaching out to families with the message of women's empowerment, education, democratic participation and fighting evil practices like dowry. If a woman wants to go out for studies or work, she ought to be encouraged. If a woman decides to enter public life, she should be supported. We are seeing this change quietly sweep across the country in a uniquely Indian manner.

DIGNITY AND SECURITY

It is a logical corollary, that wherever ABVP units are strong, those campuses are safe for female students. When the brutal Nirbhaya incident happened in Delhi on 16 December 2012, it shocked the nation and a massive social anger burst forth. ABVP was at the forefront of this struggle,[129] and shadowed Nirbhaya's parents in their fight for justice in getting the most dreadful juvenile criminal sentenced by the juvenile court. ABVP fought alongside Nirbhaya's parents for pushing amendments in the Juvenile Justice bill.[130] During the course of this struggle, an idea germinated for making the female students of our country fearless. This was concretized as 'Mission Sahasi' with grandmaster Shifuji Shaurya Bhardwaj. A reputed trainer for women's security, Shifuji had made a name for imparting self-defence skills through his 'Mission Prahar'. Mission Sahasi started in 2018, and training programmes were run in five destinations in Mumbai. On 6 March 2018, the demonstration of the learnt skills took place in BKC (Bandra Kurla Complex Ground), Mumbai, in a mega gathering of 6,000 girls. The chief minister of Maharashtra, Devendra Fadnavis, a guest at the event, witnessed the fearlessness of the girls.[131] ABVP gave Mission Sahasi a national scope with the result that eight lakh girls in a thousand places all over the country were trained in self-defence skills. Public demonstrations during 30–31 October 2018 at different locations saw a participation of 5.5 lakh girls. This programme was commended at the highest level by the sarsanghchalak himself. During the question-and-answer session at his lecture series, 'Bhavishya Bharat Ka: An RSS Perspective', held in Delhi on 18 September 2018, Mohanji praised and extolled ABVP's efforts for organizing self-defence training camps for girls as it had a big socio-psychological impact on the freedom of movement of girls.[132] It promoted the belief that women are not helpless, they

---

[129]"ABVP to Organise Nationwide Protests on Jan 4', *The Times of India*, 31 December 2012.

[130]"Pressure Mounts on Govt For Passage of Juvenile Bill', *Deccan Herald*, 21 December 2015.

[131]"ABVP Invoking the 'Shakti' Through Mission SAHASI', Organiser, 19 November 2018.

[132]RSS, 'Bharat of Future–An RSS Perspective (Day 3)', rss.org, 20 September 2018.

are fearless. India is a country of Shakti worshippers. When the ultimate power is in the form of a goddess, how could women be weak? This goddess is Durga in her divine form and has appeared as the brave Indian queens, Rani Lakshmibai and Durgavati, in human form. These role models should be internalized not only by women but also by men. The Sangh views programmes like Mission Sahasi as having great potential as it makes women self-confident and also changes the perspective of an entire society.

IN THE WORKFORCE

Securing work-life balance is most applicable for women in the workforce. It is a task for our entire society. As urban centres multiply and an increasing number of women climb up the education ladder and enter the workforce, their sustainability and achievements are contingent upon the arrangements present in society. Women have to travel distances, excel at work and shoulder all responsibilities of the domestic sphere. It is a work of several lifetimes. The word 'multitasker' is genuinely feminine. The working woman strikes a fine balance between emotion, aspiration and familial duties. She is to be celebrated and supported. If families and society fail to understand this and support her, there is a real possibility of a negative m-curve, which is faced by many developed countries where educated career-oriented women are postponing their decision to become mothers or are averse to it.

Many women in the urban world are employed in physically laborious work at retail stores, petrol stations, domestic housekeeping tasks and as labourers at building and road construction sites. In rural areas, they do back-breaking work as farmhands from sunup to sundown. All allied occupations of the agri-sector, like dairy, animal husbandry, pickle making, embroidery and stitching, and village and cottage industry, are overlaid with female labour, most of which goes unacknowledged. Combined with this is their role in the upkeep of the family, a contribution whose significance cannot be stressed enough. Everyone needs to recognize this, for it will create respect for women in society.

In many of our tribal societies and mountainous regions, we see women as equal stakeholders in decision-making in family matters. Financially, too, they are empowered. We have always relied on family values and social awareness to establish the equality of women. Government structures have performed a secondary role. The complementarity of men and women is the lifeblood of Hindu traditions. This ideal has to be lived in day-to-day life. This is the big challenge for us. It is because this hallowed precept was denuded, many times even forgotten, that we see so many of the problems that we face today as a society.

Young mothers who are professionals need to be supported. The need to have women in leadership roles in important to truly represent the state of accomplishments that women have achieved after having come a long way. Reservation in local bodies to the tune of 50 per cent is creating a new crop of leaders who are doing good work.

In any Parivar organization, a common query for any programme is the number of women who participated. Gender-sensitive cities and gender parity in schools and colleges are their demands. India cannot become a great power if the women of India—half of the country's population—fall behind. The Sangh is making sustained efforts to develop and promote women's participation and leadership in every sphere. When the story of India as a superpower is written as it is certain to be written, it will be in large measure the story of the achievements of Indian women. This is good news for the twenty-first century.

*Ravi Shanker Kapoor, 'Opposition to Scrapping of Anti-Women Article 370 Shows Hypocrisy of Left-librals', News18.com, 13 August 2019.

EPILOGUE:
A GUIDING, PROVIDING AND
PROTECTIVE FORCE

A letter written by Guruji, dated 2 April 1973, days before he passed away, reads: 'The motto of our work has been "worship the nation, worship the ideal."'

His influential work, *Bunch of Thoughts*, which also includes questions that he was asked from time to time and his response, reflects the kind of swayamsevaks that were being trained in the Sangh and the ends that they would achieve. On the topic of political theory and system, he was asked what ism he believed in. Guruji's answer was, 'I do not believe that human intelligence has by now gone [so] bankrupt that it should be straitjacketed in some ism.' There was a poser on democracy: 'Is democracy a Bhartiya concept?' Guruji replied, 'We have tried all experiments including democracy, even prior to the West.'

Guruji was given to clear conceptions and logical consistency. He responded to questions, even those that seemed uncomfortable, in a simple and straight manner. So, when he was asked whether he preferred an honest despot to a democracy run by dishonest men, he answered, 'With despots it is difficult to continue the tradition of good governance generation after generation. And so, we need some arrangements. Democracy is one such arrangement. Any type of government will do. When the men running it are honest and selfless, it all boils down to the quality of human beings.'

At the heart of all these answers is the fundamental Sangh conviction of 'vyakti nirman' and a realization that even the best systems can be waylaid if not serviced by men and women of sterling values. From the throes of change that rage from time to time, new systems can and will be created. There shall be no dissonance between needs and requirements, but all this can be done provided man-making is in mission mode. This is our main work. Swayamsevaks schooled in the shakha system will branch out in diverse fields to face challenges and create adequate systems.

Half of the twentieth century was spent slaving under foreign rule. At the midpoint of that servitude, in 1925, the Sangh was formed. It is only in the other half that we became a free and a democratic country. In this phase, when India was swerving towards an authoritarian rule, a struggle was launched to save democracy and fight the imposition of internal Emergency and the Sangh led from the front. Restoration of basic freedoms and civil liberties, resuscitating constitutional morality and re-establishing democracy were the high points in our country's political history of the twentieth century. This history of saving democracy was primarily a Sangh contribution. Doctorji's instruction that society should be prepared and it should have the generative capacity to defend our independence was proved in the anti-Emergency struggle.

During the twentieth century, the Sangh was persecuted continuously. It was under surveillance, was the target of vilification campaigns and calumny, and was banned thrice. It weathered all these massive political storms as swayamsevaks, having studied in the shakha system, dug in with their devotion and dedication to India. Politically, too, the attitude was adverse. The so-called secular politics ringed in by the Congress and later other parties used to gang up against the Sangh and single it out for discriminatory treatment. These political parties and their cliques tried their best to make the Sangh and all Parivar organizations untouchables in every field. They labelled the Sangh 'communal' and used it as an abuse at all times. They negated the Hinduness of India and Lord Ram.

We are well into twenty years of the twenty-first century and today the people of India perceive the reality. Those political parties which made anti-Sanghism their political prism and ruled over the nation did little to bring it out of pervasive poverty and lack of education. Our rural areas were prone to extreme distress and squalor dominated our cities. We did not count, in any significant manner, in global trade. In almost all states of India, such politico-social systems were challenged and overthrown through a democratic process.

Much has been achieved since. However, now there are many new issues. Urbanization is proceeding at a breakneck speed. Technology, communications, satellite technologies and digitization have impacted our social life, changed businesses, influenced politics and transformed the way in which we receive and transmit knowledge. Access is poised for another giant leap with artificial intelligence. A better quality of life through disease prevention and control, advances in genetics and medical science are our current stages of advancement.

MAKING THE TRADITIONAL CONTEMPORARY

Parallel to this progress, we have organized our traditional knowledge systems and brought it into sharp focus—almost on an industrial scale—in the international arena. India's yoga has become a sine qua non for healthy living. There is a phenomenal increase in interest about Sanskrit and other Indian languages. Our history is being liberated and decolonized.

Textbooks are being corrected and, at long, last many suppressed facts are coming to light. It is the time to end all hypocrisies. The students of the next generation deserve to learn history in the right perspective and the world is taking note. Renaming of roads by removing the colonial-era names of British viceroys and Mughal invaders are part of this process. The revival of temples which began with the reconstruction of Somnath was halted after the demise of Sardar Patel. But we have to re-establish our icons. That is why Ram Mandir will be a pre-eminent cultural agenda of the twenty-first century.

There is also the big challenge of making the traditional contemporary. Deendayal Upadhyaya called this adjustment 'yugaanukul', or syncing something with the present idiom. The Sangh is preparing its cadre with all the necessary requisites for resolving modern questions. It is consistently expanding the front organizations.

A certain core vocabulary is taught through repetitious practice, like 'sarvasparshi karya' (work benefitting all), 'saksham Hindu samaj' (competent Hindu society), 'samras Hindu samaj' (harmonious Hindu society), 'swayam purna Hindu samaj' (self-reliant Hindu society), 'secularism in its true sense in the twenty-first century' and 'environment-friendly and human-friendly model of economic development'. These coinages are expressive of the Hindu way of thinking in all spheres of life.

BUILDING BONDS

There are certain relationship matters which are critical. What is our relationship with the past? Several dimensions have been discussed and many are yet to be expounded upon. What is our relationship with India's eternal knowledge and how do we pass on its benefits to the world? What will be the order of our relationship within society with different religious practices and faiths? We have to work towards a situation where the bond with the nation will overlay all other identities of language, gender, caste and faith.

What will be the relationship between men and women and the nature of the family? What will be our relationship with the environment? What will be our relationship with other countries and nationalities? What will be our relationship with human values and technological innovations?

These are the big challenges of the twenty-first century and in all these domains, the Sangh can be a guiding, providing and protective force. The responses will be borne out responsibly. Indeed, it is a difficult task. There are no off-the-shelf solutions. It will require relentless work on the part of all countrymen and women. Equally, there are no illusions that all responses can be found in India's past. The past can and does offer vital clues but every age produces its own experiences and definitions. The Sangh's belief is that it is not an excess of laws, but 'lok shiksha', or people's awakening, that is the harbinger of change. Therefore, the Sangh is action-oriented.

India in the twenty-first century leans towards the youth. It is an India which does surgical strikes and air strikes to defend itself against terrorist attacks. It is the India with N-power which makes missiles like the Brahmos. It is a generation of youngsters who have grown up watching *Chhota Bheem* and *Jai Hanuman* on TV channels and Indian productions like *Baahubali*. Every Indian respects India dearly and wants to serve the motherland. They look up to the RSS as an inspiration and a platform for action which matches their spirit. The twenty-first-century RSS will be owned by these young, dedicated and fully-equipped swayamsevaks.

Once when Dattopant Thengadi was on a visit to the Parliament, someone told him, 'There are so many popular leaders here, where is Doctorji's presence?' A friend accompanying him quipped that the popularity of leaders should be calculated by the length of the shadow, meaning the influence is to be assessed by how many people are following the beliefs and means of the leader, long after they are gone. If this 'length of the shadow' parameter is used, then Doctorji would be right there among the top echelons. He actuated his motto, '*Matribhoomi ka paramvaibhav*' (Great glory of the motherland') through the RSS, and today, crores of swayamsevaks in different fields remain steadfast. Today, the whole world has seen the length and breadth of his shadow, and this is only expanding in all regions. The call of the motherland is irresistible and as the mother beckons, the sons and daughters of Bharat, that is India, plunge in to universalize Sangh values and methods. Thus, the mission continues.

The purpose of my writing this book is to call upon all those who desire to do something for the country. For those who are familiar with the Sangh, this book will add to their understanding. For those who are unaware, it will acquaint them with the Sangh. Together, we all will build a strong India.

Many a time, I visualize India as Bharat Mata standing upright in all her majesty and her many sons and daughters adorning the finery of knowledge and prosperity, waiting upon her, serving her. Such is my conception. It is an image which all Indians bear in their hearts.

ANNEXURE:
BEING CANDID

Most people generally think of the RSS as a political organization due to which there is a lot of misreading in their perception as they believe that the RSS works like a political party. This is totally erroneous. As an organization, the Sangh is sui generis—unique. No other body has shown such enormous staying power in voluntary service for the nation. For decades, generation after generation has instinctively chosen austerity and devoted itself to the national cause through the Sangh. Such an organization is difficult to fathom for people who are driven only by political consciousness. In the order of the frankness with which this book has been written, certain facts need to be stated with candour to set at rest the questions that are repeatedly asked. Many of these questions are even flung like accusations. So, it is necessary to clear the web of lies and misinformation.

NO POLITICS

To begin with, the RSS does not engage in party politics. There are some swayamsevaks who are in a particular political party—BJP—and work in politics. Of course, this does not mean that the Sangh is apolitical. It is not. The Sangh has a well-articulated view on politics—that it should be nationalist and political work should be according to Indian culture and should benefit society. Therefore, it keeps a keen eye on the political developments in the country and expects swayamsevaks in politics to be custodians of India's welfare and security. But at the same time, it neither interferes in the functioning of the BJP nor does it have any inclination to do so. Who will get which posts? Which locations will rallies take place in? The Sangh does not concern itself with such details.

In terms of ticket distribution, only if the senior BJP functionaries seek the Sangh's assessments—because swayamsevaks work on the ground level—such feedback is provided with accuracy. Beyond this, it does not influence electoral decision-making. It does not determine election strategy, which is the exclusive mandate of the political party. Just because there are several swayamsevaks in any BJP government, it does not mean that the Sangh interferes in its day-to-day work. That is their independent functioning.

The frequent colloquialism of 'remote control of Sangh' is a misnomer. The Sangh does not have any mechanisms of control. It conducts a dialogue with swayamsevaks and inspires them to do good work. As for the government, it works within a constitutional framework. It runs by its statutes, rules of conduct and conventions. It is responsible to the people through the Parliament of India.

During the lecture series of the RSS in Delhi, Mohanji was pointedly asked about the Sangh's relation with politics and why swayamsevaks were found in only one party. To this, Mohanji replied,

> This is not our question. Why swayamsevaks do not want to go to other political parties is a question they [other parties] have to mull [over]. By ourselves, we do not tell the swayamsevaks to do the work of any one particular party. We simply tell our swayamsevaks to stand in solidarity with those who work in national interest and for those who frame policies to serve that end.

We have seen that in the name of secularism, many political parties engage in minority appeasement and take extremely feeble positions which compromise the security interests of our country and harm its unity and integrity. All these things are watched carefully by the people of India as also by the swayamsevaks and this impacts their choice of the political party.

POLICIES AND AWARENESS CAMPAIGNS

The Sangh does not support any political party. It supports policies for which the touchstone is national interest. So, when the Sangh grows in strength, the party that is nationalist benefits.

During election season, the Sangh and Parivar organizations engage in awareness campaigns for increasing voter registration and voter turnout. For the year 2019, ABVP did the campaign, 'Nation first, Voting must.' For the 2014 election, the campaign of Youth Against Corruption (YAC) was started in 2011, as the UPA-II government became beset with massive corruption in 2G spectrum and coal allocations. For elections held after the Emergency was lifted in March 1977, the Sangh and Parivar organizations openly canvassed for the coalition of the Janata Party. This was an extraordinary situation. Ordinarily, swayamsevaks do not campaign for any political party, but it is a fact that all shakha-attending swayamsevaks go for door-to-door campaigning and appeal to people to exercise their franchise.

The engagement of the Sangh with democracy is deep and seeps through to the grass roots. Many people needlessly try to stir up a controversy about the RSS and the Constitution of India. After India's independence, a constituent assembly was formed, which unanimously accepted the Constitution of India, framed by the drafting committee under the chairmanship of Dr Ambedkar. The Sangh places a high premium on performance of constitutional duties. It is important to note that two words, 'secular' and 'socialist', were incorporated later into our Constitution. The constituent assembly had accepted 'sovereign' and 'democratic' only.[133]

Similarly, upon independence, India got its national flag after

---

[133]The Constitution of India, Appendix-II, p. 231, http://legislative.gov.in/sites/default/files/COI-updated-as-31072018.pdf

considerable discussions. Our national flag, or 'tiranga' as it is known in Hindi, is dear to all of us. The tiranga was hoisted at the RSS headquarters in Nagpur the day India became independent on 15 August 1947, and on 26 January 1950, the day India became a republic.[134]

Having participated in the Republic Day parade in 1963, the RSS instils respect for the tiranga in all the localities of India. Just like many organizations and even government departments, the RSS, too, has its own flag—the Saffron Flag or the 'Bhagwa Dhwaj.' The Saffron flag for centuries has been representative of India's cultural DNA. Following the liberalization of the rules governing the flag code in 2004,[135] the tiranga has been regularly flown with the highest standards at Sangh headquarters and hoisted in the Sangh headquarters in Mahal, Nagpur, and other parts of the country on Republic day and Independence Day; on these festivals, the Bhagwa Dhwaj is hoisted as well.

GROWING IN STRENGTH

The Sangh is a people's movement and people are getting attached to it in large numbers. It is also true that opposition to the Sangh comes from a few cliques with vested interests—profiteering NGOs, certain academic syndicates and those who engage in cheap politics. The establishment view is based on negating everything that was Hindu. India was systematically being made un-Hindu, through the teaching of distorted history and likewise the indoctrination by popular culture. Anything that was Hindu in identity was to be shunned. The Sangh challenged this because the denudation of our Hinduness would make us a cultural wasteland. What then would be left of us other than some

---

[134]Praveen S. Thampi, 'Nothing Anti-India Should Be Tolerated: Dr Manmohan Vaidya, RSS', *The Economic Times*, 28 February 2016.
[135]Union of India vs Naveen Jindal and Anr, indiankanoon.org, 23 January 2004.

fragmentation theories? With simple, ordinary people and crores of its swayamsevaks, the Sangh has stood up as a colossus against this.

Therefore, if someone practises caste politics, the Sangh talks of Hindutva to end the politicization of caste. If someone practises regional politics, the Sangh expands national Ekatmata or oneness. If some start a linguistic division, the Sangh celebrates unity and excellence of all Indian languages. There are some, who, in the name of secularism, work like terror apologists. The Sangh vociferously opposes them. When, on the same ground of secularism, religious conversions done by some Christian Missionaries through inducements and deceptive campaigns are silently allowed to bloom, the Sangh acts against this. The Constitution also prevents it. Those Left-wingers and their cohorts who do power politics from the 'barrel of the gun' ought to know that they will be stopped in their tracks by the Sangh. The reflection of national spirit in economic policies is a priority for national power. Manufacturers of certain countries, who want to dump their goods, have been and will be opposed.

So, all these elements whose nefarious activities are threatened by honest swayamsevaks get together at every possible corner and behave like flash mobs against the Sangh and they project it as a societal protest. This is false. The truth is that the Sangh has the support of the entire society and the more these stray groups of people spread rumours and drum up hysteria, the more the Sangh grows in strength.

INTELLECTUAL MOVEMENT

The Sangh's idea of India is an intellectual assertion for which it has spearheaded a struggle to free the discourse from distortions and colonial influences. Although the entire contestation mounted by the Sangh is intellectual, the direction of the country is not the sole preserve of the intellectual elite or policy mandarins. The RSS is an intellectual movement, where ordinary people are equal stakeholders. For long, the establishment in academics suppressed those who came from the Sangh school of thought through a conspiracy of linking the Sangh with the Gandhi assassination case and then there were repeated bans to suppress the idea of Hindutva. Hence, the roll call of decorated intellectuals within the Sangh-fold is few as they were kept away from higher academic positions, awards, publications and media importance. However, ornaments will be ornaments, whether on display or not. One needn't boast about something of good quality, as people always discover their merits. So, it is with Sangh thinkers, like H.V. Sheshadri, former Sarsanghchalaks Guruji and K.S. Sudarshan, the workers' movement leader Dattopant Thengadi, thinker-scholars and senior pracharaks like Ranga Hari, Padma Vibhushan Shri P. Parmeswaran and many more, who, despite all the onslaughts, brought the Sangh thought to vast audiences.

The establishment of intellectuals with its set phrases, foreign regurgitations and their tendency to be all-knowing certifiers, today lie in the dust. The people of India have rejected them. So, these frustrated, worn-out establishments of intellectuals levy the criticism that the Sangh only knows its parade orders 'daksh', meaning attention, and 'aram', meaning at ease. It does not have any intellectuals or thinkers. Those who are tutored in Marxist thinking and believe in 'nation in making' and follow Western models, have difficulties in comprehending and cannot understand Sangh thought, which is basically the grand Indian scholarship tradition spanning several millennia. With more time, they, too, will understand what the people of India already do.

The Sangh thought is not some specially created canon to be imposed on people. It is the eternal knowledge flow of India, which is explained in simple terms for the common people. The Sangh is a great simplifier. Those wanting to understand the reasons for Sangh expansion should count this as an important factor.

LINGUISTIC UNITY FOR EXPANSION

Multiplicity of languages is another added advantage for Sangh expansion, as swayamsevaks come from all language groups. There should be no discrimination based on language, and opportunities for development of all languages must be equal. In the Sangh, swayamsevaks make a conscious effort to learn each other's languages. Most senior functionaries of the Sangh are multilingual and have competence in four to five Indian languages. In the Sangh training camps, swayamsevaks learn poetry, literature and songs in different languages and competitions take place. Thus, there is mutual respect for languages and an underlying linguistic unity. If non-Hindi-speaking people in the south and other parts of India learn Hindi, it is also expected that Hindi-speaking people of the north would make an effort to learn languages of other states or at least show an aptitude for picking up the languages conversationally.

Literary translation and language familiarization are the prevalent idioms and will be taken forward. For example, Kannada novelist S.L. Bhyrappa's works have been translated in many languages. ABVP and other organizations have agitated for all-India exams to accord a respectable place to Indian languages. This will promote our integration. It is for this purpose that the Sangh urges the spread of Sanskrit language because Sanskrit is the common root, the mother language. All languages have a bank of common vocabulary rooted in Sanskrit. Therefore, interlinkages between languages can happen, as also between the people speaking them. Sanskrit is a critical part of our Ekatmata.

UMBRELLA OF HINDUTVA

Associated with Hindutva is the concept of Hindu Rashtra. Many people see it through an anti-Muslim lens. This is absolutely incorrect. Mohanji settled this issue in our times with a defining comment in his lecture series 'Ours is a Hindu Rashtra. This in no way means that Muslims are excluded. The day it is said that Muslims are not wanted, Hindutva will cease to exist.' This is the clearest exposition about Hindu Rashtra and the place of Muslims in it. The Sangh conception is that the ancestors of Muslims were Hindus. Therefore, Hindus and Muslims share a common ancestry. Since the Sangh always searches for integrating factors, it focuses on this aspect. Greater cognition of this fact by Muslims and Christians in India will result in better community relations. The reverse is also true. If the 'alien' dimension is cultivated, then these communities will be prone to be targeted by foreign conspiracies.

CONCERNS AND CHALLENGES

At the same time, no one can overlook certain evidence and trends. Undeniably, the growth rate of Muslims is outstripping the Hindu growth rate and some sections of the Muslim community are using this as leverage. The history of the Partition of India and the eviction of Kashmiri Pandits from the valley in independent India, are all memories deeply ingrained into the Indian psyche.

In districts like Dhubri and Barpeta in Assam, illegal infiltration of Muslims from Bangladesh is creating unease among local communities. Due to the large increase in their numbers, virulent Muslim parties like The All India United Democratic Front (AIDUF), which are non-Assamese in character, have planted themselves on the soil of Assam. They openly canvas on a communally divisive agenda, encourage infiltration and have even got the names of illegal migrants into the electoral rolls. The entire Assam is dealing with it. This issue has become alarming and has led to land grabs from Hindus and indigenous tribes. In Kerala, growth of the Muslim population has led to separatist organizations like the PFI, which, though innocuous sounding, is harmful. Therefore, demographic changes are a matter of grave concern for the Sangh. To tackle this, the Sangh has undertaken awareness campaigns for pushing required changes in government policy.

Hindus consider all faiths to be equal. The Hindu thought process and everyday conduct is respectful towards all forms of worship. This is also the tradition of the Sangh. But this should not be interpreted as weakness by other faiths, to do as they will, and to convert through inducement or terror. There is no place for any kind of fundamentalism in Hindu Rashtra. Appeasement, too, has no space.

In matters of safeguarding the country from Left-wing terror, the Sangh holds a public position. Hundreds of swayamsevaks and Parivar activists have been martyred while defending the country against red terror. Leftist ultras have to be exposed and isolated. Naxalism has to be fought by the administrative-security apparatuses and also in the realm of ideas. A make-believe theory had been circulated that Naxalites are pro-people and work for resolving the problems of the poor. This has been busted. People now know that all that the Naxalites and Maoists of every category do is keeping the poor poorer, through the thraldom of the gun. Law must also reign upon the urban Maoists in universities who are the protectors of the Maoists in jungles. Alongside security operations, mega administrative-cum-development roll-outs are required. This is being done on a fast-track basis. Public initiatives by mainstream organizations are the need of the hour so that the deceptions created by Leftist brigades can be dispelled.

FREEDOM OF EXPRESSION

There are a host of miscellaneous issues that have been raked up against the Sangh from time to time by opponents. These are mostly related to freedom of expression. The allegations have no basis in reality. The Sangh greatly respects artistic freedom and freedom of expression. It does not suffer from any Victorian prudishness, as it is often made out to be. We are a country of the *Natya Shastra*, of male and feminine sculptures, of Ravi

Varma's paintings, of romantic classics like Abhigyan Shakuntala, Meghadūta and many great Sanskrit plays, poetry and literature. We deeply appreciate and understand art. Only on the rarest of occasions, when some art forms, including films for political purposes, cross the line of decency and wilfully insult symbols considered sacred, the Sangh raises its voice against it because it is duty-bound to reflect the opinion of Hindu society.

LEADERSHIP FOR SANGH CENTENARY

Going forward, 2025 will be the year of the Sangh centenary. As newer platforms germinate and grow to full stature and as its activities permeate multiple layers, coordination will be a key feature. The Sangh believes that not just in politics but in all spheres of public life, leadership is required. Identifying capable people, organizing their discussions with top functionaries, giving them responsibilities and preparing them for future roles—an ongoing process—will acquire further depth as new skills and fields will be added. The volume of Sangh work has increased, and with it, the expectation that the Sangh will develop exceptional activists. India is fertile in terms of talented sons and daughters ever eager to serve the country. Others might have studied about India; the Sangh has meditated on India just as a sage meditates on India's mystical symbol, Om.

The Sangh was born out of a 'desh bhava', or a meditative experience about India. Forward planning, meticulous designing of initiatives and inspiring rich contributions from activists is a Sangh speciality, and twenty-first-century India will see a lot of it.

THE RSS STRUCTURE: ORGANOGRAM

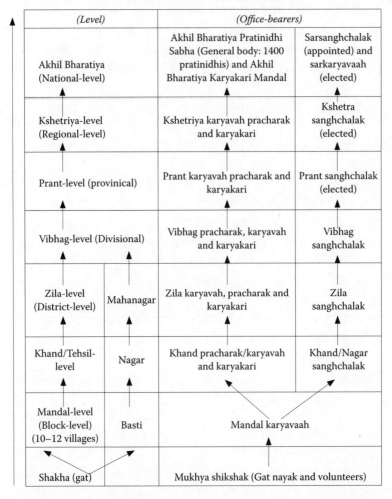

Each shakha has a list of swayamsevaks. It is in proportion to the number of volunteers in these shakhas, the prant (provinical). Pratinidhis are appointed and these pratinidhis in turn create the prant karyakari for each province. Prant karyakari is the executive wing/body of the organization at the provincial level. It normally consists of ten to twelve pratinidhis from across the province.

Akhil Bharatiya Karyakari Mandal consists of the following:

a. Prant sanghchalaks and their deputy
b. Prant karyavahs and their deputy
c. Pracharaks and their deputy
d. Pratinidhis from prant karyakari

GLOSSARY

The Sangh glossary is suggested to be organized as the Sangh structure, positions, terminology, people, organization, principles and values.

Sangh Organization

Akhil Bharatiya Karyakari Mandal Baithak (ABKM): ABKM is the All-India-level body where sanghachalak, karyavah, pracharak and their deputies from all zonal/kshetra- and state/province-level bodies meet.

Akhil Bharatiya Pratinidhi Sabha Baithak (ABPS): Top-most decision-making body like the general body of any public organization, having representations proportionate to the number of representatives. They are called 'pratinidhi' and are proportionate to the number of swyamsevaks from each province. All office-bearers of provincial executive are called 'prant karyakari'.

Sangh Structure

Shakha: The shakha as the basic unit of the RSS, and is fundamental to its working. Shakha is a place where all swaymsevaks assemble daily and receive instructions and perform physical drills and games. The functioning and objective of all shakhas are the same. As per Balasaheb Deorasji, it is a university that trains the appropriate workers so that they are available for the requirements in the various fields of life of the nation. The medium to achieve this is the games played on the grounds of RSS Shakha.

Sangh Terminology

Sangh Ganavesh—Uniform
Sangh Siksha Varg—RSS training camp
Samwaad—Dialogue
Sangh Dhwaj—Saffron Flag
Sangh Pariwar—Sangh-inspired or family organization

Sangh Positions

Pracharak: An individual who is inspired by the mission and objective of the Sangh and dedicates all his time to carry forward this mission is known as pracharak in the RSS parlance.
Sarsanghachalak—Friend, guide and philosopher
Sarkaryavaha—RSS general secretary
Sah sarkaryavah—Joint General secretary
Sangh Samanvay—Coordination
Mukhya Shikshak—Head of primary unit

INDEX